ROTARY

W9-CFV-584

BookClub
ROTARY CLUB OF EVANSTON LIGHTHOUSE

Presented in Honor of

D. J. Hoek

Assoc. University Librarian N.U.

April 25, 2017

Rotary Club
of Evanston Lighthouse

COUNTING DOWN
THE BEATLES

Counting Down

Counting Down is a unique series of titles designed to select the best songs or musical works from major performance artists and composers in an age of design-your-own play-lists. Contributors offer readers the reasons why some works stand out from others. It is the ideal companion for music lovers.

Titles in the Series

Counting Down Bob Dylan: His 100 Finest Songs by Jim Beviglia, 2013
Counting Down Bruce Springsteen: His 100 Finest Songs by Jim Beviglia, 2014
Counting Down the Rolling Stones: Their 100 Finest Songs by Jim Beviglia, 2016
Counting Down Southern Rock: Its 100 Best Songs by C. Eric Banister, 2016
Counting Down the Beatles: Their 100 Finest Songs by Jim Beviglia, 2017

COUNTING DOWN THE BEATLES

Their 100 Finest Songs

Jim Beviglia

ROWMAN & LITTLEFIELD
Lanham • Boulder • New York • Toronto • Plymouth, UK

Published by Rowman & Littlefield
4501 Forbes Boulevard, Suite 200, Lanham, Maryland 20706
www.rowman.com

10 Thornbury Road, Plymouth PL6 7PP, United Kingdom

British Library Cataloguing in Publication Information Available

Library of Congress Cataloging-in-Publication Data

Names: Beviglia, Jim.
Title: Counting down the Beatles : their 100 finest songs / Jim Beviglia.
Description: Lanham : Rowman & Littlefield, [2017] | Series: Counting down | Includes bibliographi-
    cal references and index.
Identifiers: LCCN 2016032749 (print) | LCCN 2016033693 (ebook) | ISBN 9781442271548 (hard-
    back : alk. paper) | ISBN 9781442271555 (electronic)
Subjects: LCSH: Beatles—Criticism and interpretation. | Rock music—History and criticism.
Classification: LCC ML421.B4 B55 2017 (print) | LCC ML421.B4 (ebook) | DDC 782.42166092/
    2—dc23
LC record available at https://lccn.loc.gov/2016032749

Printed in the United States of America

In remembrance of my father, Robert Beviglia Sr.

The long and winding road that leads to your door
Will never disappear

CONTENTS

ACKNOWLEDGMENTS

Every time I get the chance to write one of these books, I tell myself I'm going to keep this section brief. I'm following through on that this time around, but trust me when I say that if I mentioned everyone to whom I'm beholden on both a professional and personal level, the acknowledgements would run longer than the list itself.

Many thanks to my publishers Rowman & Littlefield for giving me the chance to continue the Counting Down series, which, I'm proud to say, is now branching out to other authors. I must also thank Bennett Graff for giving me my first shot at being published and Natalie Mandziuk for her excellent editing on my last two releases. My friends at Ascot Media continue to do a great job of publicizing my work far better than I could possibly do on my own.

In terms of research for this book, you can check out the endnotes and bibliography to find the many valuable sources I used. But I must make special note of a website that collected many of these sources as well as crucial information on the recording, instrumentation, and general history of each song. It is known as the Beatles Bible (www.beatlesbible.com). If you are a fan of the Fab Four and haven't already found this invaluable site, check it out now and thank me later.

On the personal side, I'm blessed with a loving group of friends and family. From the latter, I have to thank my brothers, Bob and Rich, who endured my love of the Beatles growing up; and my mom, Diane, who indulged it by purchasing for me not just Beatles music but also the

Beatles' solo music, Wings' music, the Travelling Wilburys' music, and so on.

Although my daughter, Daniele, has long since moved on to modern music, she still harbors enough love for the Beatles from our days of watching *Yellow Submarine* together that she plans to read this book; I appreciate her for that and because she's such a great kid. As for my wife, Marie, let's just say that I never truly understood "In My Life" until I met her.

Finally I'd like to thank the Beatles. I know that two of them can only hear me on some cosmic level and the other two are probably too busy to ever read these words. But I still have to say it, because their music not only has brought me immense joy over the years but also helped shape my outlook on life, always for the better. That's powerful stuff, and I'm grateful that I've had the chance to listen to music like that. That I get to write a book about it, well, my eight-year-old self would never have believed it possible.

INTRODUCTION

Although I chose the Beatles as the fourth installment of the Counting Down series, they were actually the inspiration for the format of the books in the first place. Years ago I decided I was going to make a mixtape, back when people still did such things manually, of the finest songs of the Fab Four. Wanting to be thorough, I had the idea of going through their catalog, picking out what I thought were their very best songs, and then ranking them to ensure that only the finest would make the cut.

Like every music-loving child who grew up in the seventies and eighties, I was a huge fan of Casey Kasem and his countdown shows on radio and television, so I decided then to put the twenty-five or so songs that fit onto the ninety-minute cassette into descending order so that the first song on the tape was number 25 and the last was number 1. I remember thinking that it would be neat to go through and rate the entire Beatles catalog in such a manner. I also thought that it would be cool to read a book like that, never envisioning that I would be the one to write it.

The other reason that the Beatles are responsible for the Counting Down series is, without them, I wouldn't have become the rabid music fan I am now. As an eight-year-old kid I discovered their music from an album of their greatest hits that my older brother had bought in the wake of John Lennon's death. After a morning, afternoon, and evening of listening to that album, I had memorized the lyrics to all the songs and had pretty much inherited the album from my annoyed brother. My love of pop music and all its permutations can be traced back to that day.

Because they recorded for such a finite period of time (only about eight years' worth of singles and albums, which is less than one-sixth as long as the Rolling Stones have been putting out records) and because they were so great, the Beatles left behind a pristine legacy. One song followed the next, each one more ambitious than the one before, each one brilliant. In terms of their albums, they didn't really have any clunkers from which they needed to rebound. You could probably point to a misstep here and there if you really wanted to be picky about it, but, for the most part, their music was spotless.

As you might imagine, trying to separate songs of such impeccability was quite the task, but one that I wouldn't trade for anything. Not that I needed a reason, but it afforded me the opportunity to dig deep into their catalog again. And whenever you listen to the Beatles, you find out something new about the songs, about the world, about yourself, even if you've heard them a million times before.

Okay, now some ground rules. The Beatles' official, original studio recordings, as released between 1962 and 1970, are the basis of the list that's about to unfold before you. That means no alternate versions or outtakes, official (as released on the Anthology series or *Let It Be . . . Naked*) or unofficial (as you might find circulating on the Internet) were considered, nor any particular live performances. (Nor did I consider the "Threetles" songs "Free as a Bird" and "Real Love.") As with the other books that I've written in the Counting Down series, only songs composed by members of the group make the list, which means no iconic covers like "Twist and Shout."

If a song was released multiple times in slightly different versions—like, for example, the single and album releases of "Let It Be"—I chose what I thought was the best possible recording when ranking them on the list. In the case of the three versions of "Revolution" and the two versions of "Sgt. Pepper's Lonely Hearts Club Band," however, I ranked them all because I felt that the differences between them were significant enough to warrant separate consideration.

As always, these rankings are based solely on my opinions of the songs, not any chart success or cultural impact or anything like that. I also strove to put aside any personal associations I might have with the songs when ranking them, although I must admit that task was much harder with this subject than it was in my other books, so long has the music of the Beatles been a part of my life and so much has it meant to me.

So I invite you now to check out the list and see what you think. Whether or not you agree with my choices, I fervently hope that you have the chance, as I did, to go back and listen to it all again. What you'll find, I guarantee, is that the music of the Beatles is nothing less than proof of magnificence in a tarnished world.

THE COUNTDOWN

100. "Your Mother Should Know" (from *Magical Mystery Tour,* 1967)

Released at the end of 1967, barely six months after *Sgt. Pepper's Lonely Hearts Club Band* conquered the Summer of Love, *Magical Mystery Tour* found the Beatles trying to ride the momentum of that groundbreaking album by tackling another out-there project. You'll hear some folks refer to this undertaking as a flop, and if you're only considering the seemed-like-a-good-idea-at-the-time film made by the group, that statement is not that far out of bounds.

But the six songs the Beatles recorded for *Magical Mystery Tour* certainly don't need anyone to apologize on their behalf. These songs took off from their *Pepper* predecessors in even more whimsical and psychedelic directions in what was really the last time that the group would write and record from that Day-Glo head space. The American version of the album, which included killer singles from the era like "Strawberry Fields Forever," "Penny Lane," and "All You Need Is Love" to go with "I Am the Walrus," "The Fool on the Hill," and the rest of the movie songs, can go toe to toe with any of the group's albums in terms of classics-to-tracks ratio.

From the movie soundtrack, Paul McCartney's "Your Mother Should Know" dials down the psychedelia, turns up the whimsy, and glides along effortlessly on pure goodwill. McCartney, always aware of his audience, made it a point throughout the band's career (and certainly into his solo stuff) to include sing-along material that could be bellowed out at a pub right before last call. These songs could be childlike ("Yellow Submarine"), rousing ("All Together Now"), or moving ("Hey Jude"); the common ground they struck was that they could induce with ridiculous ease a large gathering into swaying and singing.

Macca keeps it simple in "Your Mother Should Know," essentially repeating a single verse and refrain throughout the song, which makes it easier for people to get on board and wail along after hearing it once or twice. Throw in the typical McCartney melodic fluidity, with swoops and dives in the tune leading to the catchy refrain, add some "da-da" vocals as well as high-flying backing harmonies from John Lennon and George Harrison, and you've got a song that practically begs for audience participation.

On top of all that, McCartney bases the song around a mother, the family member who often rouses the most sentiment in those who are fully grown. Paul wrote many songs that could be described as matriarchal odes, including "Lady Madonna" and "Let It Be." Even though "Your Mother Should Know" doesn't dig too deep with the lyrics, the idea that there is wisdom inside a typical mom who may be underappreciated by a younger generation is the ultimate driver for the song.

There are many reasons that Lennon and McCartney were such simpatico songwriting partners. One of the most underrated might be the fact that Lennon's somewhat fractured family background, which led to some of the searingly honest soul baring that often characterized his work, contrasted McCartney's deep family roots, roots that likely were a big reason why he often looked back to a rosy past in his music. It could also be why he was unafraid to write songs that sound like they came from a prerock era; "Your Mother Should Know" certainly fits in that vein.

And yet the song isn't quite all sweetness and light. There are brief instrumental interludes, with McCartney's piano swirling around in uneasy territory, that suggest all isn't well in the family. Although it could be argued that this is just a way to heighten the impact of the move back into sunnier musical territory, those passages suggest that maybe the group sing-along is a way to hide some lingering pain. The fact that McCartney lost his own mom to cancer when he was a teenager can't be ignored even when considering this most benign of mother tributes. (And check out the harmonium-laced, dirge-paced version of this song on the *Anthology 2* collection for an example of just how much weirder and darker it could have been.)

In the *Magical Mystery Tour* film, "Your Mother Should Know" serves as the closing number, featuring the Beatles in white tuxes descending a spiral staircase and attempting some clumsy choreography. It certainly is a song well suited for a big production number and a grand farewell. And, as noted, its simplicity and charm make it ideal for a rowdy crowd of voices to join in the party. Just don't be surprised by the slight tinge of melancholy that lingers when those voices are stilled.

99. "She Said She Said" (from *Revolver*, 1966)

Odd circumstances surrounded both its origin and its recording, yet "She Said She Said" wears that strangeness well. One of the first Beatles' tracks that can truly be labelled "psychedelic," it reflects both the widening of the world around the group and their expanding willingness to plumb that wider world for song material.

In the early days of the band, before the first flush of fame and world domination, there would have been no outlet available to them by which a song like "She Said She Said" could have been inspired. That all changed in 1965, when the ruthlessness of their itinerary let up just a tad. As that coincided with the band's experimentation with drugs like marijuana and LSD, songwriting avenues theretofore blocked opened up for their investigation.

John Lennon, in particular, had a penchant for stumbling into experiences somehow both extraordinary and mundane, such as the one that birthed "She Said She Said." During their US tour in 1965, the band rented a private house on Mulholland Drive in Los Angeles, where they proceeded to trip out on LSD with members of the Byrds and a bunch of Playboy bunnies. One of the revelers was a pre–*Easy Rider* Peter Fonda, who tried to comfort a paranoid George Harrison with his own childhood near-death experiences. This did not impress John Lennon.

"He was describing an acid trip he'd been on," Lennon told David Sheff in 1980. "We didn't want to hear about that! We were on an acid trip and the sun was shining and the girls were dancing and the whole thing was beautiful and Sixties, and this guy—who I really didn't know; he hadn't made *Easy Rider* or anything—kept coming over, wearing shades, saying, 'I know what it's like to be dead,' and we kept leaving him because he was so boring! And I used it for the song, but I changed it to 'she' instead of 'he.' It was scary. You know, a guy . . . when you're flying high and [whispers] 'I know what it's like to be dead, man.' I remembered the incident. Don't tell me about it! I don't want to know what it's like to be dead!"[1]

When it came time to record "She Said She Said" for *Revolver* a year later, a studio argument caused Paul McCartney, who had skipped the tripping at Mulholland that fateful day anyway, to barge out of the studio. According to Paul's recollection, he took no part in the final track, leaving bass duties to George Harrison. In the past it would have been extremely unusual for a track recording to have continued without a key group member. (This was not so much the case on future albums as the individual members' relationships and reliance on each other began to fracture.) But the demands of finishing the album won out.

There is a part of "She Said She Said" that does indeed exude a "You had to be there" vibe; without knowing the story, a listener might be at a loss to make anything of the lyrics other than stream-of-consciousness ramblings. But Lennon's ingenuity and the liveliness of the recording atone for that to a great extent. In terms of the music, Harrison's lead guitar is front and center, tough and trippy all at once. And if he did indeed play the bass, the droning low notes he played provide a resonant bottom to allow his guitar the chance to soar.

This is one of Ringo Starr's finest instrumental showcases as well, as he manages to keep the beat while providing plentiful accents and flourishes at unexpected times throughout the song. When you add in the dreaminess of Lennon's vocals, there's no doubting that "She Said She Said" is a headphone highlight.

If Lennon's lyrics keep the listener a bit at arm's length here, his sly humor and melodic inventiveness certainly pick up the slack. His willingness to let the natural stops and starts of conversation invade his song lyrics, a tactic that he would use to great effect on subsequent songs like "Strawberry Fields Forever," can be traced back to this one. And the sudden shift in the bridge from the narrator's frustrating verbal tête-à-tête with this morose girl to his out-of-nowhere observance "When I was a boy / Everything was right" suggests a desire to escape heady situations like this and return to innocent pleasures.

The unspoken implication of "She Said She Said" is that such a return was impossible for the narrator, which pretty accurately represented the situation in which the four men who comprised the Beatles found themselves once worldwide renown interrupted their previously insulated world. At the very least though, as this intriguing oddball of a track proves, they could always make their newfound circumstances sound fantastic.

98. "Baby's in Black" (from *Beatles for Sale*, 1964)

"Baby's In Black" was never released as a single, yet it was a steady part of the group's repertoire from its release on *Beatles for Sale* in 1964 right up until the group ceased touring in '66. As Paul McCartney explained to Barry Miles in *Many Years from Now*, they liked the song as an effective change of pace in concerts: "And that was 'Baby's in Black,' we used to put that in there, and think, 'Well, they won't know quite what to make of this but it's cool.'"[2]

You could say that the entire *Beatles for Sale* project was one that confounded some fans who were used to an upbeat, hit-making Beatles machine. Yet the album fascinates today as an odd combination of bluesy, off-kilter originals and wild and wired cover songs. Although John Lennon and Paul McCartney couldn't reach back and fill out a whole album with originals as they had with *A Hard Day's Night*, released earlier in '64, the songs they did produce were more contemplative and questing.

Tracks like "I'm a Loser," "I'll Follow the Sun," "I Don't Want to Spoil the Party," and others hint at a time in your life when some of your wildest dreams come true and you become despondent at not having anything left to dream anymore. Throw in rip-snorting covers like "Rock and Roll Music" and "Kansas City/Hey-Hey-Hey-Hey," and you get the party and the hangover all in one sitting.

"Baby's in Black" deals with the topic of death, one that wouldn't enter many Beatles' songs, even as they got older and their lyrics became more profound. The song's narrator bemoans the fact that the "baby" in the song can only think of another guy who'll "never come back." "Oh, how long will it take / Till she sees the mistake she has made?" he queries in the middle eight, suggesting that her mourning period might eventually eradicate the possibility of new romance.

This "whim," a nagging inability to put the tragedy behind her, creates a kind of endless chain of sorrow, since the narrator is missing her even when she's with him, because she can't completely commit. Although you could say that the guy's being a little bit callous in not respecting her feelings, the frankness of his admission is refreshing, and you can't deny the anguish he's feeling.

What helps to magnify the anguish are the stunning harmonies concocted by John Lennon and Paul McCartney. Lennon tackles the lead melody, which takes precedence in the song's main sections, as McCartney simply supports. In the bridge, however, McCartney goes towering over the top of Lennon to uncork the emotion that the narrator can't quite bottle. If you're looking for the song that most closely reflects John and Paul's love of the Everly Brothers' close-harmony singing, look no further.

Musically, the song could have been an exercise in straightforward balladry if it weren't for the idiosyncratic guitar work of George Harrison. Right from the opening notes, which seem to stagger with unsure feet onto the sonic pavement, that guitar seems to signal that something is amiss, especially up against the steadfastness of Lennon's acoustic strumming and Ringo Starr's shuffling waltz beat. Even the solo is a wild ride of high and low notes. Some might find this playing to be a bit odd, but in the context of the song and the narrator's predicament, it calls to mind a kind of drunken rebellion against the harshness of his reality.

The song ends with the narrator still at sea about his quandary, his final question, "What can I do?" hauntingly unanswered by his listeners. "Baby's in Black" works very well as a soulful dip into unexpected subject matter. It also well represents an unheralded odd duck of an album that deserves more recognition and a better reputation.

97. "Day Tripper" (from *Past Masters, Volume 1*, released as a single in 1965)

Although the term "riff-rocker" wasn't yet in vogue (then again, other than with music critics, has it ever been?), songs that could easily fit that category were making a major imprint on the rock-and-roll scene by the mid-1960s. The Rolling Stones released the seismic single "(I Can't Get No) Satisfaction," featuring Keith Richards's indelible riff, in the summer of '65, while their British countrymen the Kinks had scored huge success with the back-to-back electric wallop of "You Really Got Me" and "All Day and All of the Night" a year earlier.

So by the time the Beatles headed into the studio to record their single for the 1965 holiday season, these songs were in the air. Whether or not they influenced John Lennon when he created the riff that drove "Day Tripper"—the song that would become part of a double A-side single (along with "We Can Work It Out")—is up for debate. What's clear is that the Beatles put their own spin on this burgeoning genre.

Whereas the Stones' and the Kinks' songs are frenzied and just shy of out of control, the Beatles keep their composure on "Day Tripper" even while ratcheting up the noise level. It's like they found a way to rock out without breaking a sweat. So pristinely is Lennon's riff rendered, both at the beginning of each verse and in the instrumental break, that it doesn't really resemble the aforementioned songs at all. If anything, there's some similarity to Roy Orbison's "Oh, Pretty Woman," which came out in 1964 and possessed a similar engine-starter of a riff that didn't lose control of the situation.

That's not to say that the song is tame. By contrast, the band makes impact by steadily upping the musical intensity from beginning to end. Each verse begins with that climbing riff in the first bar, followed by a second bar in which the riff is seconded by Paul McCartney's bass. In the third bar, Ringo Starr joins in on tambourine before snapping everyone to attention with his sturdy drum beat in the fourth. Even before the vocals enter the picture, we're already severely hooked.

The instrumental break also pushes things to the brink, the guitar notes ascending in tandem with some "Twist and Shout"–style backing vocals. It all leads back to the reiteration of the main riff, which emerges from the cacophony pristine and potent. Even with some funky subject matter in the lyrics, the sound of the record alone assured this one of being a hit. (It was a chart topper in the United Kingdom and a Top 5 single on *Billboard* in the United States.)

Lennon uses the song to take a poke at a dilettante who can't quite commit to the wild side. On "Day Tripper," this tug-of-war between straight society and its seedier underbelly is played mostly for fun, but it's interesting that interpersonal relations within the band would fray not too long after the song's release, in part because of McCartney's initial reluctance to join his fellow group members in partaking of LSD.

The two main songwriters share the vocals on the song niftily, with McCartney starting off each verse before Lennon slides in artfully to take charge in the chorus. "Taking the easy way out" is the first accusation levelled against the girl in the song. When Lennon calls her a "day tripper" in the refrain, it's just vague enough that he can get away with it sounding like a reference to physical travel, thereby sneaking the drug reference into the mainstream.

In the second verse, the boys continue with their mischievous word-play. "She's a big teaser," McCartney sings. The original line was "She's a prick teaser," which makes more overt the theme of sexual frustration. The following line ("She took me half the way there") again has a loose connection to the travel theme, keeping things at face value on the up-and-up while surely intending to be code for a different kind of prema-turely ended trip. They pulled off this sly trick well as far back as "Please Please Me" and return to it here. In this context, the way that Lennon stretches out the word "so" in the phrase "It took me so long to find out" is particularly agonizing.

These kinds of in-song hijinks may strike some as sophomoric, but the cheekiness to this subtle rebellion against staid societal mores charms more than grates. If anything, it's in keeping with the song's theme of keeping up appearances while occasionally sneaking down the back alley. And the music of "Day Tripper" balances on that thin line between proper and prurient as well, as the Beatles do a little musical headbanging with-out a hair falling out of place.

96. "What You're Doing" (from *Beatles For Sale*, 1964)

The early 1960s were a prime time for musical innovation, as musicians and producers attempted techniques and strategies that deviated from the typical rhythmic, instrumental, and structural tendencies of early rock-and-roll songs. Many of these deviations were so effective that other musicians quickly jumped on board and copied them, and they became go-to sounds of the era.

Many of those go-to sounds make their way into "What You're Do-ing," one of the pleasant surprises that pop up throughout *Beatles for Sale*. The Beatles' collective ears were always open, and they weren't above "nicking," as they put it in inimitably Liverpudlian fashion, from other artists. (And, since they were nicked as much as anybody, it was generally a case of quid pro quo.)

Yet when they borrowed a bit from others, as they do on this song and a few others, their own talents and sensibilities remained intact and usual-ly carried the day. All of these disparate, subtle influences disappear into the whole, and "What You're Doing," for just one of many examples, becomes a prototypical Beatles song, with all of the wonder and magic that label implies.

The first thing you hear on the track is a thumping drum pattern from Ringo Starr, the kind of showy, stuttery start that Phil Spector was so fond of using around that time in classic Wall of Sound productions like "Be My Baby." It's a bit unusual for Starr to be out in front of the production like that, but it grabs attention at the start of the song and Ringo takes well to the hitch-in-the-giddyap rhythm.

That's quickly followed by the twangy guitar of George Harrison, which picks out a precise little riff that separates itself from the rhythm section to form an indelible hook. Around that time the Searchers were churning out hits like "Needles and Pins" and "When You Walk in the Room," songs that utilized the same kind of melodic guitar lines to pull in listeners. Harrison's use of the twelve-string guitar also comes at a time when the instrument was about to explode into public consciousness thanks to the Byrds, who in turn would influence a later Harrison-penned Beatles' track called "If I Needed Someone."

The final distinguishing musical quirk in this song is the way the backing vocalists (John Lennon and Harrison) save their chiming in for the first word of each line and then go silent as lead singer Paul McCartney completes the thought. It's a technique the Beatles also had used on "P.S. I Love You," and the syncopated quality of it is very reminiscent of the vocalizing on girl-group hits from the era like "Leader of the Pack."

What's impressive is how all of this disparate source material is synthesized into a cohesive whole, and McCartney's soulful lead vocal gets the credit for centering it all. "What You're Doing" is one of the first of several songs that he would write in the middle of the decade that were inspired by then girlfriend Jane Asher, and these songs always brought out performances from Paul that were animated with emotions that seemed to be brimming on the surface. For a songwriter and performer who tends to shy away from the personal and confessional, it's interesting to hear these early songs about Asher and experience just how urgent and exasperated he seemed to be about the relationship at times.

This song doesn't feature anything fancy lyric-wise from McCartney, save for a couple of interesting rhyming pairs and his usual attention to flow and meter that revs up the catchiness factor. Yet his voice betrays the kind of frustration that's emblematic of jilted lovers everywhere. There isn't a lot of sadness evident in "What You're Doing," but the aggravation the narrator feels is embodied by the way McCartney's high notes spike. You can tell that it wasn't much of a stretch for him to get into character for this song; there are raw feelings aplenty here that elevate the performance and stand apart from any musical flourish.

On the *Love* soundtrack, which features Beatles' mash-ups coordinated by George Martin and son Giles to backdrop the spectacular Las Vegas–based Cirque du Soleil performance inspired by the Fab Four that opened in 2006, "What You're Doing" pops out of a medley that also includes "Drive My Car" and "The Word." Casual fans may have been surprised by how the song stands out in that presentation, but rabid Beatles fans already knew its potency. So will anyone else who hears it, thanks in small part to its clever mixture of '60s musical signposts, and in large part to a piercing Paul McCartney performance that clearly hit close to home.

95. "All My Loving" (from *With the Beatles*, 1963)

The old adage in the rock-and-roll world is that you have a lifetime to write your first album and a few months to write your second. That's a bit of an exaggeration in many cases, but it wasn't too far off for the Beatles. Their debut album *Please Please Me* arrived in March 1963 in the United Kingdom, and their follow-up *With the Beatles* followed eight months later to the day in November.

Such an abbreviated interim between first and second albums often leads to the dreaded sophomore slump. The Beatles didn't suffer any such plummet; if anything, *With the Beatles* solidified the excellent beginning *Please Please Me* had forged. Although there wasn't much difference between the two albums in terms of the types of songs included, and *Please Please Me* probably has the slight edge when comparing the best songs on each, the ease and assurance that come to the fore on *With the Beatles* showed the progress being made. While the first album often sounded like a raucous live show sans an audience, the second resembled a polished effort by a band that seemed like they had been in the studio for years instead of months.

The other thing staving off any letdown was the burgeoning songwriting prowess of John Lennon and Paul McCartney. They had only just gained confidence in their original material right before the release of *Please Please Me*; recall that producer George Martin initially wanted them to record a cover for their second single because he didn't think that any of their songs were up to snuff. Yet the pair hit their stride so quickly that it seemed like an endless stream of hit songs flowed from their pens from the moment they wrote "Please Please Me" on forward. That meant there was plenty left in the tank for *With the Beatles* even with the relatively short turnaround time.

If you're looking for a signature song from the second album, you can't do much better than "All My Loving." The recording displays the band's growing comfort level in the studio, how they had reined in the excess energy from their live shows to create something focused and yet still powerful. And the songwriting progression is evident as well, with Paul McCartney writing a deceptively simple little ditty that charms and seduces every step of the way.

"All My Loving" features a rhythm guitar part by John Lennon consisting of quickly strummed chords. The trebly backing rides high over the rhythm section and gives the song a feeling of weightlessness; indeed the guitar at times mimics the fluttering hearts of young lovers. Although McCartney envisioned the song as a countryish jaunt when he wrote it, it ends up sounding more Detroit than Nashville, with the backing "oohs" from Lennon and George Harrison playing up that vibe.

McCartney claimed after the fact that "All My Loving" was a rare song among those that he wrote for which the words came first. Often when writers have the lyrics before the music the melody suffers, but that's far from the case here, as Paul writes a rangy tune that rises and falls effortlessly.

The opening couplet is unassumingly brilliant. The Beatles were always aware of their audience in the first few years of their career, writing songs that seemed directly aimed at the hordes of teenage girls who formed the core of their following. These songs also acted as a kind of wish fulfillment for those girls. When McCartney opens with "Close your eyes and I'll kiss you," it tiptoes the line between sweetly romantic and hot and heavy. By following up with "Tomorrow I'll miss you," he makes sure he comes down on the sweeter side of that line. In two lines he has provided the ultimate would-be boyfriend for the screaming girls, one at whom they can level both their fantasies and their trust. And his puppy-dog vocals only up the ante.

The song plays out as a pledge of devotion from a guy forced to be separated from his girl. With striking efficiency, McCartney leaves no doubt as to where his heart lies, even if his body might be in some distant land. He might be out touring the world, but everyone harboring a crush on him could hear the song and imagine some kind of a reunion with him, even if they'd never actually met in the first place. And Paul actually doubles up on his commitment in the final verse when he harmonizes with himself, a relatively new technique by the band at the time. (They were already double-tracking vocals during this period, but in most cases it was simply to strengthen the lead vocal rather than provide harmony.)

Most US fans remember "All My Loving" as the first song the Beatles played during their historic debut on *The Ed Sullivan Show* in February 1964. Considering the gigantic audience in both the studio and in family rooms across the country, the song choice was wise. McCartney's message of romantic devotion received the biggest possible platform, and you can bet that every swooning girl who heard it that night believed it.

94. "I'll Follow the Sun" (from *Beatles for Sale*, 1964)

In the rush to record enough songs to squeeze *Beatles for Sale* into a holiday release in 1964, the Beatles had finally seen their well of originals dry up just a bit. It was their fourth album release in just two years, and their previous album, 1964's *A Hard Day's Night*, had featured nothing but Lennon/McCartney numbers. As a result, *Beatles for Sale* would once again include a few cover songs, and the group even went looking into the past for material of their own.

It's a good thing that they did, because it allowed Paul McCartney to dust off a song he had written in the nascent stages of the band at the turn of the decade when Stuart Sutcliffe was still on bass. The song he unearthed was "I'll Follow the Sun," and when rendered on *Beatles for Sale*, it became one of the first Beatles' studio recordings to feature mainly acoustic instruments. It also provided quite a contrast on the album, following in the running order the band's wild and woolly cover of Chuck Berry's "Rock and Roll Music."

"I'll Follow the Sun" is a hushed beauty, one of the first times McCartney allowed his self-reflective vibe to emerge with the band. He had a knack for marrying dreamy songs like this one to accompaniment that pulled back the reins and allowed "the beauty of the melody," to borrow a phrase from "Rock and Roll Music," to trump the forward thrust of the rhythm. In this case the acoustic guitars, interrupted only by a brief, elastic solo from George Harrison on electric, achieve this effect. Even Ringo Starr pulls back on the reins, keeping time during the song by tapping on his knees.

In discussing the song shortly before his death in 1980, John Lennon took on a slightly jeering tone. "That's Paul again," he said. "Can't you tell? I mean, 'Tomorrow may rain so I'll follow the sun.'"[3] The intimation, based on the line Lennon chose to highlight, seems to be that his writing partner tended at times toward a Pollyanna positivity that borders on the naïve. Considering that John wrote a bunch of songs, within and without the Beatles, about the power of peace and love to conquer all and made us believe them, there seems to be a bit of selective memory at best and hypocrisy at worst to the implied eye-roll in his comment.

The criticism also misrepresents the melancholic core of "I'll Follow the Sun." McCartney's very first line is "One day you'll look to see I've gone," and that spells out the theme of departure that girds the song. He also suggests with the line "One day you'll know I was the one" that the person he's addressing might be underestimating the impact his leaving will have somewhere down the road, if not right at the moment.

In the lovely bridge, Lennon joins up for some sighing harmonies with McCartney: "And now the time has come / And so my love I must go / And though I lose a friend / In the end you will know." These lines suggest that the protagonist's choice to leave will hurt him as well in terms of the loss of a friendship. McCartney doesn't specify exactly what it is she'll know in the end, but the unsmiling undertow of the music leads us to believe that there will be tears shed once that knowledge arrives.

Looking back at the lines that Lennon quoted, they certainly could be read as the worldview of a person who thinks he can stay ahead of any encroaching darkness, however foolhardy such expectations might be. But you can also hear in those lines the admission that his heart is filled with wanderlust, a word to which McCartney would return in a solo song from 1982. The gentle sorrow of the music doesn't promise any happy endings when he reaches the sun, nor does it absolve him of the nagging memories of those he left behind. But it's nonetheless an honest assessment of how the narrator chooses to live his life, and that honesty is what pushes the song above being just a sweet little trifle and gives it some real meat. "I'll Follow the Sun" may have been written well before the fame-and-fortune days of the group, but it nonetheless provides a telling portrait of McCartney the superstar artist as an extremely self-aware young man.

93. "You Can't Do That" (from *A Hard Day's Night*, 1964)

On *A Hard Day's Night*, the 1964 Beatles' album that coincided with the release of their first film, John Lennon and Paul McCartney pulled off the then unheard of feat of writing every song. While auteurs like Chuck Berry and Buddy Holly had been the principal songwriters for their own music, it was unusual for a band to compose even a majority of its songs, let alone all of them.

One reason that the Beatles' two songwriters (at that point George Harrison was rarely composing) could pull this off was that they pulled from a pretty diverse set of influences to inspire their writing, meaning that an album like *A Hard Day's Night* stays fresh instead of falling into a rut. When the duo started becoming heavily invested in writing their own songs in the early 1960s, rock and roll was in a bit of a funk, as the first wave of stars had circumstances befall them that prevented them from releasing music of the same caliber in that time period as they had in the halcyon days of the mid- to late '50s. Lennon and McCartney had no choice but to listen elsewhere for inspiration, which partially explains why their music contained hints of country and western, folk, and even vaudeville and Broadway standards, in addition to the Merseybeat sound they helped to initiate.

No form of music cast a longer shadow in the early '60s, in terms of potency and popularity, than what emanated from Motown Records in Detroit. Thus it makes sense that so many early Beatles' tunes, both original and cover, sounded like homages to the music that Berry Gordy oversaw. On *A Hard Day's Night*, the Beatles found room for their own take on up-tempo Motown girl-group sass with "You Can't Do That." You can almost imagine McCartney and George Harrison doing rudimentary dance steps as they sing the backing vocals.

On the Beatles' previous album, *With the Beatles*, they had closed out the affair with a rollicking cover version of another Motown hit, Barrett Strong's "Money (That's What I Want.)" The swagger and grit the boys brought to the recording matched that of the original. They must have thought a lot of "Money," because "You Can't Do That" bares more than a passing resemblance to it, from the circular riff that drives the song to the answering backing vocals.

More than anything though, "You Can't Do That" shares with "Money" that somewhat intangible but crucial element that sets the best R&B numbers apart from their counterparts: the groove. The right groove can move the backsides of listeners without their even knowing it's happening, and it's something that can't necessarily be planned. For whatever reason, the twisting of the guitar line, the timing of McCartney's bass notes, and the persistence of the cowbell creates a doozy of a groove here.

Lennon said that he was trying to channel Wilson Pickett with the song, but it doesn't get into the thick of it quite like Pickett's hottest sides. "You Can't Do That" is more surface area, flashy more than gritty, but executed so well that you can't help but enjoy the ride. Lyrically it's your basic jealous lover making veiled threats, but those threats never get too ominous (as they do in "Run For Your Life," a *Rubber Soul* rocker that Lennon penned and later disowned).

The song chugs along with the groove at the forefront, providing special moments here and there. Among those are the whoosh of the harmonies in the middle eight, Lennon's unhinged guitar solo contrasting the suavity of the rhythm, and the way Starr breaks down the beat with a quick snare–kick drum combo to send Lennon hurtling into the chorus. And speaking of Lennon, he sings with gusto here, proving that he could do far more than leather-jacketed rock-and-roll shouting even in the early days.

"You Can't Do That" found its way onto the second side of *A Hard Day's Night* along with a bunch of other songs that weren't heard in the movie. The Beatles seemed to use that side as a launching pad for some sounds and ideas that strayed just a bit off the path they had successfully trod over their first two years of recording. Not heeding the song title, by early '64 this special band was proving it could do just about anything and do it extremely well.

92. "I'm a Loser" (from *Beatles for Sale*, 1964)

In 1964, there were approximately 1.6 billion male human beings on the planet. It's safe to say that a good portion of them would have traded places with John Lennon in an instant. Travelling the world singing songs, making oodles of money, and basking in the adulation of screaming fans at every turn, this seemed like a life that would engender confidence and self-esteem of practically bottomless levels.

But Lennon was an interesting case. While he certainly had supreme belief in himself as a musician and performer, he also suffered from bouts of insecurity and doubt to which the common man could relate. Those nagging feelings often worked their way into his music, where he tended to hide in plain sight. The Beatles' smiling façade and buoyant music helped to mask cries for help that were hardly concealed by the lyrics.

"I'm a Loser," found on 1964's *Beatles For Sale*, was the first of these semiautobiographical plaints from Lennon. The fact that it arrived not too long after Lennon was first introduced to the music of Bob Dylan (and to the man himself as well) is not coincidental. But where Dylan, even at that young age, preferred obfuscation even when naming songs after himself, Lennon directly addressed his issues with only the natural effervescence of the sound created by his band as a filter. The ironic thing was that people looked long and hard for some kind of clue to Dylan's personality to little avail, while Lennon broadcast his frailties to the world in no uncertain terms and most missed it.

If there were any doubt, the song begins with the title sung a cappella by Lennon with Paul McCartney in harmony, his buddy standing by him for this depressing admission. Musically there isn't too much to "I'm a Loser," just a genial little folk-rock ramble enlivened by those harmonies every time the refrain comes around. Some timpani from Ringo Starr add a little drama to the percussion, while George Harrison bends his notes into a countryish twang. Since Dylan inspired this number, it's no surprise that Lennon takes impassioned harmonica solos in the break and the outro.

Lennon borrows a bit from the classic doo-wop song "The Great Pretender," written by Buck Ram and recorded for a No. 1 US hit by the Platters in 1956. "And I'm not what I appear to be," Lennon sings, while the protagonist of "The Great Pretender" admits, "I seem to be / What I'm not, you see." In addition, the narrator of "I'm a Loser" claims to "act like a clown," which is also a direct callback to the Platters' hit. (Smokey Robinson would mine similar territory a few years later with his classic "Tears of a Clown.")

As he was still a relative novice in terms of revealing himself in song instead of simply using craftsmanship to build pristine hit singles, it's perhaps understandable that Lennon clings to clichés a bit in the lyrics ("girl in a million," "My tears are falling like rain from the sky"). But it's fascinating to listen as the song progresses and transforms from a kind of battle of wills between two lovers into a dark-night-of-the-soul monologue. And his bravery in laying bare his pain is a precursor to the kind of songwriting he would do down the road both with the Beatles and in his solo career.

In the first verse he presents love as a zero-sum game; since he is the loser, the girl comes out on top: "I should have known she would win in the end." Yet slowly but surely he seems to realize that it might not just be the absent girl who is causing his doldrums. "Is it for her or myself that I cry?" he asks at the end of the second verse, suggesting that his is a malaise that might have existed even if she had stuck around.

The final verse completes this transformation within the song, as the girl doesn't even enter the picture. "I realize I have left it too late," he says regretfully, and this is the one line that stays interestingly vague. Lennon doesn't specify just what "it" is he left, but one can only speculate that there was some choice he made, either in the relationship or apart from it, that was like a personal Rubicon that, once crossed, allowed no turning back, even though he wished he could. In the final line of the final verse, Lennon claims to be telling this tale of woe to prevent the friend he's addressing from suffering a similar fate. But it seems more likely that "I'm a Loser" is meant to be self-revelation rather than cautionary tale.

One can only wonder, now that the initial song is more than a half-century old, what the initial reaction of listeners was when they spun the disc and heard "I'm a Loser" for the first time. Did they just bounce along to the rhythm and rise and fall along with the tune? Or were they aware that John Lennon was singing those words from the heart rather than embodying a character? We know the truth now, and, as such, this one cuts surprisingly deep.

91. "I'm Only Sleeping" (from *Revolver*, 1966)

Because of their myriad accomplishments, it's easy to forget how young the Beatles were during their amazing run. By 1966, they were just in their early and mid-twenties, and anyone who's lived through that age knows it's the first time since early childhood when sleep starts to become a priority. The demands of working and families begin to devour and extend our waking hours, so those who like to slumber cling to that pastime with everything they have when the opportunity to partake arises.

John Lennon loved to sleep. In the 1966 *Evening Standard* article that included his infamous "bigger than Jesus" comment, journalist Maureen Cleave wrote about his somewhat ravenous desire for beddy-bye. "He can sleep almost indefinitely, is probably the laziest person in England," Cleave wrote. "'Physically lazy,' he said. 'I don't mind writing or reading or watching or speaking, but sex is the only physical thing I can be bothered with anymore.'"[4]

One can only imagine how the rigors of being a full-time Beatle and a husband and father must have encroached on that yearning for sleep. Hence it's understandable that Lennon wrote one song about sleeping ("I'm Only Sleeping") and one song about being tired ("I'm So Tired") in his time with the group. It's the former that enters the countdown here, perhaps one of the most accurate musical interpretations of nodding off to dreamland ever laid down.

"I'm Only Sleeping" was the third track on 1966's *Revolver*, and what a diverse collection of songs that disc was. Just take a listen to the wild, wonderful roller coaster ride that kicked off the album: the stutter-stepping sarcasm of George Harrison's "Taxman"; the Victorian melancholy of Paul McCartney's "Eleanor Rigby"; and then the hazy dreamscape of "I'm Only Sleeping." And that was even before detours like "Love You To" and "Yellow Submarine" appeared on side 1. Even though they were still touring at this point, the group, with the indispensable assistance of George Martin, had so mastered the studio that there were no stylistic or genre boundaries they needed to respect anymore. Their fertile, drug-boosted imaginations could be given free rein.

On "I'm Only Sleeping," the band evoked that weird nether region between deep slumber and eyes opening up, that point when it's difficult to tell if you're still dreaming. The very first guitar chord heard on the song even sounds like the kind of thing that would introduce a dream sequence in a movie or TV show. Paul McCartney's bass line creeps around as if afraid to wake anyone, especially in the connecting segments when it's the only instrument you hear. By contrast, Ringo Starr's snare drum seems determined to keep everyone at least partially awake, lest they not get anything done.

The most famous instrumental quirk of all in the song is George Harrison's backward guitar. Harrison had been noodling about with possibilities for the instrumental break when a tape operator accidentally loaded a tape machine the wrong way. The playback intrigued the band, and they somehow knew that it would be a perfectly bizarre insert for this track. (Besides, anyone who's ever watched *Twin Peaks* knows that backward talk is a hallmark of dream worlds, so backward guitar makes perfect sense.)

Lennon concentrates as much on the sound of his lyrics here as he does on the meaning, with rhymes like "ceiling" and "feeling," "morning" and "yawning" adding to the effect of weariness that he successfully conjures. (There's even an audible yawn from one of the group members when the music drops away at one point.) While the narrator hasn't exactly gone full-on hermit ("Keeping an eye on the world going by my window"), he also wonders why others around him can't see the folly of constant activity: "Running everywhere at such a speed / Till they find there's no need." He'd prefer to stay "miles away," and the way the title is phrased is an indication that he can't understand why anyone would find fault with that preference.

So he awaits that precious "sleepy feeling" with the anticipation of a kid waiting on a wonderful present. Years later, John Lennon would again utilize the "lazy/crazy" rhyme found in "I'm Only Sleeping" on his solo song "Watching the Wheels." In the latter song, released on *Double Fantasy* just before his death in 1980, he's also wondering why he has to apologize for the way he chooses to spend his time, although in that case it was his decision to step away from the recording "merry-go-round" and live the life of a husband and father that was in question. "I'm Only Sleeping" isn't asking for such a long-term retreat, just forty winks or so for a busy, busy guy. And it asks for it so seductively that anyone who hears it might feel the urge to pull the covers over their head themselves for a nap of their own.

90. "When I'm Sixty-Four" (from *Sgt. Pepper's Lonely Hearts Club Band*, 1967)

"Rock'n'roll wasn't all I liked in music. Kids these days must find it hard to imagine a time when rock'n'roll was only one of 'the musics.' Now it is *the* music. There is a huge spectrum, from pop to serious blues players. Back then I wasn't necessarily looking to be a rock'n'roller. When I wrote 'When I'm Sixty-Four' I thought I was writing a song for Sinatra. There were records other than rock'n'roll that were important to me."[5]

The "back then" in the above quote from Paul McCartney found in *The Beatles Anthology* retrospective would be about 1957, since Paul also stated that he wrote "When I'm Sixty-Four" around age fifteen. The Beatles would return to the song in their Cavern days as an occasional change of pace. And this early morsel of a song would later adorn the group's most famous album, 1967's *Sgt. Pepper's Lonely Hearts Club Band*, creating a jarring juxtaposition as a sort of show tune following up George Harrison's mystical musings on the Indian instrument-drenched "Within You Without You."

Some have made the case that "When I'm Sixty-Four" doesn't belong at all on *Pepper's*, since it isn't remotely trippy or psychedelic. The first argument against that is that there are several songs which would fall into that category on the album, from the genial pop number "With a Little Help from My Friends" to the classical turn on "She's Leaving Home." In addition, since *Sgt. Pepper's* was supposed to be an expansion of rock's boundaries to such an extent that those boundaries ceased to exist, no song could be considered unsuitable.

More than anything, "When I'm Sixty-Four" belongs because it easily fits into the way the album showcases stories of everyday people going through their routines, enjoying their minor victories and suffering their occasional defeats. As far-out as the music could be at times, the stories all remained stubbornly relatable to common folk who would never cross paths with a rock star in their lives. And there's nothing more relatable than the fear of growing old alone.

McCartney mentioned a Frank Sinatra–style standard when he described his thought process for "When I'm Sixty-Four." In truth, the song contains more of a vaudevillian vibe. You can almost imagine it coming in the middle of a bunch of old-fashioned pie-in-the-face comedy skits when the main comedian steps out to give the audience a little song and dance. (You can even envision the guy doing a lively little kick or making an outsized facial expression when Ringo Starr hits the chimes in the breakdown after the middle eight.)

Knowing the antiquated sound he was seeking, McCartney chose clarinets as the instrument to carry the load for the song. The only slight concession to a rock sound is the brief introduction of Lennon's jaunty electric guitar to the mix in the final verse. This being *Sgt. Pepper's* though, they had to come at the track a little sideways: The recording was sped up in pitch a half note, which gives McCartney's protagonist a little more twinkle and mischief than might have otherwise existed.

The pleasures that McCartney describes in the song might seem mundane, but, as anyone in the glow of a loving relationship knows, the mundane can seem magical. As such, Sunday morning rides, mending fuses, and digging weeds engender warm feelings from the narrator: "Who could ask for more?"

This guy has more than a little bit of the scamp in him. The fact that he would even need to ask the question, "If I'd been out till quarter to three / Would you lock the door?" indicates that it's a possibility the girl might have to prove her answer one day. And he has a sense of humor too: "Yours sincerely, wasting away" is how he addresses his paramour. But there's a genuine sweetness in there as well, especially evident when he imagines grandchildren the two might have and when he makes his promise: "You'll be older too / And if you say the word / I could stay with you."

Paul McCartney is now a decade past the age milestone listed in the song and still releasing great music and putting on breathless stage shows for his adoring fans. But "When I'm Sixty-Four" nonetheless rings true. It's an old-fashioned song about getting old found on the most groundbreakingly novel album of its time, and it makes perfect sense right there.

89. "I Should Have Known Better" (from *A Hard Day's Night*, 1964)

Considering that they are the most widely acclaimed band of the rock-and-roll era, it's hard to claim that any aspect of the Beatles, concerning the group as a whole or the individual members, is underrated. Yet it's fair to say that the members of the group tend to be underrated as instrumentalists. With the exception of Paul McCartney being listed as one of the top bass players in most rock rankings devoted to instrumental prowess, it's rare to hear people who discuss the Beatles begin by talking about how well they play their stuff.

Part of that is because the band members tended to play only what was needed for the song to succeed rather than going off in showy displays meant to display their virtuosity on their respective instruments. (This was true of McCartney as well, but his style of playing melodically instead of just chunking along to the rhythm revolutionized the instrument and is impossible to ignore.) The other part is that the songs themselves are so memorable that the instrumental backing tends to get a bit lost in the shuffle.

John Lennon usually gets the worst of this underrating when it comes to the individual members, because he tended to strictly play rhythm guitar on most songs. When he did play lead guitar in place of George Harrison, it was usually memorable, but those occasions were rare. But where he really gets underrated is in terms of his harmonica playing.

In the early recording days of the band, a good chunk of their songs contained Lennon's harmonica; some ("Please Please Me," "Love Me Do") are iconic, while others ("I Don't Want to Spoil the Party," "There's a Place") are hidden gems. "I Should Have Known Better," found on 1964s *A Hard Day's Night*—and featured in the movie of the same name, in which the boys played it on a moving train—is simply hard to imagine without Lennon's harmonica riff driving the song.

Lennon first heard the music of Bob Dylan in 1964, and Dylan's early acoustic music leaned heavily on the harmonica, so that's probably where some of the inspiration came from. But Lennon had used the instrument often before that, in part inspired by the work of a young Delbert McClinton on the Bruce Channel hit song "Hey Baby." From all these disparate sources came a style that he made his own, a hard-charging method of playing that nonetheless displayed the same uncanny ear for hooks that he displayed in his songwriting.

In "I Should Have Known Better," that harmonica is the first of many hooks that the listener can discern, which is especially impressive when you realize it's a song without a chorus. Lennon's first elongated enunciation of the word "I" plays off the hustled words in the rest of the verse to create a grabby vocal moment, as do the rising high notes he hits as he soars to the end of each verse.

George Harrison takes a quick guitar solo that sticks to the main melody before adding a ringing tone on the final note that kind of explodes the rest of the instruments away until they rise back up for Lennon's final vocal salvos. Harrison adds trebly chords in the bridge as Lennon, who also strums along on acoustic guitar, shows off his vocal range. All the while McCartney and Ringo Starr are steadfast in providing the rhythmic engine so that the showier vocal and instrumental parts can make the proper impact.

With the song sounding so great, there's really not much fancy that Lennon needs to do with the lyrics. The title is clever in that it sets you up to expect a guy who's regretting falling for someone. In actuality, it's just his way of saying that he didn't realize just how far he would fall. Yet ultimately, he's pretty confident that she'll reciprocate his feelings.

Lennon's talents are all over "I Should Have Known Better." It's no surprise that he sings the daylights out of it and writes a catchy up-tempo track. But anyone who is surprised by his harmonica wailing, well, they should have known better as well.

88. "Drive My Car" (from *Rubber Soul*, 1965)

Questions of authorship of the Beatles' songs, especially those credited to Lennon/McCartney, continue to hound band experts and fans alike. John Lennon put his two cents in first with his landmark interviews with *Rolling Stone* and *Playboy*, while Paul McCartney gave his side of the story largely in his official biography, by Barry Miles, *Many Years from Now*, as well as in various interviews throughout the years. Contradictions between the two main sources have kept folks searching for clues for many years.

A song like "Drive My Car" makes it clear why such questions would be impossible to answer even if all the participants were alive today and could sit in a room and clear it up. Even if we possessed a time machine and could go back and view every moment from a song's inception to its completion, the picture would still be a bit muddy.

On "Drive My Car," the safe assumption has always been that Paul McCartney wrote the bulk of the song. As a general rule that admittedly contains several exceptions, a Beatles song's lead vocalist is usually the one who wrote it, and, since McCartney sings the lead vocal line here, albeit with John Lennon singing low harmony throughout, it would seem to fall to him.

But Lennon noted and McCartney later seconded that Paul came into the session with a refrain that originally went, "You can buy me golden rings." Whether Paul knew that the line was lousy to begin with or John told him it needed to change is where the tales differ. Nonetheless, the two brainstormed and eventually came up with the refrain, "Baby, you can drive my car." As McCartney noted in *Many Years from Now*, "'Drive my car' was an old blues euphemism for sex, so in the end all is revealed. Black humour crept in and saved the day. It wrote itself then. I find that very often, once you get the good idea, things write themselves."[6]

Only it didn't quite write itself from that point, at least not without the intervention of George Harrison on the musical end. Harrison came up with the bass line for the song, a thumping approximation of the same one used by Donald "Duck" Dunn on the Otis Redding version of the soul classic "Respect." He then doubled it up on guitar while McCartney played the bass. Just as it's doubtful "You Can Buy Me Golden Rings" would have been a proud moment in the Beatles' catalog, it's also tough to envision "Drive My Car" sounding so gritty and vibrant without that bass line running through it.

Once all of that was in place, the lyrics about a would-be starlet with extracurricular job demands for her driver came together beautifully. The song provided the perfect bluesy kickoff for the group's superb 1965 album *Rubber Soul*. Whereas lyrical introspection tended to be the name of the game on the rest of the album, "Drive My Car" balanced out some of the balladic elements with a good old blast of sex and rock and roll.

The recording pops at every turn, from McCartney's singeing guitar solo in the break to Ringo Starr's playful cowbell on top of his peppery drumbeat. One thing the song does share with the rest of *Rubber Soul* is a proclivity for soaring three-part harmonies from Lennon, McCartney, and Harrison; the way they arrive in the chorus on the heels of the talk-singing of the verses renders those intertwined voices even more memorable.

In a time before women's rights were on everyone's lips, the way the song flips the scenario of a typical sexual power play is eye-opening. It's the girl in charge here, taking advantage of a young guy in return for decent pay and a glimpse of the good life. But the final verse takes some of the sting out of the situation by revealing that the girl hasn't yet secured this good life (she doesn't even own a car), but "I found a driver and that's a start."

The "beep-beep beep-beep yeah" chant in the outro adds one more bit of cheeky innuendo to the track before it fades out. Who wrote how much of "Drive My Car" is immaterial. What matters is that it somehow made it to its final, fun-filled form, and it remains one of the best Beatle rockers released during their mid-'60s apex.

87. "Lucy in the Sky with Diamonds" (from *Sgt. Pepper's Lonely Hearts Club Band*, 1967)

A few songs back on this humble list, the question of whether "When I'm Sixty-Four" deserved its spot on *Sgt. Pepper's Lonely Hearts Club Band* was discussed. "Lucy in the Sky with Diamonds," on the other hand, is generally considered to be one of the album's signature songs. In actuality, it's a bit of an outlier.

Many folks (John Lennon being the most prominent of those) have noted that, for a supposed concept album, *Sgt. Pepper's* lacks much continuity or anything resembling a through line. Yet the album does hold together in thematic terms even if Billy Shears doesn't make a grand return after his memorable entrance. *Pepper's* is a group of stories about ordinary life, full of simple pleasures, unexpected heartbreaks, and the bittersweet in-between. Those stories are then rendered musically in the most fantastical ways that the imagination of the four Beatles and George Martin could conjure.

Except for "Lucy in the Sky with Diamonds," that is. Oh, it has the musically fantastical part down pat, for sure. From the almost eerie altered organ that opens, the song is the perfect soundtrack for a surrealistic boat trip in search of an elusive phantasm of a girl. The verses sound like a dream sequence, a slow-motion journey amid impossibly bright, towering fauna and non sequitur creatures and objects. The choruses, signaled by three bass drum thumps from Ringo Starr, resemble jovial chase music.

On the lyrics, Lennon took his Lewis Carroll flavored wordplay and spun it through a psychedelic washing machine. (Paul McCartney apparently helped with some of them.) The euphony of the words as they're thrown together strikes more than any meaning they might have; it's okay to imagine what "plasticine porters" and "newspaper taxis" might look like, but it's what they sound like that really takes you away, to paraphrase one of the lines.

Lucy, unobtainable, runs through it all, and yet the triumphant chorus, with each line containing a melody of mostly a single note, suggests that just her presence is enough. When Lennon analyzed the song in later years, he speculated that he was having a kind of premonition about a woman coming around to change his life, and that came true when he met Yoko Ono. While it's hard to say if any second sight was going on with the song, there is an undeniable sense of romance in spite of the fact that there's no evidence that the narrator and Lucy ever even get the chance to speak to each other or touch. Just the hint of her "kaleidoscope eyes" creates a world of magical, inviting warmth.

Lennon sings it all in ethereal tones, his voice soaring far from reality and basking in the wonder of the reverie. He had a knack for catering his vocals to his subject matter in just the right manner that few rock singers have ever possessed, and his ability here to so convincingly float off into the ether is the song's most charismatic aspect.

Yet the fact that the song exists in that ether is what makes it the odd song out on *Sgt. Pepper's*. Lennon defended himself until his death against claims that the initials of the song's title were a coded way of promoting LSD. But there can't be any denying that the imagery on "Lucy in the Sky with Diamonds" was influenced in some way by the songwriter's experimentation. The title may not have partaken, but the song itself seems unlikely to have existed without Lennon's own tripping experiences.

Now that doesn't work against the song quality-wise in any way, but it does make it an uneasy fit among its brethren on the album. If we could see what the iconic folks on the cover of *Sgt. Pepper's Lonely Hearts Club Band* were looking at, we'd probably have all of the characters that inhabit the songs, the salt of the earth who have stepped away from their daily routines to enjoy an afternoon in the park listening to this magical imaginary band. "Lucy in the Sky with Diamonds," however, would be hovering way above them all the way out of view.

86. "Don't Let Me Down" (from *Past Masters, Volume 2*, released as a B-side in 1969)

The entire *Let It Be* project was a mess in a lot of ways, but the idea behind the project wasn't to blame. After several years of creating music that was beholden to recording-studio techniques for its realization, the Beatles intended to "Get Back" to their original method of sitting down in a room with their guitars and drums to see what would happen, much as they had in the early days.

Alas, the acrimony that had built up between group members meant that sitting in the same room was a recipe for disaster, causing the band to shelve the project and find their footing again with swan song *Abbey*

Road. By the time the four men got around to dealing with the music that would become *Let It Be*, their breakup was in process and it was hard to get any of them to bother with the giant slab of sessions recorded for the album. That's when Phil Spector entered the process and a lot of odd decisions were made.

One of the strangest was the decision to leave one of the band's strongest-ever blues numbers, "Don't Let Me Down," off the finished album, relegating it to a B-side of the "Get Back" single. While there are no out-and-out clunkers on *Let It Be*, certainly "Don't Let Me Down" deserved a spot over slighter throwaways like "Dig a Pony" or "One After 909." Considering the song contained one of John Lennon's most impassioned performances at a time when he was showing less and less interest in the band he founded, the omission is particularly glaring.

It's also confusing because "Don't Let Me Down" features the Beatles' instrumental excellence shining like it failed to do at other times on *Let It Be*. In typical Lennon fashion, the song spirals through sections so distinct they practically sound like minisongs of their own, yet the band stays with every identity shift and manages to tie it all together beautifully. Billy Preston, who joined the band as a special guest during the sessions for the album, takes center stage with soulful electric piano work, but the Fab Four also represent themselves beautifully.

Paul McCartney's bass locks deep in the groove during the verses then adds gorgeous melodic counterpoint in the refrains and the middle eight. George Harrison keeps his playing to a minimum, but his contributions, including the gritty opening lick and the lilting descending notes in the verses, are essential. And Ringo Starr is right on top of every change in mood, delicately handling the hi-hat in the verses before crashing in on the cymbals in the choruses.

"Don't Let Me Down" comes as close as any song to the solo work that Lennon would do immediately after he left the band, right down to the soul-baring screaming singing style that would distinguish his first album with the Plastic Ono Band. But the screaming also gives way to his tender, delicate assurances in the verses and the joyous, gospel-like fervor he displays in the middle eight, celebrating a "love that lasts forever / It's a love that has no past." Lennon's performance shows all the glorious good and potential bad in jumping into a new relationship.

If his lyrics seem a bit simplistic, they were meant to be. He was leaving behind the surrealistic dreaminess of his work in 1967 and '68 to go for a more direct approach. As he told *Rolling Stone*'s Jann Wenner, this reflected his need to express his raw feelings for Yoko Ono. "When it gets down to it, when you're drowning, you don't say, 'I would be incredibly pleased if someone would have the foresight to notice me drowning and come and help me,' you just scream ," he said.[7] That kind of forceful, pain-tinged declaration of his feelings hits home because Lennon's vulnerability is on full display. His need for Ono in the song is comparable to his need for air.

The Beatles played "Don't Let Me Down" during their rooftop concert that temporarily put the *Let It Be* project to bed in early 1969. During the song, Lennon muffs the lyrics at one point, switching to gibberish to get through the line. McCartney somehow stays right with him, the old chemistry resonating when they lock back into the harmonies at the end of the line. What made the moment somehow even more moving is the fact that it came during a song that shows Lennon courting the new love that would require him to leave McCartney and his bandmates behind.

85. "Piggies" (from *The Beatles*, 1968)

"The creatures outside looked from pig to man, and from man to pig, and from pig to man again; but already it was impossible to say which was which."[8] So ended George Orwell's *Animal Farm*, in which anthropomorphized farm animals gain their independence from man only to become corrupted by the power they gain, eventually turning on each other.

In George Harrison's "Piggies," everyone is a swine, for lack of a better term, but they've assimilated into a system of haves and have-nots very similar to the one the human race has unofficially implemented. Harrison's black humor cuts deeper than the relatively benign commentary he levels on the song, which wears its weirdness like a badge of honor and is a perfect fit on the anything-goes aesthetic of the White Album.

Harrison by that point had established himself as the most willing social critic in the band among the songwriters. Considering that he had less opportunity to get his originals on albums dominated by Lennon/McCartney classics, this meant that a large percentage of his work had the wider world beyond romance in its sights. "Taxman" from *Revolver* was a biting critique of unfair British tariffs, while "Within You Without You," found on *Sgt. Pepper's Lonely Hearts Club Band*, concentrated on a vaguer yet just as trenchant societal ill: the foolhardy pursuit of materialism as a substitute for genuine human connection.

So it was that Harrison continued this streak with "Piggies," which also stood out for its odd instrumentation. Chris Thomas, who at that time was a kind of assistant producer for the band behind George Martin, decided on a harpsichord to adorn this odd satire. It provided just the right touch, its Victorian dignity contrasting the down-in-the muck behavior of the song's characters.

A string section seconds that kind of disconnect between the haughty music that supposedly classy members of society might enjoy and the low-down things they do to get to such a lofty place in life. Snorting pig sounds scuffling about the music drive this point home.

Harrison also sings the song with the precious diction of a royal troubadour, the perfect way to tackle a melody so prim and proper. He efficiently lays out his worldview with three verses and a bridge. The first verse sets up the hard-luck "little piggies," for whom "life is getting worse." The greatest reward in their measly existence is the dirt they "play around in."

In the second verse, the "bigger piggies," who dress in "starched white shirts," make their presence felt. This clean attire establishes they are nowhere near the lowly environment of the little piggies. The next line suggests that these animals are in control of their less fortunate brethren: "You will find the bigger piggies stirring up the dirt."

Harrison's voice takes on a disembodying effect in the middle eight to add a neat little flourish to a song rife with them. It also plays up his urgency and frustration at the situation he describes: "In their sties with all their backing they don't care what goes on around / In their eyes there's something lacking." His anger then boils over: "What they need's a damn good whacking."

The final verse insinuates that the song is not pure fantasy, since anyone could see the piggies on display if they would just open their eyes to see. John Lennon allegedly contributed the final twist to Harrison's song in the last line, when it's revealed that these animals are devouring themselves: "Clutching forks and knives to eat their bacon." In that last verse, Harrison's vocals are multitracked, each voice more exaggerated in its dismay than the next, until it sounds like a precursor to a Monty Python anthem.

Harrison cleverly tiptoes a fine line on "Piggies." The story is an Orwellian nightmare, but it's delivered like a Pythonian farce. It ends up being purely Harrisonian, which is more than enough to make it a winner.

84. "Hey Bulldog" (from *Yellow Submarine*, 1969)

The Beatles were contractually obligated to produce some new music for the soundtrack to *Yellow Submarine*, the 1969 animated film about their imaginary exploits in Pepperland fighting off the Blue Meanies. The band was frustrated both at their lack of involvement in the picture and at the need for new songs, which is why they somewhat halfheartedly tackled the task.

In the end, they put forth four new songs to be used beside classics like the title track and "Eleanor Rigby" in the film. George Harrison wrote two of them, of which "It's All Too Much" was a fun, psychedelic freak-out and "Only a Northern Song" a bored inside joke. (Considering he usually received, at most, two writing credits on a full album, Harrison's heavy involvement is a dead giveaway of the band's lack of involvement in the project.) Paul McCartney's benign, if simplistic, singalong "All Together Now" served as the movie's fade-out tune.

The best of the four songs by far is "Hey Bulldog." John Lennon came up with this one; considering he was the most ardent in his objections to the film, he clearly channeled his frustrations into this spicy little number. McCartney had suggested John write something since the band was scheduled to be in the studio to be filmed for a "Lady Madonna" promotional video and thus could get some actual work done in the process. Lennon pulled some lyrics together, and the band went to work.

"Hey Bulldog" features one of the most memorable opening riffs in the band's catalog, played initially by Lennon on piano as if he was trying to bust up the strings on the instrument. Harrison then doubles the riff on guitar in the second bar as Ringo Starr taps out a boogie beat. McCartney then comes aboard on bass for the third bar before the whole band surges into the main section of the song.

McCartney niftily bounces around the lower depths of the song as Starr keeps up a steady tempo. Harrison fools around occasionally at the fringes while mostly staying silent, until he unleashes a fuzzy solo that's very much in keeping with the song's inherent wildness. That's the funny thing about "Hey Bulldog": it's played tightly, and yet there's an unhinged quality to it, as it maintains tension throughout while letting loose at the same time.

Lennon's lyrics when read from start to finish are hard to decipher (and probably weren't meant to be deciphered anyway). Yet there are individual lines that really cut through with urgency, suggesting that the song is more than just ramblings about sheep dogs and wigwams.

The couplets at the end of each verse combine intriguing philosophical musings with harsh accusations of whomever it is the narrator is addressing. "Some kind of innocence is measured out in years," Lennon sings. "You don't know what it's like to listen to your fears." And then later: "Some kind of solitude is measured out in you / You think you know me but you haven't got a clue." In their own way, these lines possess a Dylanesque harshness, as if Lennon's "Bulldog" spent a lot of time on Bob's "Positively 4th Street."

And yet the narrator turns abruptly on a dime in the chorus and assures this person, "If you're lonely you can talk to me." These tonal shifts in the lyrics mimic the music's split personality. And, as if the roller coaster ride hadn't already been established, Lennon and McCartney indulge in some playful barking theatrics at the end of the song, a studio improvisation of sublime silliness.

Yellow Submarine turned out to be a charmer of a movie, one that still acts as an introductory course to the music of the Beatles for toddlers worldwide. "Hey Bulldog," with its goofy title and animal noises, works on a kid's level if you want to keep it down there. But keep alert as you listen, and you'll notice that it also has a little bite to go along with that bark.

83. "I've Just Seen a Face" (from *Help!*, 1965)

You often hear the Beatles' 1965 album *Help!* referred to as a "transitional" album in the group's catalog. Sometimes "transitional" is rock-critic code name for "letdown," but the term doesn't seem to have any negative connotations here. After all, it's hard to find too much fault with an album that included bona fide evergreens like the title track, "Yesterday," "Ticket to Ride," and "You've Got to Hide Your Love Away." But it does feel at times like the album has one foot in the band's moptop past and another in its trippy future, so transitional seems a fair assessment.

The album's relative lack of a lofty reputation among the Beatles' other releases can partly be blamed on the movie of the same name, the group's second motion picture, which contained its share of loony charm but was a far cry for *A Hard Day's Night*, their first celluloid effort. Not to mention that this was another album that was butchered up by Capitol Records in the United States to squeeze out more Beatles' product; the song we're about to discuss, as a matter of fact, actually ended up being the leadoff song for the US version of *Rubber Soul*.

More than anything, *Help!*, through no fault of its own, suffers a bit in comparison to the albums that followed it: *Rubber Soul* and *Revolver* reached dizzying heights, and *Sgt. Pepper's Lonely Hearts Club Band* did nothing short of revolutionize the LP format. *Help!* is nothing to sneeze at, but there isn't quite as much depth in the lineup behind those afore-mentioned standouts as on the subsequent albums.

The pleasures to be had if you delve deeply enough into the album are of the simpler, sweeter kind, examples of excellent songcraft, if not for-ward-reaching tracks. Many of these are straightforward love songs with no agendas other than to say how they feel to someone special. That's always been in Paul McCartney's wheelhouse, and he delivers with "I've Just Seen a Face," which combines loving feelings with feisty music to catchy effect.

The band throws us off guard with a fluttery acoustic intro that seems just this shy of dainty. That gambit turns out to be a bit of misdirection, meant to prop up the impact when the hard-charging rhythm of the main section kicks into gear. "I've Just Seen a Face" proves that acoustic doesn't need to mean soft; this one rocks in its way.

Any bluegrass band wishing to cover the Fab Four should start here; just slap a couple of banjos on this one, and it can't miss. McCartney manages to breathlessly deliver the fast-talking lyrics without losing track of the darting melody. The walled acoustic guitars are accompanied by Ringo Starr's brushed drums, and George Harrison takes a stomping solo in the break while McCartney scats along behind him.

The idea behind "I've Just Seen a Face" is that love can happen in a moment, or it might never happen at all; fate and chance play a great role. The narrator of the song is lucky in that he happens to stumble across this girl who changes his life in an instant. He realizes his good fortune and how easily he could have missed out on it: "Had it been another day I might have looked the other way / And I'd have never been aware but as it is I'll dream of her tonight."

This is the kind of song that McCartney has always been able to toss off with such effortlessness that it's easy for others to overlook just how skillfully the thing is put together. There's not a wasted moment, and even if the words don't dig too deep past the blush of love at first sight, they capture the headiness of that experience without fail. And the whoosh of the music delivers that same kind of rush to the listener.

In the chorus, McCartney harmonizes with himself, singing the word "falling" over and over as the narrator relishes his loss of control over the situation. You can also hear the genuine surprise in his voice at the fact that "she keeps calling me back again." McCartney plays the role of the underdog coming up a winner in love to the hilt.

"I've Just Seen a Face" never plugs in but still nearly wears us out with the relentlessness of its attack. New love can sneak up on you with the speed of its approach, but Paul McCartney and the rest of the band prove here they're more than ready to keep up.

82. "And Your Bird Can Sing" (from *Revolver*, 1966)

As anyone who's ever seen *High Fidelity* can tell you, there is an art to making mixtapes. The rules that govern this practice, somewhat outdated now in the age of playlists, aren't as hard and fast as John Cusack's character might have led you to believe, but if you've ever tried to make them, you know when you've made a good one and, by contrast, when you've made a hash of it.

One rule that seems almost counterintuitive is that it's usually not a good idea to insert a Beatles' song into a mix of any kind. You would think that inserting as much great music onto a mixtape is the goal, and, since the Fab Four have a higher batting average of great music than any band that's ever existed, that you'd want them on there as much as possible. The problem though is that the Beatles' greatest songs achieve such a level of perfection that they tend to break the spell of your average mixtape. Everything surrounding a Fab Four song on the tape or CD or playlist tends to sound just a little less special compared to it.

You can pull this gambit off though if you choose wisely enough. Don't go for the masterpieces; look instead for less ambitious numbers onto which the Beatles ladled just a dollop of their strange magic. For example, any mix or playlist of peppy rockers would be immediately enlivened by "And Your Bird Can Sing," a charming if somewhat inscrutable oddball found on 1966's *Revolver*. It's just modest enough that it won't intimidate all the other songs around it on your preferred method of assembling your favorite music into one tasty batch.

"And Your Bird Can Sing" comes from the prolific pen and magpie mind of John Lennon. He later dismissed the song in his post-Beatles interviews, but that shouldn't be held against it; most groups would be thrilled to have produced a greatest hits album full of the songs that Lennon poo-pooed after the fact. It's definitely a strange one, for sure, but it demands your attention while it's on and lingers benignly after it's over.

The song possesses an indelible instrumental hook that starts it off and keeps reappearing so that the momentum doesn't flag. George Harrison and Paul McCartney play harmony guitar lines that follow each other through a long spiraling dive and then back up again into perkier territory. It's an example of how one idea can transform a song; while "And Your Bird Can Sing" might have succeeded with just one guitar playing the riff, the addition of the second adds an irresistible flavor. McCartney's kicky bass lines also keep things lively every step of the way.

Speculation about Lennon's meaning for the song has been running rampant among Beatlemaniacs for about a half century now, with no real clarity emerging. Theories throughout the years have posited that the song was a dig at, variously, Mick Jagger, Frank Sinatra, or even McCartney. But seeing the song as primarily accusatory seems to be misjudging the tone a bit.

Let's not forget that Lennon wrote several songs and spoke in interviews about being on a lonely plane of existence that he felt no one else could reach. He at times saw that level as a soaring peak and at others a lowly valley ("I mean it must be high or low," he famously sang in "Strawberry Fields Forever").

It seems like you can interpret "And Your Bird Can Sing" in similar terms, with Lennon in this song feeling a bit defiant about his place in the world. Over and over he refutes the bold statements made by whomever he's addressing by telling that person that he or she still come up short of relating to him on any meaningful level. They can't hear or see him, no matter how many wonders they've experienced or the talents of their mysterious "bird."

But the song also makes room for some goodwill from the narrator. In the middle sections, Lennon envisions a day when the other person can no longer count on these things about which they previously boasted. Yet instead of turning his back on them, he promises steadfast friendship: "Look in my direction / I'll be round."

Thus "And Your Bird Can Sing" ends up conjuring far more good vibes than bad, yet another reason for it to find a home next to some other positively themed rockers you may fancy. It's still the Beatles though, so you might have to adjust your expectations a bit for the rest of the songs filling out the running time.

81. "Ob-La-Di, Ob-La-Da" (from *The Beatles*, 1968)

Paul McCartney's perfectionism in the studio occasionally rubbed his bandmates the wrong way. At no time was it more apparent than during the recording of some of his more fanciful songs, ones about which John Lennon and George Harrison were ambivalent in the first place.

For example, his attempts to turn "Maxwell's Silver Hammer," a bizarrely upbeat-sounding song about a mass murderer found on *Abbey Road*, into a hit drove his musical partners to distraction. In that case, however, the song itself was too slight and cloying to be worth the trouble.

In similar fashion, there was an apparent dustup during the making of the White Album about McCartney's quasi-reggae track "Ob-La-Di, Ob-La-Da." McCartney kept recording different versions of the song to find the right fit, even after he had recorded the take that would prove the basis for the final version. This didn't sit too well with Lennon and Harrison.

Yet the battle was worth it on "Ob-La-Di, Ob-La-Da." No matter how many permutations the song endured (and there's a pretty good conga-style version to be found on *Anthology 3*), it's difficult to argue against the notion that McCartney muscled his way to an energetic, enduring finished product. And Lennon and Harrison turned out to be good sports as well, giving solid contributions to the song.

McCartney borrowed the title phrase from a Nigerian musician named Jimmy Scott who was fond of using it as a kind of shorthand philosophy. He then concocted a tale about a hard-working youngster named Desmond and an aspiring songstress named Molly. In the course of three verses and a bridge, they meet, court briefly, get engaged, build a home, have kids, and then switch jobs just for fun (a scenario caused when McCartney accidentally messed up the names during the take and decided to leave it the way it was just to throw people off a little bit, a decision that probably elicited a sigh of relief from the other members of the band that they didn't have to go through yet another revision).

The lyrics might seem too good to be true, that these people from such humble beginnings could stumble into an idyllic life, but the buoyant music makes you believe it could happen. The bass line McCartney plays, which dips its foot in the ska pool without quite diving in fully, keeps heads bobbing, while the tempo, prompted by Lennon's maniacal piano, never flags, suggesting that life doesn't just go on; it speeds by, so you better grab the wondrous moments with the kids in the yard for all they're worth and sing every song with gusto.

"Ob-La-Di, Ob-La-Da" is a great song to listen to with headphones, through which you can hear all kinds of mischief from Lennon and Harrison, probably venting their frustrations in this manner, as they answer McCartney's lines in the background. Every instrumental flourish is a winner as well, such as the tinkling piano that sneaks into the latter verses and the saxophones gliding through the chorus. For somebody who was supposedly hard to please concerning his song, McCartney certainly allowed an anything-goes aesthetic to creep into the mix, and it works well for the song.

From time to time, critics will come forth to bash "Ob-La-Di, Ob-La-Da"; look hard enough on the Internet, and you'll find lists that call out the song as being one of the worst in the Beatles' catalog and even, believe it or not, one of the worst of all time. This is an odd phenomenon to befall such a harmless song. Maybe people don't like whimsy or happy endings; more than likely, the song's genuine embrace of sentiment and happiness doesn't jibe with our ironic age.

Yet it holds up far better than, for example, "Good Day Sunshine," another McCartney paragon of positivity that plays more like an advertising jingle, forcing the warm feelings down our throats. "Ob-La-Di, Ob-La-Da" comes by it all quite honestly. It may have its critics, including some aggravated members of the band that recorded it, but the story of Desmond and Molly still gives the rest of us hope that life's forward progress will lead us somewhere special.

80. "Being for the Benefit of Mr. Kite!" (from *Sgt. Pepper's Lonely Hearts Club Band*, 1967)

The Beatles had a way of picking songs out of the air, songs that were waiting to be written but seemingly could only be located by the members of the Fab Four. They tackled songs about the everyday, found the fantastical within it, and could reverse that equation if need be.

There is no more old-fashioned entertainment than a traveling circus, one that rolls into town and leaves a trail of wide-eyed, mouths-agape children (and probably a few adults as well) in its wake. It predates the modern forms of distraction with which we fill up our time these days, and yet it still has the power to excite and amaze.

So it was that the circus made the perfect topic for this group who managed to routinely make the routine sound otherworldly. John Lennon walked into an antique shop one day and stumbled onto a poster of a nineteenth-century circus, and "Being for the Benefit of Mr. Kite" was born, eventually to be included as the side 1 closer of *Sgt. Pepper's Lonely Hearts Club Band* in 1967.

If you ever get a chance to see the photo of Lennon standing near the poster, you'll see that most of the elements in the song were right there for him. He made a couple changes here and there, most likely for rhyming, rhythmic, and metrical purposes (and here it must be noted that Paul McCartney has claimed that he assisted in the songwriting as well), but otherwise there wasn't too much imagination needed in this case.

For that reason, Lennon was later somewhat meek about the song in interviews. Yet he should be commended for having the initial vision to see that the poster could be turned into something special with the right musical backing. And the timing, right when the Beatles were at their most musically adventurous in the studio, couldn't have been better for "Mr. Kite" to be brought to life.

In this effort, the Beatles were extremely lucky to have George Martin at their disposal. Whereas McCartney tended to be precise about his musical instructions to the producer, Lennon generally spoke in abstracts about his songs, leaving Martin to translate these intangible notions into concrete ideas. "He would talk in metaphors about his ideas," Martin told Lennon biographer Ray Coleman. "I'd have to get inside his brain to find out what he wanted. It would be more of a psychological approach.

"He'd say—for example, on 'Being For The Benefit Of Mr. Kite!'—'This song's about a fairground. A little but mystified. I want to get the feeling of the sawdust and the feel of the ring. Can you do something about it?' I'd then have to think how that imagery could be transformed into sound."[9]

Martin concentrated thus on the instrumental passages in the middle and at the end of the song to work the wonders Lennon imagined. He took tapes of calliopes playing marching songs, cut them into tiny pieces, mixed them up, and then reassembled them randomly with the help of engineer Geoff Emerick. The resulting soundscape, pasted as it is on top of the main rhythm of the song, mimics what it would be like for a young brain at the circus imbibing all those sights and sounds at once, mesmerizing and even a little frightening.

An army of harmonicas, organs from Lennon and Martin, and a harmonium paint bright melodic colors all across the landscape. Meanwhile, Ringo Starr's oompah beat steadfastly keeps to its task while McCartney crawls along underneath on bass as if he's trying to sidestep a charging elephant. Lennon plays the ringmaster through it all, his double-tracked voice cutting through this sonic wonderland and luring all those within earshot to this antiquated extravaganza.

It's hard to find a song more suited to an album than "Mr. Kite" is to *Sgt. Pepper's*. (And it's another example of the Beatles' uncanny knack for wild juxtapositions, with its vividly psychedelic touches coming right on the heels of the classical melancholy of "She's Leaving Home.") Here was an album that took a bunch of everyday folk and elevated their mostly mundane exploits to rivetingly mysterious realms. You can imagine some of those folks visiting this circus and walking out with their minds blown.

John Lennon may have later felt that "Being for the Benefit of Mr. Kite" was little more than glorified plagiarism of a poster, but he was missing the point. With the Beatles as their house band, Mr. Kite, the Hendersons, Henry the Horse, and all the rest manage to put on a performance that can legitimately stake its claim as the greatest show on earth.

79. "Julia" (from *The Beatles*, 1968)

Songs by rock artists about their mothers are relatively few and far between. Those that do exist tend to go to one of two extremes. You'll get the occasional gushing tribute, à la Bruce Springsteen's "The Wish," in which he thanks his mother for supporting his rock star dreams. On the flip side of that coin are the rockers who take umbrage with the way they were raised, such as Roger Waters in Pink Floyd's scathing "Mother," which could have been more accurately renamed "Smother."

The Beatles' "Julia" leans to the softer side of these maternal odes, a kind of impressionistic meditation by an earthbound man on the ethereal presence of a woman calling to him yet hovering out of his reach. Or at least that's how it sounds removed from any context. In actuality, the man, John Lennon, was writing the song as an indirect tribute to his deceased mother, Julia, which makes this one of the more oddly fascinating entries into this subgenre of music.

For those who don't know the backstory, Lennon's mother was only a sporadic part of his life once his father left the family when John was an infant. The two got closer in Lennon's teenage years, but that ended abruptly in 1958 when Julia, while crossing a street, was hit by a car and killed.

The Beatles rarely referenced their personal lives, at least directly, in song in their early years. But by the time the White Album rolled around in 1968, all subjects were game, as Lennon and Paul McCartney wrote oodles of material (with George Harrison and, on one song, Ringo Starr also contributing), so much so that a double album was deemed necessary to contain it all. In his 1980 interview with *Playboy* magazine, Lennon explained that the band's retreat to India to be spiritually enlightened by the Maharishi Mahesh Yogi provided ample opportunity for songwriting, and "Julia" was a byproduct of that.

"'Julia' was my mother," he said. "But it was sort of a combination of Yoko and my mother blended into one. That was written in India. On the White Album. And all the stuff on the White Album was written in India while we were supposedly giving money to Maharishi, which we never did. We got our mantra, we sat in the mountains eating lousy vegetarian food and writing all those songs. We wrote tons of songs in India."[10]

Lennon is the only Beatle to perform on the track, solo efforts having become commonplace within the Fab Four around this time. Using a finger-picking style he learned from Donovan while in India, he plays delicate arpeggios around his fragile yet somehow soothing vocal melody. There is an undeniable loneliness evident in his voice, even amid the double-tracking that he preferred.

He borrowed some of the lines from the poem "Sand and Foam" by Kahlil Gibran, including the opening couplet: "Half of what I say is meaningless / But I say it just to reach you." It must have been strange for fans to hear the leader of the biggest band in the world co-opting a line that evokes ineffectuality, but Lennon was always about upending expectations. The bulk of the lyric consists of poetic imagery that speaks of beauty and distance: "Silent cloud"; "Morning moon"; "Her hair of floating sky."

Lennon's contention that he intermingled the memories of his mother with his then current emotions for his wife, Yoko Ono, is hard to hear in the finished product. What you do hear is the combination of mantra-like calm and profound yearning he conjures each time he sings his mother's name. It's as if he hopes the longing vibes he emits can somehow reach his mom in the afterlife and that this will forge the connection with her that he lacked when she was still alive.

About two years later, with the Beatles in his rear-view mirror, Lennon recorded "Mother," a harrowing excavation of his deep-seated feelings of abandonment concerning his parents. He screamed his vocals on that song with the fervor of a man determined to vomit out the cause of an infection.

But that approach wouldn't have worked with "Julia." It is, after all, a "song of love," and, regardless of where that love was meant to be directed, nobody did those kinds of songs better than this man and this group.

78. "Not a Second Time" (from *With the Beatles*, 1963)

Considering that the Beatles wrote many of the most memorable ballads of the rock era, it's somewhat surprising to note that it took them a little bit of time to get into the swing of it. There are slow songs on their first two albums, *Please Please Me* and *With the Beatles*, but they were all covers of the material of others, like "Anna (Go to Him)" and "Till There Was You."

What's ironic is that their biggest rivals for British rock supremacy, the Rolling Stones, took a little bit quicker to the slow stuff than the Beatles. Despite being known for the brashness and bluesy abandon of their original material, the first song that Mick Jagger and Keith Richards essentially wrote together was "As Tears Go By," which would be given to Marianne Faithfull before the Stones did it themselves with a "Yester-day"-style string section a year or so later. It was a ballad, as was "Tell Me," the group's first original song to chart in the United States.

By contrast, the Beatles' string of early hits and the bulk of their 1963 albums featured quick tempos, bright melodies, and pounding rhythms. It wasn't until *A Hard Day's Night*, their third album, released in 1964, that featured "And I Love Her" and "If I Fell," that the band started to get in touch with their sensitive side on the songs that they wrote themselves.

But *With the Beatles* does contain a kind of balladic precursor in "Not a Second Time." No, it doesn't really slow the tempo down too much, with John Lennon, who wrote the song, jumping into the vocals almost immediately and hustling the band through a pair of verses and refrains. Nor does it take a softer touch rhythmically, as Ringo Starr lays heavy on the hi-hat to prod along the verses while adding some crackling snare shots to connect the different sections of the song.

Despite those qualities, "Not a Second Time" feels partially like a ballad because it seems to come from a more personal place. Throughout the first couple albums, the Beatles wrote plenty of songs praising differ-ent types of girls in their efforts to create a kind of wish fulfillment for their throngs of teenage female listeners. Rarely did one of their early songs ever come off as accusatory toward the object of affection, but this intense rumbler certainly does.

Moreover there are far more clouds than sunshine in the melody. The song is a bit odd structure-wise, a not uncommon trait of Lennon's song-writing, lurching about from section to section without concern for what might be expected of it. Lennon instead worries more about conveying the depth of the narrator's wounds and how reluctant he is to suffer them again than about how it will all hang together musically. Hence you get some minor keys where you would expect the triumphant majors to be, along with George Martin's hushed piano solo in the instrumental break instead of ringing guitars.

Lennon's character in the song is drawing a line in the sand to prevent any hopes of reconciliation with the girl he's addressing, lest there be more pain coming his way. "And now you've changed your mind / I see no reason to change mine," he asserts. "My cry is through." It's a bit of an odd line; you'd expect "My crying's through." But Lennon's choice works, as it makes the act sound more like a primal plea rather than just your average tears.

"You're giving me the same old line," he continues in the chorus. "I'm wondering why." Enough skepticism has arisen inside him, based on her past behavior, to ensure that he won't fall for those old promises again. "You hurt me then, you're back again / No, no, no not a second time." Lennon sings this last line beautifully, starting out by expressing his torment with the repeated "no" before coming back down into a steadier, more assertive tone for the title phrase. That's the way it was, his voice suggests, and now this is the way it's going to be.

"Not a Second Time" may seem humble next to the more polished ballads the group would eventually write and perform. Heck, it might not even seem like a ballad at all, with its percussive feel and scarcity of lyrics. But it does point the way, rather effectively, to the more expressive songs from the heart in their near future. Known for saying "yeah, yeah, yeah" to all the pretty girls up to that point, the Beatles proved with this unheralded track that their ability to say "no, no, no" to a damaging relationship was equally convincing.

77. "Got to Get You into My Life" (from *Revolver*, 1966)

Among the formidable bands and artists in rock-and-roll history, the Beatles are relatively unique in that they recorded most of their music in the same location. The vast majority of the band's output was recorded at Abbey Road studios in London (the most notable exception being the *Let It Be* album). Even on the rare occasions they left Abbey Road to record elsewhere, it was only to venture somewhere else in England.

Considering the product that emanated from the band within the hallowed Abbey Road studios, it's hard to argue that their decision to stick within those friendly confines was ill advised. Yet one wonders what might have happened had they ventured to some other famous location to lay down some tracks, à la the Stones recording "Brown Sugar" at Muscle Shoals in Alabama.

It turns out that the Beatles were actually considering just such a recording change of scenery at one point. In 1966, the band looked into recording at the Stax Studio in Memphis, Tennessee, the same place from which some of the finest soul music of the decade, including classic sides and albums by Otis Redding, Sam and Dave, and many others, originated. The band's manager, Brian Epstein, looked into the possibility, but, as a newly unearthed letter from George Harrison shows, the Fab Four's reputation doomed their chances.

"Did you hear that we nearly recorded in Memphis with Jim Stewart?" Harrison wrote to Atlanta-based disc jockey Paul Drew in May 1966. (Stewart was co-owner of both Stax Records and the studio.) "We would all like it a lot, but too many people get insane with money ideas at the mention of the word 'Beatles,' and so it fell through."[11]

The album that the group was recording at the time of Harrison's letter was *Revolver*, which included "Got to Get You into My Life," the first Beatles' song to feature prominent brass instrumentation. While the Abbey Road version of the song is an undeniable winner, it's fun to imagine what kind of grit and groove might have been added by the maestros at Stax had the original plan come to fruition.

In any case, "Got to Get You into My Life," written by Paul McCartney, while George Martin provided the horn arrangement with McCartney's help, is a gleaming gem. The brass magnifies the exultation of the lyrics, blasting above everything else in the mix. From the opening notes, bursting with possibility, to the crescendos reached in the outro, these horns are sky-high.

And that's only fitting, because the song is McCartney's unfettered tribute to pot. He has admitted this in various interviews, but the lyrics aren't that hard to parse. If you just heard the chorus you might assume that the "you" in the song is a girl, but the verses make clear the intention. McCartney sings about "taking a ride" looking for "another road" where he could discover "another kind of mind."

"You didn't run, you didn't lie," he sings, comparing his drug of choice to the fickle humanity that lets him down. He also expresses his desire to avoid spending another day away from this entity he's addressing. There are even parts of the lyrics that simulate the kind of confusing logic that only someone stoned could truly understand: "If I am true I'll never leave / And if I do I know the way there."

While the content of the lyrics might raise eyebrows, the skill with which they're assembled should be lauded. This is another fast-talking McCartney track, à la "I've Just Seen a Face," in which the rat-a-tat words, instead of seeming jumbled and hurried, interlock until they're airtight. McCartney's nimble delivery assures that.

The musical structure is dominated by the horns to such an extent that only George Harrison's brief yet crackling guitar part pokes out to show its face; the rhythm section is largely subordinated here. Some might find fault with that mixing decision, but, again, those horns are such a weapon that trying to compete with them might have messed things up unnecessarily.

Brass accompaniment would become an increasingly bigger part of the band's studio repertoire in the years to come, to the point that parodies or approximations of the Beatles' signature sound these days usually include some sort of harrumphing horn or tripping trumpet. Yet "Got to Get You into My Life" might just be the Beatles at their brassiest, and not just because they were singing a love song to a recreational drug.

76. "You're Going to Lose That Girl" (from *Help!*, 1965)

Perspective is an underrated weapon in the songwriter's arsenal. By altering the perspective every now and again, a songwriter can make songs of similar subject matter sound different. The Beatles utilized this trick most famously on "She Loves You," which is written from the perspective of a would-be matchmaker trying to get a reticent guy to wise up and apologize to a girl who's still sweet on him.

There were actually many occasions when the Beatles would switch up the person speaking or the person being addressed, especially in the early years when they needed some way to produce variety. On their first five British albums or so, most of the songs concerned mostly the good and occasionally the bad of love and romance. As a result, finding different ways to attack the topic was paramount, and these guys were clever enough to figure that out early in the game.

On the *Help!* album, perhaps the last on which this kind of manipulation would be needed, the Beatles came at relationships from all kinds of angles. "Another Girl" had a guy addressing the girl he was about to dump for someone new; "You've Got to Hide Your Love Away" featured a brokenhearted sap commiserating with a crowd of onlookers about his crumbling love; and "You Like Me Too Much" took the cake in terms of perspective playfulness, with George Harrison singing in the first person but essentially putting words into the mouth of his paramour, making it kind of a combination of a love song and an act of ventriloquism.

John Lennon's "You're Going to Lose That Girl" also indulges in a skewed approach to a song about romance. Lennon plays the guy on the outside of a love triangle about to bust his way in. He lets his rival know his intentions and still comes off as somewhat innocent because he reveals that the shortcomings of the other guy, in terms of his relationship skills, are the reason this switcheroo is about to take place.

Lennon gets able backup in this mission from his bandmates Paul McCartney and Harrison, who provide refreshing responses with their backing vocals to the lead singer's not-so-veiled threats. For example, when Lennon sings, "I'll make a point of taking her away from you," the other two join in harmony and then quickly follow it up with "Watch what you do." The men's ability to so convincingly mimic girl-group vocals might seem surprising, but only to those who hadn't heard them do it on earlier cover songs like "Soldier of Love" and "Please Mr. Postman" with such aplomb.

While those vocals definitely dominate the recording, the musical backing pumps with freshness throughout as well. McCartney delivers his typically tuneful work on bass, upping the melodic quotient immeasurably when his lines bob to the surface out of the blue. Harrison takes a quick but piercing guitar solo, and Ringo Starr handles the song's swagger just fine with his backbeat. (As for his bongos, well, they must have seemed like a good idea at the time; at least they're buried in the mix for the most part.)

This is another song on the *Help!* album that seems to be leaning back to the early Beatles rather than pushing forward into their next era. The playful attitude the song evokes makes it a fun listen time and again. And it shows that they weren't hung up on gender roles in song; aside from the aforementioned flavor of the backing vocals, the sass and spunk Lennon delivers in his lyrics and vocals are a far cry from the macho posturing he could have taken. Why some female group or artist didn't dive on this one and change it around to "You're Going to Lose That Guy" back in the day is a mystery, but the opportunity still exists for it to happen.

The narrator's insinuations wouldn't have been possible without the neglect the other guy has shown toward the girl, so he's kind of on the right side of the argument anyway, even if his taunting is a little beyond the pale. "You're Going to Lose That Girl" rises above any such concerns thanks to the spunk of the performance and the novelty of the perspective.

75. "I Want You (She's So Heavy)" (from *Abbey Road,* 1969)

In 1969, Led Zeppelin released their self-titled debut album, thereby signaling that heavy metal had officially arrived from the primordial ooze from whence it came. Other bands had toyed around with the kind of thunderous approach to blues riffing that characterized the genre (the Beatles themselves had released "Helter Skelter," a wild, wailing mass of guitars and drums, the previous year on the White Album), but Zep attacked most of their early songs with the same reckless abandon for decorum, and there was no turning back once they hit the scene.

How much those sounds influenced the Beatles as they sat down to record "I Want You (She's So Heavy)" for *Abbey Road* later that year is up for speculation, but the coincidence is undeniable. John Lennon's evocation of romantic obsession, rendered in simplistic lyrical terms and mammoth musical terms, isn't all that far removed from the breezy-to-bludgeoning aesthetic of "Babe I'm Gonna Leave You" and other early Zeppelin stompers.

"I Want You (She's So Heavy)" belongs high on the list of most polarizing Beatles' songs. Some true believers likely hear the band at its instrumental zenith, giving musical life to the unquenchable fire in Lennon's loins for Yoko Ono. Others likely hear indulgence and monotony, the band straying from what they did best.

The definitive worth of the song probably lies somewhere in between those two extremes, which makes sense since it's probably best to analyze the song as two distinctly different movements shoved together. What you would call the verses, the bluesy, somewhat restrained sections of the song featuring Lennon's pleas of "I want you so bad / It's driving me mad," unfortunately validate the opinions of the song's detractors.

There is nothing really that the band does in those portions of the song that couldn't be pulled off by halfway decent blues noodlers around the world. Yes, Paul McCartney's bass runs are impressive, and Lennon's soloing is suitably soulful, if a bit low-key. But were the song to have stayed on this low boil the entire way, it's likely that no one would have given it too much attention in the long run.

Luckily, the band snaps out of that self-imposed torpor for the refrains, and those parts are where "I Want You" achieves true glory. Lennon and George Harrison's multitracked guitars keep blasting away at the same arpeggios as if the force behind playing them will bust down the doors holding the narrator back from the object of his lust. McCartney and Ringo Starr push the rhythmic rock steadily up the hill while some freaky organ swirls invade the dense tangle of sound created by the band.

You could argue that the verses build the tension and then the choruses achieve the release, but, in truth, the choruses provide the tension and release all at once, leaving the other portions somewhat superfluous. It is a pummeling sound that they create, one that is only intensified by the white noise from the Moog synthesizer that washes over them in the closing moments.

In typically inventive fashion, the band decided, instead of doing a typical fade-out, to have the song cut out completely when things had reached their most cacophonous point. It's startling even when you've heard the song a million times and should expect it.

Some might find fault with the one-note nature of Lennon's lyrics, but his all-in pursuit of Ono necessitated the directness he displays here. Many years down the road, Elvis Costello would follow a similar path on "I Want You," which adds a lot more lyrics but maintains the repetitiveness of the main phrase. The idea is that the single-mindedness that envelops someone in the throes of a torrid, all-consuming love affair can afford no tangents or sidetracks. Over and over and over again, the basic desire must be expressed, because the verbal manifestation of that desire is the only set of words that make any sense.

It's telling that "I Want You (She's So Heavy)" is one of the only Lennon contributions to *Abbey Road*; aside from "Come Together" and it, the rest of the writing he adds to the album were the fragments, many of which he already had lying around before recording was begun, that are stitched together in the side 2 medley. Part of the reason for his inaction was a car accident that kept him out of the studio for some of the sessions, but a bigger part seems to have been that he had already checked out of the band mentally and had turned all his attention to his life ahead with Yoko. This song is like the turn signal letting his fans know that he was about to veer off the Beatles' long and winding road.

Whatever the motive behind it, "I Want You (She's So Heavy)" likely will continue to spark debates about its merit for years to come. It's halfway meandering, halfway masterful, but you can't deny its heaviness.

74. "Paperback Writer" (from *Past Masters, Volume 2*, released as a single in 1966)

They weren't always world-beaters. Although they may have seemed to have simply burst onto the scene as fully formed superstars in the United Kingdom in 1963 and then the United States and just about everywhere else the following year, the Beatles had battled their way from obscurity to beat the odds and achieve huge success from humble beginnings.

During those leaner years prefame, enthusiasm would often sag and doubts would creep in about whether the big time would ever be within their grasp. According to John Lennon, the band would then need a little pep talk to get them going again. He is quoted in *Anthology* as saying, "When the Beatles were depressed, thinking, the group is going nowhere, and this is a shitty deal, and we're in a shitty dressing room . . . I'd say, 'Where are we going, fellas?' They'd go, 'To the top, Johnny!' And I'd say, 'Where's that, fellas?' and they'd say, 'To the toppermost of the poppermost!' and I'd say, 'Right!' Then we'd all cheer up."[12]

Still, the memories of those harder times must have persisted within the members of the group for some time even after they had reached that hypothetical apex. Clearly those memories inform "Paperback Writer," which depicts a guy with a desire for fame and fortune that seems to be a long shot gamble at the very best.

Paul McCartney came up with idea behind "Paperback Writer" and then received help fleshing it out from John Lennon. The two conceived the song as a long letter written from a would-be author to a publisher asking them to consider his new novel. As anyone who has ever endured this process knows, it requires a combination of boasting, flattering, and groveling, which makes it difficult to keep one's dignity intact. That self-debasement only makes rejection sting that much more if it arrives, which it does much more often than not, according to the percentages.

"Paperback Writer" captures all of those tactics as well as the creeping desperation that one who has poured his heart into a piece of work inevitably feels when its fate hangs in the balance. The narrator quickly blurts out that his book "took me years to write," as if that will have any bearing on the publisher's decision, and then also claims that "it's based on a novel by a man named Lear," which immediately calls into question his originality.

The second verse spouts out clichés that seem lifted from the hackiest book jacket, although he gets points for including a character wanting to be a writer as well, showing a little self-reflexivity well before it was popular. He later reveals that the book is a bit of a doorstop at one thousand pages, and he shows the lengths to which he will go to see his dream fulfilled: "I can change it round." In the final verse, his bravado ("It could make a million for you overnight") is contrasted by his grasp of cold reality ("If you must return it you can send it here"). You can get whiplash following this guy's train of thought, but such is the eager-to-please, frantic behavior of someone trying to catch his or her big break.

This all could have been musically framed in a folky kind of way, à la a Ray Davies slice-of-life Kinks song, but the Beatles chose to turn up the heat with some of the most crunching rock and roll of their middle period. "Paperback Writer" gives a master class on how to generate interest in a song right from the start. McCartney, Lennon, and George Harrison form an a cappella, multitracked chorale on the title to start, coming at it from all angles high and low. Harrison then tears into a meaty riff, and Ringo Starr comes busting out of the gate with a go-go beat. McCartney's bass then flickers to life, which signals that it's time for the main portion of the song to begin. The group must have known they had something juicy in that beginning, because they ended up repeating it twice more in the song.

After that it's just a matter of McCartney's character making his futile case while his buddies have some fun behind him. (Listen closely in the second half of the song for Lennon and Harrison singing a falsetto version of "Frère Jacques" for backing vocals.) The urgency of the churning music dovetails beautifully with the narrator's need for publication. "Paperback Writer" finds the Beatles coasting along at the "toppermost" of their game, even as it hints at a previous time when they feared they'd never escape the bottom.

73. "Octopus's Garden" (from *Abbey Road*, 1969)

As the Beatles headed into the making of 1969's *Abbey Road*, which would turn out to be the last album they recorded (*Let It Be* was recorded prior but released after), their drummer, Ringo Starr, had but three songwriting credits to his name with the band. There was "What Goes On," a jovial, if routine, country number from 1965's *Rubber Soul*, on which he received writing help from John Lennon and Paul McCartney; "Flying," a slight instrumental from 1967's *Magical Mystery Tour* that was credited to all four members of the band; and "Don't Pass Me By," a lurching oddity of a track that could only have been found on 1968's White Album and was his first solo songwriting effort.

None of those songs were classics, to put it kindly. Although the fairy dust that was sprinkled on all Beatles' music helped, nothing about these tracks indicated that the world would be missing an essential songwriting voice if Starr had simply clammed up and left the writing to others from that point. Luckily for us, if a bit unpleasantly for him, a spat with his bandmates inspired him to write a truly winning Beatles' track in "Octopus's Garden."

Starr briefly walked out of the sessions for the White Album in 1968 when the heaviness between the group members became a little too much for him to bear. During his couple weeks away, he took a holiday on a yacht provided by actor Peter Sellers. It was then and there that a conversation with the boat captain left Starr feeling he had something in common with the octopuses below him in the sea. "He told me that they hang out in their caves and they go around the seabed finding shiny stones and tin cans and bottles to put in front of their cave like a garden," Starr remembered in *Anthology*. "I thought this was fabulous, because at the time I just wanted to be under the sea too."[13]

For all of the rancor that led to the song's creation, "Octopus's Garden" engenders nothing but the warmest of feelings on playback. Part of this is due to Starr's naturally good humor and sweet disposition on the microphone. But the song itself is a surprisingly sturdy construct, simple chords around an affecting melody with just a little bit of melancholy clinging to the goodwill in the lyrics.

His bandmates also chip in with charismatic performances of their own. George Harrison's guitar work—including the stop and start intro and a crisp, chipper solo—takes some Chet Atkins licks and skims them across the ocean surface. Starr and McCartney form a choogling rhythm section while Lennon and McCartney provide the sighing backing vocals, all "oohs" and "aahs" that are relaxation incarnate. The group even adds underwater effects in the instrumental break, thanks to some studio trickery; you'll swear on listening that you can smell the salt air.

Starr imagines an idyllic existence below sea level, full of dancing and laughing and sleeping on the ocean bed. The octopus host "knows where we've been," a phrase that hints that the former world these travelers left behind wore them down. "We would be warm below the storm," he sings, and you have to believe that the metaphorical storm above is considered far more problematic than anything the weather can conjure.

Although the main verses float along in tranquility, the sudden chord change before the refrain is somewhat startling. It forces Starr to raise his vocal above the gentle croon he maintained in the verses, and at these points in the song, you can hear that his urge to get away from it all has as much to do with what he's escaping as it does with his new destination. He sings, "We would be so happy you and me / No one there to tell us what to do," and it's easy to locate in those lines Starr's own personal feelings about his place in the band and the toxic atmosphere that had crept into what was once a tight unit.

But that brief moment of tension quickly dissipates with the refrain, as he joins his musical brothers in harmony to once again express his desire to be back in the garden. "Octopus's Garden" gave just a taste of what could be expected of Ringo Starr as a songwriter and front man; his solo success in the early 1970s, which often outdid, commercially anyway, the efforts of his bandmates (who, it must be noted, provided Ringo ample assistance in those exploits) proved it was no fluke. How ironic that it took a near band breakup for him to find his voice.

72. "Let It Be" (from *Let It Be*, 1970)

For the record, there are three versions of "Let It Be" from which Beatles fans can choose: the version released as the Beatles' final single until the *Anthology* reunion twenty-five years later, the version used on the *Let It Be* album, and the version found on *Let It Be . . . Naked*, Paul McCartney's attempt to de-Spectorize the album over which he had lost control decades earlier. That's not to mention an early take found on *Anthology*— and heaven knows how many alternate takes are circulating around the Internet.

All of this illustrates in some weird way how the *Let It Be* album, or *Get Back*, or whatever you want to call it, never had any chance of realizing its full potential. There were about nineteen different people making decisions on the group's product in those sad final days, and none of those voices seemed to be in agreement. Hence the mishmash of out-takes and overdubs and after-the-fact production decisions that made it hard to hear what in tarnation the original songs were supposed to sound like.

Let's be clear though: "Let It Be" has flaws in any version, which is why a song so hallowed by many occupies a relatively modest spot on this list. First of all, the song strives for anthemic status à la "Hey Jude" but doesn't earn it naturally. Second, the incorporation of the full band into this ballad never occurs smoothly in any of the existing versions; there always seems to be a struggle between the intimate emotions the song wants to express and the guitars and drums and brass muscling into the picture.

Which leads us to the other major issue that plagues the song, which is the writing itself. "Let It Be" works when it's about a man struggling with pressure and receiving some sort of spiritual aide in the times when he needs it most. Yet in the second verse, Paul McCartney, who wrote the song, tries to pull the whole world into the picture, uniting all the "brokenhearted" and promising them that "There will be an answer." It feels presumptuous and as though it's too big a leap for the song to make. (The clichéd rhymes in that section don't help matters either.)

Yet for all these flaws, the potency of "Let It Be" at its finest moments is undeniable, and it still possesses that power to encourage and uplift all these years later. McCartney, struggling internally with his band's gradual dissolution and the pressure he felt in trying to keep it together, saw his mother, Mary McCartney, who had passed away in 1956 when Paul was just fourteen, in a dream. The song the dream inspired was as close to gospel as the band would ever come. (John Lennon claimed in interviews that McCartney was trying to rewrite "Bridge Over Troubled Water," but, considering recording on "Let It Be" began in early 1969 and that classic Simon and Garfunkel song didn't arrive until 1970, the timing makes this unlikely.)

"When I find myself in times of trouble / Mother Mary comes to me / Speaking words of wisdom / Let it be," McCartney begins. She is there for him in his "hour of darkness." Later he speaks of a light shining on him in cloudy skies. And he wakes from his dream "to the sound of music." These are simple, moving lines, his own experience directly expressed and yet resonant to all who seek succor in the midst of trying times of their own. Calling on the whole world to join him in the second verse is just redundant; his own personal experience is enough to draw anyone listening into the tale and make clear his belief in something beyond the physical realm that can soften the world's harshest blows.

If you have to choose a version of the song, your best bet is probably the version found on the *Let It Be* album. George Harrison's guitar solo is a jangly gem on this take; Billy Preston's organ parts the heavens; and Phil Spector's production tics, so maligned (and often with good reason) by McCartney, George Martin, and other Beatle enthusiasts over the years, actually work well here, as the echo on Ringo Starr's drums magnifies the portent of McCartney's pronouncements.

Alas, none of the versions, even the supposedly stripped-down *Naked* take, really capture the fragile, yearning tone that would have best suited the song. Maybe the only thing that could have would have been a McCartney solo performance on piano. The Beatles might have preached "Let It Be" to the world in one of their final musical statements, but it turns out that practicing what they preached in those tumultuous times was much easier sung than done.

71. "I'm Down" (from *Help!*, 1965)

Long before they were studio craftsmen, the Beatles were live aces. From Germany to Liverpool and all points in between for a span of five years or so, they honed their performance skills in front of audiences that ran the gamut from rabid to hostile to indifferent. And they learned well how to construct a live show, when to dial up the energy and when to pull it back, and what kind of set list was be needed for a particular type of crowd.

They also learned the importance of a great showstopper, which was often a raucous piece of rock-and-roll or rhythm and blues history that was more screamed than sung. The group could drop this song in at the end of a show to leave the crowd wanting more or at any point the enthusiasm of the audience might be waning. Since they patterned their early albums as more precise but still animated versions of their concerts, it's no surprise that both *Please Please Me* ("Twist and Shout") and *With the Beatles* ("Money (That's What I Want)") ended with these types of songs. Even as far into their career as *Help!*, the Beatles decided not to close things out with "Yesterday," instead inserting a bombastic version of "Dizzy Miss Lizzy" as the final number.

All of the aforementioned songs were sung by John Lennon, but Paul McCartney proved he could knock out a good screamer or two with his wild and woolly takes on "Long Tall Sally" and "Hey-Hey-Hey-Hey." McCartney decided in 1965 that he'd try his hand at writing one of his own belters so that the band wouldn't remain beholden to cover songs to fill that space in their concerts. And wouldn't you know he killed it at first asking with "I'm Down," which raises the roof without skimping on cleverness or craft.

McCartney's clear inspiration for "I'm Down" was Little Richard, whose whooping and hollering style is mimicked in Macca's vocal pyrotechnics here. But this isn't just a screamfest; McCartney makes sure to write a trio of couplets that range from authentically bluesy to charmingly cheeky, telling his tale of a suitor in the doldrums while the object of his affection takes pleasure in his suffering.

"You tell lies thinking I can't see / You don't cry 'cause you're laughing at me," he begins, setting up the extreme difference between the two. He then adds a grizzled assessment of a typical relationship: "Man buys ring, woman throws it away / Same old thing happens every day." Finally, he admits that some of his frustrations are sexual in nature: "We're all alone and there's nobody else / You still moan, 'Keep your hands to yourself.'" These lines seem tossed-off and effortless, but a closer listen reveals the nuance of the internal rhyme, an example of McCartney paying attention to detail even at his most off-the-cuff.

Of course, a song intended be to a rabble-rouser needs to have ingratiatingly insane music to back it up, and "I'm Down" easily clears this bar. After McCartney sets the tone with an a cappella bleating of the first line, the rest of the band kicks in headlong at a furious pace. Matters intensify in the instrumental breaks. First George Harrison blasts through one of his most forceful solos; usually known for the precision of his playing, here Harrison concentrates on gritty gusto. Later John Lennon takes over with an organ solo as messy as it is magical. Apparently he took McCartney's exhortation to "Hurry up, John" to heart and played like he was trying to propel his instrument airborne. Ringo Starr adds a crashing beat and some off-kilter touches (Did they have a bargain on bongos when they were making *Help!* or what?) while the backing vocals, which include Lennon's hilarious low bass note on the word "down," are wacky and wonderful as well.

The Beatles are having so much fun on the recording that they just can't seem to let it go, repeating the chorus several times over at the end before the fade-out finally interrupts. It's a good thing it did, because

McCartney was absolutely going to town in this section, pushing his vocals to places that must have impressed even Little Richard himself.

"I'm Down," which ended up the B-side to the "Help!" single, would indeed take its place in the group's live shows, most famously at their Shea Stadium gig where McCartney and Harrison cracked up at Lennon playing the organ with his elbows. They could still stop the show at that later stage, only by that time, it was with an original song that stacked up well against, and even surpassed, some of the old standbys.

70. "Happiness Is a Warm Gun" (from *The Beatles*, 1968)

John Lennon was an art school student, and that's relevant to his music because it seems like he looked at songwriting in much the same way an artist or a painter would like at a blank canvas. There aren't really any rules in place for artists, and they are bound only by what their mind's eye can imagine. Lennon had a mind's ear, if there is such a thing, that attacked his songs in the same way.

None of the Beatles were trained in music in any way, so they had few preconceived notions of how their songs were supposed to go other than by comparing them to what they heard on the radio. But Lennon seemed nonplussed by even that when he wrote songs, as his material regularly either broke rules or simply chose to ignore them. Yet he ended up writing, both by himself and with Paul McCartney, some of the most memorable and important songs in the rock-and-roll era.

"Happiness Is a Warm Gun," found on 1968's double-disc whopper called *The Beatles* but known as the White Album, demonstrated Lennon's skewed approach as well as any song. There are at least four distinct sections of the song jammed together without much concern for transition from one part to the next. Mournful folk gives way to clanging rock, which then yields to a bluesy rant, which finally relents in favor of soul testifying with doo-wop backing vocals. Time signatures change at will, tempos shift randomly. It's difficult to tell which part is the verse and which is the middle eight, and after the chorus the song ends abruptly.

Yet there's not a moment of the track that isn't fascinating, even if it's in a weird kind of way. The title of the song arose from the cover of a magazine that producer George Martin brought into the studio. Lennon thought it was a fantastic and morbid phrase, although the song ends up using it to connote sexual release rather than violence.

But that only comes at the end. First Lennon uses a clichéd British compliment ("She's not a girl who misses much") to launch into some of his most surrealistic lyrics yet. If the words in "Lucy in the Sky with Diamonds" represent a psychedelic experience at its most colorfully trippy, this section of "Happiness Is a Warm Gun" hints at the nightmarish comedown, loaded as it is with sinister characters and depraved images. The guitars in this section keep prattling loudly against Lennon's lyrics, and they're played here more for blunt force than for any melodic sweetness.

At that point, the pace drags to a crawl, and George Harrison starts bending his notes like a sorcerer, spiraling downward into the drug-fueled abyss that Lennon begins to describe: "I need a fix 'cause I'm going down." But just before he hits rock bottom, he and the music perk up on the repeated line: "Mother Superior jumped the gun." Lennon was referring to Yoko Ono, whom he called "Mother" as a term of endearment, and her presence seems to pull the narrator back toward the light.

It could have been noted at any point in the description of this song, but let's take the time here to say that Ringo Starr's ability to handle all of Lennon's swerves and feints and keep the beat intact can't be understated. The last of these moves takes us into the jubilant portion of the song, as Lennon finally gets to the title, which turns out to bear little connection to the rest of the track. Nonetheless, it inspires him to rattle off a series of double entendres about fingers on triggers and the like while the backing vocals get into the act as well ("Bang, bang, shoot, shoot").

Through it all, Lennon's vocal performance holds the song together; he's convincingly dismal and small at the start, edgy and mischievous in the center, exultant and triumphant in the closing. The last sustained falsetto note might just even be his winking way of acknowledging that his narrator has achieved the sexual satisfaction that seemed to be compelling him through this entire bizarre journey.

Someone reading this description without ever hearing the song might assume it was a total train wreck. Perhaps that's only fitting, considering Lennon's famously disdainful quote about those who attempt to analyze music. (Look it up yourselves; this is a family book, folks.) You just have to listen to "Happiness Is a Warm Gun" to believe it and appreciate it, and you'll likely wind up appreciating the idiosyncratic side of John Lennon's songwriting along the way.

69. "I Will" (from *The Beatles*, 1968)

Even though it was the third album from the last that they recorded and released, the White Album, from 1968, is the record on which you can most clearly hear the Beatles breaking up. *Let It Be*, even if it sounds uninspired and exhausted at times, gives the impression of togetherness because the concept behind the album required all four members contributing to the songs at the same time. And *Abbey Road*, drenched as it was with interlocking songs and heavenly harmonies, feigns unity between the band members so well that it's hard to believe actual relations between the four had become fractious enough that the decision to break up would come hard on the heels of its recording.

The White Album, released in 1968, featured many songs that the individual group members wrote while in India visiting the Maharishi. They generally continued working on those songs when they reached the studio almost as if they were singer-songwriters employing a backing band to help out (or sometimes completing the songs on their own without any help from the others). As a result, the double album gave a glimpse into what the early solo careers of the group's three chief songwriter's would look like.

For John Lennon, there were hints of the lacerating rock ("Yer Blues") and intensely intimate slow stuff ("Julia") that would appear on *John Lennon/Plastic Ono Band* and *Imagine*. George Harrison demonstrated an early feel for the stately, resonant work ("While My Guitar Gently Weeps," "Long, Long, Long") that would appear all over *All Things Must Pass*.

Perhaps even more than Lennon and Harrison, Paul McCartney provided the blueprint for his early solo material, in particular *McCartney* and *Ram*, the two albums he would release in the interim between the Beatles' breakup and the formation of his 1970s band Wings. And it wasn't so much the type of material that tipped his hand, even if on the White Album one could find McCartney-penned ballads, rockers, and novelty-type numbers that would presage the work he would do on his own.

What McCartney already had down pat on the White Album was his knack for making his songs sound homemade and tossed off. Even if the song took a lot of work, as was the case with the tender slow one "I Will," the end result seemed like a ditty that McCartney wrote and recorded in less time that it took for his afternoon tea to warm. And that rough-hewn, back-porch quality carried a great deal of charm.

It helped when the song on which the approach was used was crafted as expertly as "I Will." Clocking in at about fifteen seconds shy of two minutes (which only adds to the off-the-cuff feel), the song makes every moment count, riding a lilting melody all the way to heart-tugging territory. McCartney's grasp of the subtleties of a love song, such as knowing when to be playful and when to be sentimental, understanding how to inject just a bit of sorrow to the mix to make the happy ending even sweeter, and finding new ways to say something that's been said countless times before, finds a fine outlet in this understated, underrated number.

The neat thing about "I Will," the thing that you probably miss unless you follow the lyrics closely, is that it appears to be an ode to a girl that the narrator hasn't yet met. In the first verse, he asks, "Will I wait a lonely lifetime / If you want me to, I will." He then starts the second verse with "For if I never saw you / Or didn't catch your name."

Perhaps these are just hypothetical situations he's posing, but they work in any case as a testament to the devotion that those who are truly in love unconditionally display. He gets away with the clichés of the middle eight because, having set up the situation in this way, you believe he means every word of them. (Plus McCartney does his usual bang-up job of melding those oft-said words to the meter so snugly that they sound brand-new.)

McCartney's accompaniment on this journey is mostly just acoustic guitar, Ringo Starr's bongos, and his own vocalized bass notes. This last touch really ups the homespun ante: it's as if he couldn't be bothered to go get an actual bass and just improvised to get it done.

At the end of the song, as the narrator imagines eventually meeting this captivating girl, McCartney soars up into falsetto and does some impromptu scatting, once again making it seem like the whole thing was being created on the spot. The recording logs show that "I Will" took two days and upward of seventy takes to create a finished product. The audible evidence, however, sounds like a guy serenading a girl over a campfire. It's a sound to which Paul McCartney would return when he.no longer had his Beatle buddies around and he sounded like a one-man band because he actually was one.

68. "Good Morning Good Morning" (from *Sgt. Pepper's Lonely Hearts Club Band*, 1967)

In typically askew *Sgt. Pepper's* fashion, "Good Morning Good Morning" appears near the end of the show, right before the sergeant leads his band out for a reprise of their theme song and they segue into the closing number "A Day in the Life." Also typical is John Lennon's post-Beatles dismissal of this song; if we've learned anything from the list so far, it's that Lennon was perhaps the most unreliable and inaccurate critic of both his own work and that of his band.

Sometimes it takes an outside perspective to see what's going on in the song, since a person's subconscious often remains hidden to nobody but themselves. Paul McCartney provided just such a perspective on "Good Morning Good Morning" in his recollection from *Many Years from Now*: "John was feeling trapped in suburbia and was going through some problems with [first wife] Cynthia. It was about his boring life at the time—there's a reference in this lyrics to 'nothing to do' and 'meet the wife'; there was an afternoon TV soap called *Meet The Wife* that John watched, he was that bored, but I think he was also starting to get alarm bells."[14]

While it's hard to imagine a Beatle having a boring life, Lennon certainly makes a convincing case. His song, which grabbed its title from a Kellogg's commercial to really amplify the banality, starts morbidly with the death of a house husband: "Nothing to do to save his life call his wife in." The following line, "Nothing to say but what a day how's your boy been," equates the death with the trivial small talk that neighbors make when they're at a loss to say anything of meaning. In this way, Lennon quickly establishes the mood of ennui that permeates the song.

His protagonist, whom he renders in the second person to make every listener at home going through the same doldrums stand up and take notice, can't bear the thought of going to work, but a deviation through town doesn't provide much solace: "Everybody knows there's nothing doing / Everything is closed it's like a ruin / Everyone you see is half asleep." Lennon is intimating that the suburban drones know that they're living lives of quiet desperation, as Thoreau suggested, but they ignore it because the truth is too depressing to bear.

The protagonist eventually starts to perk up; it's as if Lennon couldn't bear to keep the song so dark and chose to see the bright side of the life he was describing and living. He keeps reassuring us that "it's OK" at the end of every verse. Maybe there's even some comfort to be taken from the fact that "nothing had changed it's still the same." By the end of the song, he's gladly giving out the time to passersby and getting excited about meeting a girl at a show.

If there is a whiff of boredom about this fellow's daily activity and the nagging sense that the routine of his life isn't that thrilling anymore, the music eradicates it with its irresistible forward thrust. "Good Morning Good Morning" starts with a battle charge of horns and doesn't let up for a moment. Ringo Starr provides snap-to-attention drum breaks, while McCartney takes a guitar solo that's all wiry energy finally let out of the bottle. The head rush provided by the horns is undeniable, and then Lennon takes us on a wild animal chase at the end of the song thanks to a series of animal sound effects. If nothing else, this heady mess of sound and furry fury seems destined to wake up all the neighbors from their somnambulant lifestyle.

"Good Morning Good Morning" thus works on a couple levels. You can simply enjoy the mad dash of the music, which never allows you to catch your breath and thrills at every step of the way from the first rooster crow to the moment the animal sounds morph into the opening guitar note of the "Sgt. Pepper's" reprise. Or you can dig deep into the middle of that maelstrom and hear the strangled cry of a guy bored out his skull with the old routine.

67. "Helter Skelter" (from *The Beatles*, 1968)

Let's get this out of the way right up front: whatever associations or messages that Charles Manson drew out of the song, "Helter Skelter" had no sinister or ominous intent behind it. Discussing it any further in that context might lend some kind of credence to that silly theory, so let's move on from there.

The genesis of "Helter Skelter" was an interview that Pete Townsend of the Who gave, talking up the band's latest song, which he promised would be second to none in terms of loudness and heaviness. Paul

McCartney interpreted that quote as a gauntlet being thrown down, one he and his bandmates gladly picked up. Having accepted the challenge, McCartney wrote a song that the Fab Four could suitably desecrate with their wildest, loudest, most unhinged playing ever.

After multiple furious jam sessions on the song, some of which lasted nearly a half hour, the ferocious beast that was "Helter Skelter" was eventually corralled into a four-and-a-half-minute edit and squeezed onto the second disc of the White Album, because, really, where else would it be? While it's a bit shy in quality of the song about which Townsend was boasting ("I Can See for Miles," which carried a pretty potent message in the midst of its madness), it may indeed outstrip it in terms of its deranged dedication to pushing all the needles into the red.

The opening guitar riff and drums set the tone, building to a climax as McCartney tells his tale that's ostensibly about a fairground ride but seems meant to mimic a particularly intense sexual escapade. The narrator is somewhat callous in his dismissal of this girl ("You may be a lover but you ain't no dancer"), but that doesn't stop him from going up and down that slide over and over again, the constant climaxing of the music seconding that notion in blunt fashion.

"Helter Skelter" provides an excellent showcase for McCartney to show off his wilder side. The "nice Beatle" seemed to take great enjoyment at undercutting this image when he had the opportunity, and you can tell he relishes every moment of this insane jam. There's not a moment when he's not teetering on the edge of blowing out his vocal cords, yet the inherent tunefulness of the song, even with somewhat simplistic if forceful playing and bashing behind it, keeps things from going too far off the rails.

John Lennon plays bass on this rare occasion, with McCartney helping out George Harrison on guitar. Lennon's moaning notes lay out a thick bottom half of the song, while the guitars simply freak out above him when they're not indulging in those downward-spiraling riffs in the refrain. Ringo Starr takes to the cymbals like he's trying to break them in half; no wonder he complained about his blisters at the end of the song.

That final portion of the song really stands out as it keeps fading and rising again, as if the engineers keep thinking the thing is over only to have the jamming continue unbeknownst to them. Lennon for no good reason other than to add to the anything-goes spirit of the song grabs a tenor sax and wails away briefly. The multiple false endings really do make you believe that this was a session that wouldn't end, even if the finished product comes in at a reasonable length.

The White Album often featured the band members working independently of each other to finish songs, but "Helter Skelter" is a notable exception, as everybody pitched in to try to realize McCartney's anarchic vision. Well done by the boys that they were able to bash away like they'd never done before but still keep it coherent enough that we're willing to take the ride with them over and over again.

66. "I Need You" (from *Help!*, 1965)

George Harrison's songwriting career took a while to get started, then took just a little bit longer to really hit the heights. It's important to remember that Harrison was a little younger than the Beatles' principal songwriters John Lennon and Paul McCartney. That duo attained such impressive levels of proficiency with their original songs so quickly that it was difficult for Harrison to compete.

There was a reason he was known as the quiet Beatle; speaking up in song with those two as the impossible standards he would have to meet could only result in unfair comparisons and, perhaps, a lack of confidence in his own unique songwriting voice. So waiting and developing that voice over time proved to be a wise move and one that enabled Harrison to reach, by the time the decade ended, approximately the same level of songwriting acumen as his two highly lauded bandmates. (You could make a case that the two finest complete songs on *Abbey Road*, the group's last album, belonged to Harrison.)

So it was that *Please Please Me*, the group's first album, contained no credits for Harrison. On *With the Beatles* from 1963, Harrison wrote his first tune with the band, an odd little number called "Don't Bother Me," which combined a go-go beat with some rather sour pronouncements about wanting to be alone. If nothing else, the song displayed a point of view far different from Lennon's or McCartney's, even if the finished product was lacking compared to their best early work.

Harrison then sat out, in terms of writing, both of the Beatles' 1964 albums. That time must have been spent honing his songwriting chops, because from that point forward, every Beatle album contained at least one Harrison song worthy of hanging with the best Lennon/McCartney had to offer. "I Need You," from 1965's *Help!*, was the song that started it all.

"I Need You" boasted an easy, melancholy prettiness and a vocal performance by Harrison of great warmth and vulnerability. It also benefitted from the group's growing dexterity in the studio, where they had learned to experiment with different methods of attaining the sounds they heard in their heads.

In the case of "I Need You," the key effect is Harrison's twelve-string electric guitar with the sound altered by a volume pedal. This technique gave the guitar a soft, yearning quality as it played the main four-note riff throughout the song. It also made it more of an easy fit with the smoothly strummed acoustic guitars. Paul McCartney's quick-footed bass locked in with the homemade percussion of Ringo Starr as he banged the back of a guitar case. John Lennon helped Starr out by hitting the snare drum when needed, and Ringo also added some cowbell in the bridge for a little bit of percussive flavor.

While Harrison's lyrics aren't that complicated, he sings them with such honesty that you feel like you're eavesdropping on a late-night phone call to his estranged lover. "I could never really live without you," he admits, regretting his mistakes and hoping that the girl gives him another chance. "Please come on back to me / I'm lonely as can be," he admits, and later goes even deeper into a funk: "And feeling like this, I just can't go anymore."

Lennon and McCartney sing gorgeous wordless harmonies behind him, but Harrison's vocal conveys all you need to know. When he sings "I need you" three times at the end of the song, with the reverberating guitar sound interrupting his utterances, you can hear the desperation and pain beneath the straightforwardness of the statement. When you sing a tune as sturdy as that and do it as well as Harrison does, extra words would only complicate the emotion.

As if the Beatles' music didn't already enjoy an embarrassment of riches, adding a third songwriter as great as Harrison almost wasn't fair to their rock competition. "I Need You" may have paved the way for more well-known Harrison classics throughout the years, but it shouldn't be overlooked in its own right as one of the group's finest midperiod ballads.

65. "Getting Better" (from *Sgt. Pepper's Lonely Hearts Club Band*, 1967)

By 1967, the days of John Lennon and Paul McCartney churning out hit singles by writing face-to-face in a room together were pretty much done. Yet they also hadn't reached the point where they were a songwriting partnership in name only. Many of the group's finest songs of their ridiculously rich middle period emanated from a different kind of collaboration, one in which one of the two would start a song and the other would then add his vital contribution, by editing, perhaps adding a middle eight, or sometimes just suggesting a line or two to improve the finished product.

Occasionally that process led to songs that displayed little bits of the sensibilities of both men. "Getting Better," as sure a pop shot as you'll find on the legendary *Sgt. Pepper's Lonely Hearts Club Band*, is just such a song. McCartney began the writing and started the song on a primrose path. Lennon got ahold of it and ensured there would be some thorns hidden along that path. That combination made the song's eventual happy outcome that much sweeter, because it was so hard earned.

"Getting Better" sets up as a tug-of-war between the hard-luck verses and the optimistic refrains, with the bouncy music tipping the balance to the latter. The chirpy staccato guitar part that introduces the song is an immediate, ingratiating wake-up call. McCartney's bass rubbernecks giddily from the lower depths to higher altitudes in the verses as Ringo Starr handles the herky-jerky beat. One thing that's immediately noticeable is the space left between the instruments; whereas the Beatles formerly took a full-speed-ahead, all-hands-on-deck approach to midtempo numbers like this one, the less-is-more strategy they utilize here pays dividends, amplifying both the cleverness of the instrumentalists and the sturdiness of the tune.

In each of the first two verses, the narrator explains his problems, some out of his control and some of his own doing. He complains about the poor treatment he received at school; Lennon adds the word "fools" to bookend McCartney's comment about the teachers "filling me up with their rules." The second verse finds him reminiscing about his days as an "angry young man," McCartney using the slangy "me" for a little bit of unorthodoxy. His contention that "I'm doing the best that I can" springboards the listener into the chorus.

That chorus features the dichotomy between McCartney and Lennon in a nutshell, as McCartney sings the refrain of "I have to admit it's getting better, a little better all the time," to which Lennon answers in playful falsetto, "It can't get no worse." Obviously neither Lennon nor McCartney was ever so one-sided in songwriting or in life that they could be boiled down to a simple generality, but you could do worse, if you had to shorthand to an alien what made their partnership so simpatico, than by playing him that line.

The final verse opens with the drone of George Harrison's tambura, a sudden change in the sonic texture that clues the listener in to the import of the following line. "I used to be cruel to my woman / I beat her and kept her apart from the things that she loved." It's a bracing line, one that comes out of the blue in what had seemed like a pretty benign song up to that point, and even though the narrator follows up by admitting his regrets, it very nearly disturbs the fragile balance the song had struck to that point.

What makes the line even more surprising is that McCartney sang it even though it was Lennon's experience that inspired it. "I used to be cruel to my woman," Lennon admitted to *Playboy* interviewer David Sheff in 1980. "I was a hitter. I couldn't express myself and I hit. I fought men and I hit women." Later in the interview, Lennon went on to say, "I will have to be a lot older before I can face in public how I treated women as a youngster."[15]

The fact that he was apologetic then and that the narrator is similarly sorry in the song doesn't excuse the act in any case, even though Lennon's honesty, in the song and the interview, is admirable. It's also important to remember that we currently live in more enlightened times concerning this topic and that the abuse of women engendered far more casual reactions at the time "Getting Better" was written; it's doubtful the line would have made it into the song in 2016.

In any case, the rueful tone the lyrics strike immediately after save the song from being swallowed up by the admission. Once "Getting Better" rises back into that triumphantly hopeful chorus, the shadow fades. That startling admission aside, it's a song that's immeasurably deeper than your average pop trifle because of the bitter that Lennon adds to McCartney's better.

64. "Girl" (from *Rubber Soul*, 1965)

Rubber Soul is the album that in 1965 cemented the Beatles' progression from head-bobbing rock-and-rollers to contemplative studio artists. While that may sound like a boring transition to some, the inherent charisma and copious amounts of musical ingenuity the band possessed ensured that even when they were engaging in deep thoughts, they could still make music as invigorating and indelible as anything they did when they were hammering away at their instruments and hollering out their lyrics.

If they hadn't made this transition, it's hard to imagine gentle gems like "Girl" ever existing. Written primarily by John Lennon, with a solid assist from Paul McCartney, "Girl" is one of many songs that men have written about unnamed females who frustrate, tantalize, charm, and generally befuddle them until their only recourse is to lay it all down in song and pick up the graying hairs from the bathroom sink.

Just from the previous books in the Counting Down series alone, we could take Bob Dylan's "Just Like a Woman," Bruce Springsteen's "Secret Garden," and the Rolling Stones' "Ruby Tuesday" and plop them down in the same category. Add Billy Joel's "She's Always a Woman" and, many years down the road and coming from a more positive but still wondrous point of view, Lennon's solo song "Woman." There are far too many others to mention, but you get the gist here: these songs are a dime a dozen, but, when done correctly, they offer a mixture of praise and exasperation that summarizes the efforts of men to know the unknowable about the opposite gender.

"Girl" is a downright lovely acoustic effort from the group. The verses are rendered with more than a little tension, Lennon's vocal querying and questing for answers that never come. In the refrains, the ice breaks and the sighing vocals reveal relief, with Lennon's exaggerated breath making it seem like he can intake air for the first time in months. Then it's back to the verses, and the cycle begins all over again, a stellar approximation of the ebb and flow of man's grasp of the subtleties of womankind.

Lennon begins by reaching out to his audience as if they might have heard this one before: "Is there anybody going to listen to my story / All about the girl who came to stay?" He then elucidates the first of many contrasts that this girl in particular presents to him: "She's the kind of girl you want so much it makes you sorry / Still you don't regret a single day."

In the second verse, he admits that he has attempted to get away from the cycle of triumph and torment that his relationship offers, only to be drawn back in out of sympathy for her tears. When he explains, "And she promises the Earth to me and I believe her / After all this time I don't know why," it doesn't necessarily imply that she's deceiving him so much as he's gullible for falling for promises she can't possibly deliver.

The bridge, with McCartney and George Harrison undercutting the solemnity with a refrain of "tit," adds more fuel to the narrator's ardor; her casual cruelty and disconcerted air when praised, instead of pushing him away, only makes him want her more. And again it lets out into the deep sigh of relief of the chorus, as if he was frightened for a moment that she actually had escaped his life, only to look and see her smiling from the other room.

Much has been made of the final verse's supposed dig at Christianity, with its lines about pain leading to pleasure and the necessity of suffering before salvation. Yet that final verse can also be interpreted in terms of the demands that the girl puts on him, the notion that all the various acts of kindness and heedless sacrifices he's performed, which are ultimately intended to finally win him her good graces, might only lead him to the grave. It's a cynical version of either Christianity or marriage, but either way the argument is made quite well.

There's a case to me made, however, that the most convincing argument made by "Girl" comes when the lyrics drop away for a Greek-style instrumental interlude featuring Harrison's twelve-string guitar. It's a gorgeous segment, one that suggests the intensity of the emotions, both good and bad, roiling in the narrator for this girl. It lets out eventually into another sigh and the fade-out, but the evidence the song has already put forth leads us to believe that he'll be put through the ringer soon enough again. Just an album earlier in the Beatles' catalog, Lennon had warned a cad about losing that girl; here he finds a "Girl," but realizes that his torment will be unceasing whether he loses her or keeps her.

63. "I've Got a Feeling" (from *Let It Be*, 1970)

"I've Got a Feeling" pretty well sums up what the Beatles had in mind when they first undertook the *Get Back* project, later renamed *Let It Be* when released as an album and motion picture in 1970. Featuring collaboration like it was in the old days from group leaders John Lennon and Paul McCartney and an outstanding band performance, the song shows that the spark of talent was still there for them to be a great rock-and-roll band, even if the spirit was no longer willing.

"I've Got a Feeling" is one of those rare Beatle mashups, when two songs started separately by individual members were then jammed together to form a surprisingly coherent whole. The most famous example is the *Sgt. Pepper's* closer "A Day in the Life," but there was also "Baby You're a Rich Man" from *Magical Mystery Tour* in 1967, when the band took a Lennon song and a McCartney song, swirled them together like chocolate and peanut butter, and came out with something pretty tasty.

In the case of "I've Got a Feeling," Lennon had begun a song during the White Album sessions but not completed it. This became the "Everybody had a hard year" section of the *Let It Be* track, which otherwise was a McCartney composition. That the two men could figure out that the two pieces of music would make good neighbors within the song demonstrates that their musical partnership still had legs at the time it was recorded in early 1969, even if their personal relationship was rupturing.

"I've Got a Feeling" also stands out for being the best of the *Let It Be* songs that were recorded during the Beatles' famed rooftop performance on January 30, 1969. For such a hallowed event, the performance was mostly a shambolic one. Brutally cold temperatures and the brevity of the show prevented anything too magical from happening on what would be the band's final live performance. But they managed a pretty searing version of this song, one that was edited slightly but otherwise used as it was laid down live for the album.

Considering that they hadn't performed in front of an audience in three years, the interplay and cohesion between the instrumentalists is impressive, as is the smoothness of both the harmonies and the eventual vocal interplay between McCartney and Lennon. In "I've Got a Feeling," McCartney's vision of writing, rehearsing, and then performing new music in front of actual fans instead of in a studio was beautifully realized, however briefly.

Beginning with a propulsive guitar riff, McCartney's main section is a song of exultation, practically gospel-like in its fervor. Inspired by his budding romance with Linda Eastman, who would soon become his wife, McCartney sings in husky yet exuberant tones about an indescribable, undeniable, indestructible feeling. Of course, the terms he uses are a bit more restrained and quirky ("I've got a feeling that keeps on my toes," for example), but the passion in his voice lets us in on the import. Although they're hard to hear with his screaming vocal, the lyrics in the bridge articulate how he stumbled into good fortune: "All these years I've been wandering around / Wondering how come nobody told me / All that I was looking for was somebody who looked like you."

When Lennon arrives on the scene with his more muted lines about hard years, high socks, and wet dreams, it's amazing to hear how easily they fit into the sway of the music despite how different in temperament they are to McCartney's pronouncements. Once again it's a case of the two men supporting and complementing each other in song with their own unique perspectives.

Not to be outdone, the musicians all rise to the occasion: Harrison's guitar is steady and potent, Ringo Starr's drums are the glue, Billy Preston and Lennon fill in gaps with electric piano and rhythm guitar, respectively, and McCartney displays his grasp of not only what notes to play but the exact right time to play them. For what could have been a muddled live performance (à la "One after 909," also from the rooftop), the five men display the chemistry necessary to make this nuanced song soar.

"I've Got a Feeling" only gets stronger as it goes, peaking toward the end when McCartney and Lennon sing their respective melodies at the same time before some thrilling instrumental crescendos shut the thing down. Lennon can be heard exclaiming, "It's so hard," but in fact the band made this complicated endeavor sound pretty easy. It's the sound of what might have been had all the songs on *Let It Be* been as cleverly composed and passionately performed. Alas, such a warm, delicate feeling was difficult to maintain in the band's waning days.

62. "Sexy Sadie" (from *The Beatles*, 1968)

Whether or not he actually warranted it, Maharishi Mahesh Yogi incurred the wrath of John Lennon toward the end of the Beatles' visit with him in India in 1968 for a meditation-based retreat. Maybe the maharishi was enlightened, but he must have missed the knowledge that it's never a good idea to get on the bad side of a great songwriter, deservedly or not, or else you'll have a song like "Sexy Sadie" written about you besmirching your reputation from here to eternity.

The short version of the story is that Lennon, who initially dove head-long into meditation and the maharishi's teachings, lost respect for him when he heard that the so-called Giggling Guru had made a pass at one of the female retreaters. Many who were there claim there was never any evidence of this happening and that Lennon was intentionally given bad information. In any case, he was fired up enough to write a song express-ing his disgust, changing the title from "Maharishi" to "Sexy Sadie" only when George Harrison convinced him to do so.

This wasn't the only song of disdain that emanated from his India experience; he aimed "The Continuing Story of Bungalow Bill" at an ardent hunter in the camp. But that one came off as a fun but slight novelty at best when it was released on the White Album in 1968; "Sexy Sadie," on the other hand, rose much higher on the strength of some enchanting music and the complicated mixed bag of emotions in the lyrics.

The song begins with Paul McCartney's piano intro, somehow stately and wobbly at once thanks to the effects added to it. Once the rhythm kicks in, it does so at an ambling pace, yet Ringo Starr is able to keep things from falling into torpor with effectively counterintuitive drum-ming. One of Starr's many underrated qualities as a drummer is his ability to find spaces for snare drums and other aggressive measures within songs with slower tempos, thereby enlivening the recordings of those songs. He does that wonderfully here, while McCartney flitters about the lower end on bass. Eventually Harrison takes over on the outro with precisely rendered, hefty riffs.

The music somehow manages both dreaminess and melancholy, which makes it just the right fit for Lennon's lyrics. One key in appreciat-ing the song is realizing that Lennon doesn't just go off on a one-sided diatribe, which would have been easy enough but could have come off as too snide. Instead, he adds just a hint of admiration, as if ultimately impressed that the title character has the ability to wield such power over her acolytes.

Thus every accusatory word ("You made a fool of everyone") is bal-anced out by quasi-praise ("How did you know / The world was waiting just for you?"). In fact, it takes a while as the song progresses to hear that beyond the adulation in lines like "One sunny day the world was waiting for a lover / She came along to turn on every one." The backing vocals by McCartney and Harrison, altered as they are by some studio trickery to sound like Motown call-and-response tinged with sadness, also seem to hover between praise and mockery.

By the final verse, Lennon has had enough of equivocating, finally calling her out: "You'll get yours yet / However big you think you are." Yet even the anger within that line is quickly turned around to disappointment and even a glimmer of lingering hope: "We gave her everything we owned just to sit at her table / Just a smile would lighten everything." Lennon's last falsetto cries seem resigned to the fact that he's been duped though, and he's left to repeat his threat: "However big you think you are."

There's a great moment captured in *The Beatles Anthology* documentary of Lennon being queried by a reporter shortly after his return from India about whether he thought the maharishi was on the level. Lennon, ever sharp and lightning quick with a retort, responded, "I don't know what level he's on." That sense of disillusionment and unknowing hangs heavy over "Sexy Sadie," one of the prettiest poison-pen letters you'll ever hear.

61. "I'm Looking through You" (from *Rubber Soul*, 1965)

Jane Asher has had a distinguished, prolific career as an actor on stage, screen, and television in her native England and abroad. She's found success as a writer, holds top positions in multiple charities, and even turned entrepreneur with her line of cake mixes. She need never have met Paul McCartney to have achieved any of these things.

Yet because of the Beatles' status as arguably the most famous people on a planet obsessed with fame (listen to the stories from celebrities who became tongue-tied on meeting members of the Fab Four if you doubt this assertion), and because of the songs she inspired, many of which rank among the most unforgettable the group ever produced, her relationship with McCartney, which ran from 1963 to 1968—the height of Beatlemania—will always be somewhere near the very top line of her biography.

It's interesting to note that McCartney's reputation as a songwriter reticent to reveal personal details or to take on a confessional tone takes a hit when considering the songs, both positive and negative, that his relationship with Asher instigated. Even though he's spoken since their parting in measured tones about the level of his affection for her during their relationship, it's hard to rectify that equivocating with the audio evidence left behind.

Case in point: "I'm Looking through You," an excellent tale of romantic disappointment and disillusionment that fits snugly in with the rest of the pristine and poised pop songs on the damn-near perfect *Rubber Soul*, released in 1965. A row with Asher about her commitment to the relationship led McCartney to write the song, which details how it can sometimes take a while for someone's true self to surface even in the presence of another who seemingly knows them the best, like their lover.

"I'm Looking through You" breezes through an acoustic guitar intro and then gets moving with the odd percussive help of Ringo Starr tapping on the back of a matchstick box. Mostly the music stays out of the way of McCartney's yearning melody, which is a smart thing for it to do. The exceptions come during the refrains, when staccato blasts of organ and cloudbursts of fiery electric guitar join McCartney's shouting, the aural incarnation of the song's narrator finally deciding that enough is enough.

McCartney's lyrics embody the doubt that creeps up in a person who feels betrayed by his significant other. What he sees isn't her; it's the façade she puts forth so that, in her heart of hearts, she can be where she truly wants to be, which is away from him. "You don't look different, but you have changed," he sings, his suspicions seeping into every nook and cranny of his person. Notice he doesn't sing, "I'm looking at you" but "I'm looking through you," the implication being that she's no longer as mysterious to him as she thinks.

The narrator isn't so much saying that he's leaving but rather that he's onto her disguises. He also feels that this gives him the upper hand in the relationship: "You were above me, but not today." When he tries to understand her motivations, all he can do is come up with theories about the fickleness of love, which "has a nasty habit of disappearing overnight."

McCartney's vocals run the gamut from wounded and small in the verses to fierce and cathartically charged in the choruses as he cycles through the narrator's emotions with the verity of one who didn't have to dig too deep to locate them within himself. It wasn't very long after McCartney and Asher split that he began dating his eventual wife Linda Eastman, who rarely inspired anything but the sweetest of love songs from her husband. Good for them but maybe not so good for the listening public, because a heartsick McCartney back in the day was an insightful one about romance and its perils.

Considering the infinite reams of paper that have been spent recounting the Beatles' history and accomplishments, to which these humble musings have been added, Jane Asher could name her price to any publisher in the world for the story of her time with McCartney and within the group's orbit. To her everlasting credit, she hasn't even given a single interview about the subject since the announcement of the breakup. Nonetheless, we have McCartney's own take on the relationship in "I'm Looking through You" and several other classics, a take that is undoubtedly compelling, albeit one without rebuttal.

60. "Can't Buy Me Love" (from *A Hard Day's Night*, 1964)

"Can't Buy Me Love" was the sixth single the Beatles released in the United Kingdom. Paul McCartney sang lead on the first, 1962's "Love Me Do," which reached the Top 20 in England. The following four singles, "Please Please Me," "From Me to You," "She Loves You," and "I Want to Hold Your Hand" all featured the lead vocals of John Lennon. All four went to No. 1.

When attributing actual songwriting credit for the Beatles' songs officially listed as Lennon/McCartney compositions, a good rule of thumb is that the singer also tended to be the main writer. Granted that wasn't the case 100 percent of the time, and the fact that the two collaborated much more closely in those early years muddies the picture even further. Nonetheless, the aforementioned string of singles demonstrates that Lennon was the primary hit-making force within the Beatles in their first couple years of recording.

"Can't Buy Me Love" provides the turning point away from Lennon's dominance in that regard. Not only was it written and sung by McCartney, but it also featured no harmony vocals from Lennon or George Harrison. "Can't Buy Me Love" also rose to No. 1, and although you could sniff and say that the Beatles could have released a test pattern around that time and muscled it to the top of the charts, the aural evidence shows that "Can't Buy Me Love" possesses amounts of gusto and cleverness similar to those other songs and pushes the pleasure button just as often and as effectively. McCartney proved with the song his ability to court mass audiences for the material he fronted, and the authorship split between Lennon and he would be much more even from that point forward.

"Can't Buy Me Love" also serves as a kind of mirror image to Lennon's title track to *A Hard Day's Night* in terms of its relentless tempo. It soundtracks a great scene from the *A Hard Day's Night* film in which the four members of the group take a break from their rigid schedule and frolic around a field. Yet the song was originally intended by its author to be a kind of slow grind of a blues song. You can hear a little of that intent in the version of the song included on *Anthology 1*, although the natural exuberance of the band at that point pushes even that slowed-down take into upbeat territory.

Once George Martin came up with the idea of refrains of the song title to be used as bookends, everything else started to fall into place. McCartney sings high above the low rumble of the band, as his bass line, Ringo Starr's clashing drums, and Lennon's acoustic guitar provide a sturdy, unshowy engine. The lyrics tell a tale of a guy with the capability of buying lots of fancy stuff for the girl he fancies yet wishes that she'd scorn those things in favor of what "money just can't buy."

McCartney's lyrics do their job in typically snappy fashion; the interior rhyme of lines like "I may not have a lot to give but what I got I'll give to you" lends them an inevitable flow. He briefly steps back to let George Harrison rip forth with a guitar solo, one that, oddly enough, gets a boost from unintentional tape bleed that allowed a solo he had done for a previous take to be heard softly in the background of the finished version. It thus comes off like the guitar doing a call-and-response with itself and turns out to be a happy accident.

When McCartney returns for the final verse, he's more animated in his pleas to the girl, his voice spiking as he desperately asks her to put away material things. That leads back into Martin's quasi-chorus concoction to close out the song, which ends with a full stop as the listener gasps for air in an attempt to catch up.

Although his work had been showcased on the group's previous albums, McCartney undoubtedly seized his opportunity to step into the single spotlight on "Can't Buy Me Love" and ran with it as quickly as the band tore through the recording. The friendly rivalry was on, and the increasingly amazing compositions that Lennon and McCartney poured forth were the fruits of that competition.

59. "Because" (from *Abbey Road,* 1969)

As we go through this list of the Beatles' finest musical accomplishments, it becomes clearer with each song that there were myriad reasons for their excellence. Impeccable songwriting, recording acumen, skilled helpers like George Martin, camaraderie and charisma that infused all their work, that indefinable quality we call chemistry, and so on; it all melded into an incredible package that flirted with perfection every time they made a sound.

Speaking of perfection, another reason why they stood above their peers emanated from the beautiful blend of their voices together. Whether it was simply John Lennon and Paul McCartney supporting each other, George Harrison joining Lennon or McCartney on backing vocals, or perhaps all three of them together going after it in three-part harmony, the noise they made together makes you believe in destiny. Because if these three men hadn't come together, the world would have been deprived of their blended voices, which seems unfathomable.

On *Abbey Road,* the Beatles included more of these blended vocals than they had in their previous few years of recording. While it's somewhat iffy whether the band knew for sure that they were closing out their history together when making the album, one could make the leap that the vocal togetherness was a subtle nod to their fans longing for harmony between the singers, who were in such disharmony at the time of recording. For those fans, "Because" was the crown jewel on an album filled with priceless gems.

John Lennon wrote the song based on his wife Yoko Ono's classical piano noodling. "Yoko was playing Moonlight Sonata on the piano," he told David Sheff in 1980. "She was classically trained. I said, 'Can you play those chords backward?' and wrote 'Because' around them."[16] To strengthen the Beethoven vibe, Martin played the arpeggiated chords on a harpsichord, albeit an electric one to modernize it a bit. On top of that came Lennon's lead guitar and, later on, Harrison's moog synthesizer, first imitating brass, then making raindrop-like noises. McCartney provides just a few well-timed notes on bass here and there to move the song along without interrupting the airy proceedings above him.

For the lyrics, Lennon kept it simple. "The lyrics speak for themselves; they're clear," he told Sheff. "No bullshit. No imagery, no obscure references." Those lyrics bespeak a deep appreciation for nature's beauty, as the shape of the world, the height of the wind, and the color of the sky—the kinds of things we take for granted as the most certain of truths—appear as if new. So beautiful are these forces that they invoke in him a kind of doleful wonder, a feeling embellished by the three-part harmonies.

What harmonies they are. Lennon in the middle, that cutting voice making its presence felt even as his buddies swirl around him; Harrison, steady and supportive on the lower end (although still up there pretty high, because these vocals are meant to keep us aloft); and McCartney, bouncing about on the higher end, ever the melodic spark. When they drop a bit to assert, "Love is old, love is new / Love is all, love is you," well, let's just say if you don't believe it after that, you never will.

When compiling the soundtrack for *Love*, the Beatles-inspired Cirque Du Soleil show, Martin and his son Giles had the inspired idea to begin the show with the isolated vocal tracks from "Because." Hearing those voices in this manner, unadorned, soaring, and together, will tingle spines and induce tears. And when some contrarian asks you why the Beatles were so great, you can play that for them with the speakers turned up so they can imbibe those harmonies in all their majesty. Then you can simply turn to that wise guy and say, "Because."

58. "It Won't Be Long" (from *With the Beatles*, 1963)

In the grand scheme of things, three months isn't really all that long a time, especially to those just living their lives day to day without anything that exciting to deviate from the routine. But to Beatlemaniacs in England who had made their favorite group the toast of the country in the first half of 1963, it must have seemed like an interminable wait. Three months is the amount of time the folks had to bide between "She Loves You," a single released in August 1963 and *With the Beatles*, the group's second full-length LP, which came out in November of the same year.

If there were any doubts about whether this layoff had sapped the boys of their magic, "It Won't Be Long," the opening track off *With the Beatles*, answered them with resounding authority. Even cleverer was how the song's subject matter appeared to address the breathless anticipation of their fans for new product.

"It Won't Be Long" seems to be John Lennon's baby for the most part, although Paul McCartney said he was essentially the cowriter, citing the group's clever usage of "be long" and "belong" in the song as a particular point of pride. In any case, the song, which rushes through its two-minute running time as if being chased by a pack of rabid teenagers, nods to the frenzy surrounding the group by turning the tables, as Lennon sings about the frustrating delays in getting back together with the girl he loves while remaining confident that it's going to happen eventually.

This is the kind of pace that the Beatles kept on the regular in their songs from the early days. That they can zoom like they do in "It Won't Be Long" without the song coming apart at the seams is a testament to the discipline and skill of the players. McCartney on bass and Ringo Starr on drums form a rumbling rhythm section that never seems to break a sweat even as the scenery whizzes by them. Lennon adds his customarily understated rhythm guitar wherever needed, while George Harrison stays precise on lead guitar even as he revs up the energy. The quartet also handles the twists and turns that Lennon instinctively and often unconsciously added to his songs (if indeed he was the main composer), which in this case includes a quasi-bridge that emerges from the chorus and features a structure entirely different from the bulk of the song.

What "It Won't Be Long" captures expertly is the eagerness that one desperately waiting to come together with his significant other must feel. The narrator spends his time sitting alone and crying instead of living his life, but the knowledge of her finally returning home sparks a burst of energy in him.

The chorus acts as the embodiment of this spike. It starts on a minor key to highlight the urgency before switching to the major to play up the exultation of that wonderful moment of reunion. Once again here is a Beatles' song that starts with the chorus, and the immediacy of this opening grabs listeners and shakes them into an alert understanding of the situation within seconds.

By starting the song and the album this way, the Beatles perform yet another bit of wish fulfillment for their fans, making it seem like they miss them just as much as the reciprocal of that relationship. The song flies by with abandon until pulling into the garage on some cooing harmonies, all of the spent energy having been proven worthwhile now that the separation is over. "It Won't Be Long" refuses to let up until it gets where it needs to be; after those three long months of waiting, the fans surely appreciated its hustle.

57. "Rocky Raccoon" (from *The Beatles*, 1968)

There are those who feel that the Beatles overstuffed the White Album by its release in 1968. The double album contained a whopping thirty-one songs and ran over ninety minutes. Compare that to the early days when their albums tended to hustle through a bunch of songs and were done in a half hour or less, and you can understand why some might have felt beyond satiated.

Producer George Martin expressed those views on a number of occasions. "I tried to plead with them to be selective and make it a really good single album, but they wouldn't have it," he said.[17] You can understand this view to a point; included on the album there are a few throwaways like "Wild Honey Pie," overly precious songs like "Honey Pie," and underrealized tracks like "Long, Long, Long." There was also the behemoth that was "Revolution 9," which, contrary to those who hear in it great profundity, doesn't really belong; it would have been better served on an experimental album with like-minded music, or noise, to be more accurate, all around it.

Yet Martin's view also would have meant an album more focused and narrowcasted, which likely would have deprived the world of lovable oddities like "Rocky Raccoon." With all of this space to fill, why not include a tongue-in-cheek country and western number that aspires to be nothing more than a tall tale cleverly and humorously told?

With lots of time on their hands in between meditation sessions and vegetarian meals while on their India retreat with the Maharishi in February 1968, the Beatles toted around acoustic guitars and played whatever popped into their cleared-out heads. Many of those songs made it to the White Album, with "Rocky Raccoon" being one of the silliest and yet most ingratiating of the bunch.

McCartney is clearly having a bit of a laugh at some of the conventions of country music, even adopting an exaggerated and somewhat unconvincing Southern accent in his talking-blues intro. He does all this in a loving rather than cynical way, and, in much the same way that "Michelle" was meant to tweak art songs and ended up being a gorgeous love song, "Rocky Raccoon" transcends its roots in parody to become a sneakily moving track.

More than country music, though, McCartney's target appears to be the American Western movie, as "Rocky Raccoon" contains a saloon, a gunfight, a femme fatale who sparks a conflict, and even a hoedown. It also might not be too much of a stretch to say that McCartney was making subtle reference to the Western-influenced songs on Bob Dylan's 1967 album *John Wesley Harding*, in which all kinds of cryptic events were related in this-happened, that-happened style by Bob. Like, for example, "The Ballad of Frankie Lee and Judas Priest," McCartney's song contains no chorus and ends on a somewhat unsettled note, albeit in a much more lighthearted manner.

Musically, the song sticks close to McCartney's acoustic guitar and his high-pitched vocal, with John Lennon on bass and harmonica and Ringo Starr on drums providing only window dressing. (Ringo's snare rap when the shootout takes place is a neat touch, borrowing from "I Fought the Law" and its six-gun.) The lone flourish comes when George Martin plays a saloon-style piano that makes it seem like McCartney is narrating from inside the bar while the imbroglio goes down and his piano player scores the action.

The humor is front and center here. There's the girl whose name seems to depend on who's addressing her and the drunken doctor who lies down instead of the patient. But there's also something solemn and somber about Rocky himself. That first line, "Rocky Raccoon checked into his room only to find Gideon's Bible," suggests something forlorn and seems to foreshadow the sad fate that awaits him. It's also somehow funny and sad that his single-minded mission of revenge is undercut by his slowness on the draw; certainly that's not the way it happens for the hero in the movies.

Yet Rocky stays optimistic, even as he appears to be bleeding to death. What is that revival that he enjoys at the end? Is McCartney suggesting that he's physically on the mend, or is the Bible, left behind by a skedaddling Gideon in another winking touch, the source of some kind of path to the afterlife? It's an engaging little mystery that deepens this otherwise frivolous track.

Maybe the White Album is an unwieldy mess of an album in places, but it also provided us with more Beatles music than we otherwise would have received, so that can't be a bad thing. And besides, what a tragedy it would have been had the saga of "Rocky Raccoon" remained untold.

56. "This Boy" (from *Past Masters, Volume 1*, released as a B-side in 1963)

Earlier in this list we talked about "Not a Second Time" and bandied about the theory that it could be considered the first Beatles' ballad written by John Lennon and Paul McCartney to be released on record. The song was featured on the album *With the Beatles*, which was released in the United Kingdom on November 22, 1963.

Just a week later, the group released their fifth single. The A-side was the mammoth track "I Want to Hold Your Hand," which would become the band's fourth consecutive No. 1 hit in England and the song that would eventually break in the band in America early the following year. On the B-side sat "This Boy." While "Not a Second Time" predated it by a week, that song's quicker tempo and heavier instrumentation make it somewhat of an iffy notion to categorize it as a ballad, even if the gloomy sentiment suggested it was so.

"This Boy" is indeed a slow-moving song rendered with heart-rending emotion, which certainly would seem to categorize it as a ballad. Certainly John Lennon, who appears to have been the song's principal writer (although Paul McCartney has also claimed it was a pretty strict cowrite) understood that it was an early display of songwriting versatility that even he didn't know he possessed. In interviews he cited the song as an example that he was adept at writing melodies in the early days when even he felt that he was only good at writing rock-and-roll ravers.

The melody of "This Boy" is somewhat understated in the verses, on the verge of placid. What melodic punch there is comes from the three-part harmonies, the first time the Beatles utilized this technique to which they would return throughout their career with great success. McCartney on the high end does wander about a bit with his vocal, just as his bass notes also tend to step out of the straightforward pluck of George Harrison's trebly guitar, but otherwise those verses are slow strolls in a relatively straight line.

This flat-line approach is effective because it sets us up perfectly for the emotional crescendo in the middle eight. As soon as Lennon sings, "Oh, and . . ." to cut out of the second verse, you can sense a change. The music starts to build in intensity, Lennon takes the vocal solo (albeit double-tracked), and McCartney and Harrison step away to sing wordless backing vocals ever rising up the scale.

Lennon's vocal in this portion of the song is a showstopper. Yes, he had learned well from Smokey Robinson and other soul belters, but the aching, authentic feeling that he displays here is something that can't be learned or taught. The entire segment is breathtaking, culminating with Lennon turning "cry" into a six-syllable word as everybody else stands back and lets him have his moment.

From there, "This Boy" returns to the understated vibe it had established earlier. Although the lyrics are pretty basic stuff, a guy telling a girl in the simplest terms why he's better for her than a romantic rival, the rise and fall of the song and the roller coaster that Lennon's vocals travel tell the listener everything about the protagonist's torment. You don't even have to understand English to be able to tell what the song is about.

The Beatles wisely made "This Boy" one of the staples of their early live shows, and whenever Lennon played his part in that thrilling bridge, the intensity of the screaming would somehow elevate. Maybe it's a stretch to call it the first Beatles' ballad, as the doo-wop influence certainly makes it a bit of a mixed breed. But it's safe to say, thanks to the magnetism and heartbroken majesty of Lennon's performance, it will always be regarded as one of their most beloved songs of any style.

55. "I Don't Want to Spoil the Party" (from *Beatles for Sale*, 1964)

We return again to the underrated *Beatles for Sale*, which you'll recall from earlier entries as a kind of repository for ideas and emotions that didn't quite jibe so well with the lovable, unflappable, moptop image the band had cultivated in their first few years of stardom. From that album, released at the tail end of 1964, "I Don't Want to Spoil the Party" is delivered by John Lennon in a manner befitting a meek wallflower rather than the leader of the biggest band in rock-and-roll history.

Paul McCartney recalled that he and Lennon had originally worked out the song for Ringo Starr to use as his one vocal showcase for the album. That makes sense considering the band's tendency to lend songs to Starr that had a country feel to them, but somewhere along the line that plan was scrapped; Starr ended up singing the Carl Perkins cover "Honey Don't" on *Beatles for Sale*, while Lennon took the lead on "I Don't Want to Spoil the Party," which he described as being "a very personal one of mine."

Actually the vocals are traded back and forth between Beatle members during the song, and this interplay is one of its chief selling points. In the verses, a double-tracked Lennon harmonizes with himself, the low part sung as if he's dejected beyond belief, the high part rendered with the quivering emotion of someone deeply hurt but trying to hide it. At the point when the melody rises within the verses, Lennon goes solo with backing "ooh-ooh" vocals from Paul McCartney and George Harrison.

It changes again in the middle eights as Lennon sings low support while McCartney joins on the high part that kind of acts as the main melody. This is the part of the song when the narrator sings, "I still love her," yet instead of the exultation such a line should engender, McCartney and Lennon's shared voices only project pain.

The reason for that is spelled out in Lennon's lyrics, which, if they were indeed a reflection of some actual event in his life or at least a representation of his inner feelings surrounding a relationship he had at some point, reveal something about the man that, again, most Beatlemaniacs probably missed. "I Don't Want to Spoil the Party" is, at its core, a song about insecurity, the kind that misreads seemingly innocuous signs as dire portents of separation and won't allow a guy to love himself enough to be truly loved by a woman in kind.

Anyone who's ever felt like an extra wheel at a social event can understand the sentiment in the lines "I don't want to spoil the party so I'll go / I would hate my disappointment to show." Instead of sticking around and enjoying himself, he chooses to "disappear," before revealing why he's melancholy: "If she turns up while I'm gone, please let me know."

His inner tumult comes across clearly in the mixed signals he sends in the second verse. A couple drinks don't improve his mood any, and he admits, "There's no fun in what I do if she's not there." Yet he thinks he can turn things around by finding her: "I think I'll take a walk and look for her."

If she truly felt the same way about him as he does about her, it's unlikely that she would have abandoned him to his self-doubt the way she has. And that unspoken context, which can be heard in the weary sorrow of Lennon's vocal, makes this song an unexpected grabber. It also benefits from some excellent folk-country music with a guitar pull feel, featuring nice touches along the way like Starr's thumping kick drum when the music drops away in the bridge and Harrison's homey yet probing solo in the instrumental break.

The pained lyrics and bittersweet music found on *Beatles for Sale* were in many ways test runs for what would come in the next few years of the band's career. Had a song like this been released in 1965 or '66, it likely would have been festooned with psychedelic trappings or production flourishes that demanded listeners' attentions more forcefully. You have to search a little bit for the hidden emotions on "I Don't Want to Spoil the Party" as it was recorded, much like the other partygoers likely had to search for the protagonist once he wandered off. But they're there nonetheless, and they're quite revelatory once exposed.

54. "I'm So Tired" (from *The Beatles*, 1968)

In 1966 on *Revolver*, John Lennon told the world "I'm Only Sleeping," a song that detailed how slumber was often his recreational activity of choice when not tethered to the everyday demands of Beatledom. Just two years later, "I'm So Tired" made it clear, with edgy authority, just how difficult sleepless nights can be for someone so inclined to traveling to dreamland.

As Lennon explained in a 1980 interview, his inspiration for "I'm So Tired" was the side effect of insomnia that accompanied the mind-unburdening techniques he learned from the Maharishi in 1968: "'I'm So Tired' was me, in India again. I couldn't sleep, I'm meditating all day and couldn't sleep at night."[18] Like so many other songs written by the group members in India, it found its way onto the White Album later that same year, where it provided a bluesy edge to the often way-out proceedings.

In the same interview, Lennon professed his admiration for the sound of "I'm So Tired," and you can hear on first listen what he means. The tension and release that the song achieves is brilliant, even if it's all tension for the narrator, who desperately seeks but never quite finds the sleep he so desperately needs.

Beginning with low guitar footsteps, the band settles in beneath Lennon as he recounts his insomniac's lullaby. In the verses, there's very little color, just a low rumble and churn. Some organ does filter in toward the end of the final verse, but other than that the music is just a creep along the hallway that doesn't want to wake anybody else up. It's a

hallucinatory vibe that the song captures here, something to which someone in the throes of prolonged sleeplessness could relate.

Lennon sings these verses in gentle tones, not entirely unlike the voice
he utilized in "I'm Only Sleeping." After all, we're still in the dead of
night here, and it seems as if the narrator respects the silence of the wee
hours even if they don't respect him back. These verses explain the depth
of his torment, how his "mind is on the blink," how neither alcohol nor
cigarettes can offer a solution as he turns his agitation toward Sir Walter
Raleigh.

But what's really making his head spin away from the calm needed to
provide sleep are his thoughts of someone who's not there in the room
with him. At this point, Lennon was with his first wife, Cynthia, but he
had already met Yoko Ono, so it's not too hard to surmise the identity of
this mystery person interrupting his rest.

Despite his best efforts to stay in a restrained mental state in order to
fall asleep, he eventually can stand it no more, as Lennon's voice suddenly booms forth on the line "I wonder should I call you but I know what
you would do." That's the signal for the band to kick into another gear:
Ringo Starr gooses the tempo, and George Harrison starts throwing out
chunky bits of electric guitar. Lennon's vocal intensifies throughout this
section, although it's hard to surmise by this point whether it's the lack of
sleep or the lack of his object of desire that's "doing [him] harm."

By the end of the chorus, he's practically raving: "You know I can't
sleep, I can't stop my brain / You know it's three weeks, I'm going insane
/ You know I'd give you everything I've got for a little peace of mind."
McCartney is harmonizing with him at this point, and, in the final moments, the pair repeats that last line about "peace of mind" three times as
the band comes to a false stop each time, only to be revved up again by
Starr's fills. It's as if he's just about to doze off only to be jolted awake
each time. Only the mumbling noises made by Lennon at the end give us
any hope that he might finally find some sort of rest.

As Lennon suggested, the song makes a really great noise through the
speakers, a scintillating full-band performance from the Beatles at a time
when such occasions were dwindling. "I'm So Tired" proved a fascinat-
ingly fevered chapter in the continuing story of John Lennon's quest for
sleep. Perhaps even more important than that, it provided one of the first
pieces of evidence that he was about to start writing for an entirely new

muse in Yoko Ono, one who would inspire him for the rest of his days as a songwriter.

53. "Across the Universe" (from *Let It Be*, 1970)

The information above lists *Let It Be* as the album that contains "Across the Universe," but that's only part of a long, convoluted story. Here's the short version taken from John Lennon in his *Playboy* interview in 1980: "It was a lousy track of a great song and I was so disappointed by it. It never went out as the Beatles; I gave it to the Wildlife Fund of Great Britain, and then when Phil Spector was brought in to produce *Let It Be*, he dug it out of the Beatles files and overdubbed it. The guitars are out of tune and I'm singing out of tune 'cause I'm psychologically destroyed and nobody's supporting me or helping me with it and the song was never done properly."[19]

So how did such an abysmal fate befall such an amazing song? The journey taken by "Across the Universe" from conception to recording also inadvertently tells a lot about just how haphazard the final act of the Beatles really was, hampered as they were by far too many projects and not nearly enough follow-through.

Lennon first brought the song into the studio in early 1968, but the efforts to record it didn't convince the other band members it was deserving of the single spot, which went to "Lady Madonna." From there it sat around unused until Lennon brought it up again during *Let It Be*, although the band didn't rerecord it during that fractious time. The World Wildlife Fund charity album referenced by Lennon in the interview included the song in 1969, while *Let It Be* featured the Spectorized version in 1970.

Neither of these versions was anywhere near the standard of the song itself, which ranks as one of Lennon's most beautiful meditations on love's power over the corporeal and mental. "Across the Universe" contains lyrics of such cosmic serenity and effortless transcendence that no one would have been surprised if Lennon had cribbed them from some ancient Eastern spiritual text.

The elongated lines and calming meter give the song the feel of an oversized mantra, one that you need not remember fully to recite because it seeps deep into your subconscious the first time you hear it. "Across the Universe" sets up as a tug-of-war between the thoughts and words that wish to tether the narrator to his mundane existence and the intangible, elusive emotions and feelings that pull him into a benign vortex of light and love, a vortex that reveals to him nothing less than the mysteries of the world. It's understandable then that the thoughts and words are fighting a losing battle.

Lennon's poetics are impressive throughout, his metaphors and similes creating one of the most visual songs about the unseen that you'll ever hear. We can picture the paper cup in the rain or the wind in the letter box, the recognizable imagery orienting us in this world beyond our earthly realm. The narrator eventually is able to cast away the worthless things holding him back and indulge in the "limitless undying love" that his journey across the universe promises.

"Jai guru deva om" might not mean much on paper to those unfamiliar with the translation, but the yearning turn that the melody takes when Lennon sings it makes it clear that the narrator is giving himself over to something greater than himself. With this relationship in his corner, his refrain of "Nothing's gonna change my world" makes sense because the trivial day-to-day hassles of life ring meaningless in the shadow of such a vast realization.

There is simply too much beauty inherent in Lennon's words and melody to have been completely eradicated. But, boy, do the two official releases take sledgehammers to the impenetrable building blocks the song provides. On the World Wildlife Fund version (which can also be found on the *Past Masters, Volume 2* compilation), Paul McCartney had the horrific idea to ask some teenage female fans who were hanging around outside the Apple building to come in and sing backing vocals; their squealing cheapens the song's profound pronouncements. Speeding up the tape of the recording was also a misfire, as it robs the song of some of its sonority.

Spector, unfortunately, went too far in the opposite direction when he got hold of the track on *Let It Be*. He slowed down the tape, which makes Lennon sound as if he's in a fog. And the choirs and strings clash with the inherent drone of the melody. It's the better of the two versions if only because it takes the song seriously, and this ranking is based on that take.

That said, "Across the Universe" probably would have been twenty spots higher on this list had either of the after-the-fact versions included on *Anthology 2* or *Let It Be . . . Naked* been the official release. Both of these takes get rid of the nonsense and clear the way for Lennon's beautiful song (at its proper speed). But it's still awfully ironic that a song promoting such bliss and warmth would be victimized by the disjointed-ness and disarray that characterized the Beatles' final years together.

52. "Mother Nature's Son" (from *The Beatles*, 1968)

While its role as the album that essentially began rolling the Beatles downhill from their peak toward their dissolution can't be denied, the White Album actually benefits in many areas from the acrimony that dogged the sessions. The theory that it was essentially three solo albums smushed together under a Beatles' banner might be true, but it also might not have been such a bad thing. While the democracy that the band had previously displayed certainly provided fabulous results, there was also something to be said for one member or another moving ahead with a song without having to endure the groupthink that can dilute one's origi-nal vision.

While John Lennon (with the exception of "Julia") and George Harri-son still essentially used the other group members as backing musicians on the songs they spearheaded, Paul McCartney often went further than that. There are four songs on the White Album that were one-man shows by McCartney, while a fifth ("I Will") only includes some minor percus-sion work from Ringo Starr. This practice created bad feelings within the group, but, for the most part, it's hard to argue with the quality of what McCartney produced. We've already seen "I Will" on this list, we're about to talk about "Mother Nature's Son," and "Blackbird" is still to come. As for the other two, "Why Don't We Do It in the Road?" just missed inclusion in the top one hundred (as you can see in the appendix), and "Wild Honey Pie" is just an interstitial on the album and doesn't really attempt to be anything more than that.

In the case of "Mother Nature's Son," it's difficult to see that there's anything else the other three members of the band could have done to improve what McCartney managed on his own (with the help of some brass musicians). Since the song is about a kind of loner who derives his joy out of playing music for other people, the lack of involvement from the others makes even more sense.

McCartney's do-it-yourself ability also comes from his facility with multiple instruments. The two different acoustic guitar parts he plays here evoke the bucolic mood expertly while also hinting slightly at the loneli-ness that seems to be the character's lot in life; he might prefer his solitude, but maybe he doesn't have a choice. McCartney also makes the wise choice to add the thumping percussion of the timpani, creating a kind of march in the instrumental section with the brass, which is both playful and stirring all at once.

McCartney was inspired in part by a lecture given by the Maharishi during the Beatles' time in India, but his knowledge of standards also came into play. In *Many Years from Now*, he said, "I've always loved the [Nat King Cole] song called 'Nature Boy': 'There was a boy, a very strange and gentle boy . . .' He loves nature, and 'Mother Nature's Son' was inspired by that song."[20]

Cole's "Nature Boy" was written by a fellow named eden ahbez, who actually lived the lifestyle described in the song, in essence providing an early template for the hippie movement. There's something eerie about "Nature Boy," even when cooed by Cole, but McCartney's song projects far more warmth, albeit tinged with just a touch of loneliness.

His melody is the main reason for this difference. The opening lines in the verses are somewhat desolate, but then a quick change in the style of the strum and a turn to the major chord is like the sun peeking through the clouds and shining down on the grassy knoll that the narrator inhabits ("Find me in my field of grass / Mother Nature's son").

McCartney's lyrics soothe with their sibilant internal rhymes ("Swaying daisies sing a lazy song beneath the sun"). The brass session players lend just the right instrumental touch to the song, coming on as puffy, unthreatening clouds in the verses and then pumping a little life into the instrumental breaks, as McCartney's "doo-doo-doo" refrain indicates how his character is moved to song even when he doesn't have the words to sum it up. And when he sings about the rising waters of a mountain stream, the music gently suggests the serene majesty of such a sight.

And so these wonders of the natural world inspire this character to serenade the folks who cross his path: "All day long I'm sitting singing songs for everyone." McCartney, himself a prolific songwriter and lover of nature, clearly identified with the character, so much so that he didn't request any embellishment from his bandmates on the song. "Mother Nature's Son" proves that doing it yourself can sometimes be the way to go even when you've got three of the most talented musicians in the world at your disposal.

51. "Hello Goodbye" (from *Magical Mystery Tour*, 1967)

If there are still people out there questioning Paul McCartney's musical gifts, which seems doubtful since he seems to have by now outlasted them all or simply proven them wrong time and again, it would seem their most common complaint against him is that his songs, while melodically impressive, can be lyrically slight. There are simply too many examples to list here that would refute such a notion, but, for argument's sake, let's just say that they were in the ballpark of being correct. The question then becomes whether or not it is somehow a lesser achievement to write a song that's musically brilliant with words that aren't anything special.

Classical composers rarely had to worry about attaching words to their songs, concentrating instead on devising melodies that would enchant audiences when played by the right combination of instruments, so you'd probably need to have a problem with Mozart if you have one with McCartney. And there's also the point that cumbersome, complicated lyrics, however intelligent or insightful, can sometimes only hamper a melody that calls for precision of meter, which in turn necessitates more basic wording.

In the case of "Hello Goodbye," which not only was one of the highlights of the *Magical Mystery Tour* film and album in 1967 but also topped the charts for multiple weeks on both sides of the Atlantic, its lyrics, while cleverly assembled, solve no great mysteries of the universe. As McCartney explained, "It was a very easy song to write. It's just a song of duality, with me advocating the more positive. You say goodbye, I say hello. You say stop, I say go. I was advocating the more positive side of the duality, and I still do to this day."[21]

That's all fine and good, but had that duality been rendered via a simplistic tune, the song might have sounded like the work of a grade-schooler. Instead, McCartney and his Beatle buddies give us enough ear candy to cover a lifetime of Easters and Halloweens. The song seems to constantly soar, which is all the more amazing considering it never dips to any low point from which it can ascend again.

Right from the bursting "You say yes" opening, we're immersed in an Eden of euphony, with McCartney serving as the tour guide. For all of the ebullience that the song transmits, his voice at times seems exasperated by the Negative Nellie he's addressing, wondering why she can't join him on the same positive page. All of the lines set up direct contrasts between the two, all except the one that doesn't: "You say why / And I say I don't know." Abbott and Costello would have been proud of that little deviation.

Meanwhile, the music never stops pleasing or surprising. The rhythm section of McCartney and Ringo Starr keep separating from each other, with Starr and his frisky fills especially standing out thanks to those snares miked in that magical midsixties Beatles way, only to reunite for the charging chorus with the guitars of George Harrison and John Lennon joining them on ascent. The keyboards lend a circus-like air in the backgrounds, while those violas saw away diligently as if they aren't aware of the wilder proceedings going on all around them.

Just when McCartney has reprised the refrain for the third time and you think that there can't be anything more for the music to give, the band pops out of the false ending with another burst of energy, chanted vocals and pounding drums pushing matters even farther into the sonic stratosphere.

"Hello Goodbye" need not apologize for anything, and yet its reputation as being lightweight has dogged it pretty much since it was released. Lennon didn't help matters by criticizing it in his post-Beatles years, as he did so many McCartney-penned numbers that he felt were lyrically lacking. It didn't help in this case that "Hello Goodbye" was chosen as the A-side for the single over Lennon's "I Am the Walrus," which had as much if not more going for it in terms of musical invention and far surpassed "Hello Goodbye" in terms of lyrical depth.

But falling short of "I Am the Walrus" in the lyric department is no shame, because that's an awful high bar to clear. And "Hello Goodbye" was the right choice as the single, as the huge success it enjoyed demonstrated. Instantly accessible, endlessly hummable, and musically impeccable. To quote a song McCartney wrote in his solo career to defend some of his other songs taking the rap from critics, what's wrong with that?

50. "Fixing a Hole" (from *Sgt. Pepper's Lonely Hearts Club Band*, 1967)

We've already seen several instances on this list (and there are several more to come) of songs from *Sgt. Pepper's Lonely Hearts Club Band* that concern rather mundane activities and yet glow strange and exciting when painted by the Beatles' unearthly musical brush. "Fixing a Hole" takes the cake in this regard, because what could be more mundane than home repair?

And yet in many ways it is one of the dreamiest songs on the album, a kind of declaration of mental independence composed by Paul McCartney and aimed at all of the folks who believe that every moment of every day should be filled with some sort of productive behavior or activity. McCartney's point seems to be that such a life would be devoid of the kind of mind-wandering, time-wasting, waking reveries from which works of art like, say, the greatest album in rock-and-roll history, might spring.

Yet the way he phrased it in the song caused some misinterpretation, including a false assumption that the hole being fixed referred to a person shooting up heroin. McCartney settled the issue in *Many Years from Now*: "'Fixing A Hole' was about all those pissy people who told you, 'Don't daydream, don't do this, don't do that.' It seemed to me that that was all wrong and that it was now time to fix all of that. Mending was my meaning. Wanting to be free enough to let my mind wander, let myself be artistic, let myself not sneer at avant-garde things."[22]

"Fixing a Hole" contains some of the most delicate, subtle playing on the album, almost jazzlike in its commitment to mood over bold strokes. That kind of restrained backing allows McCartney to go where he will with the melody, since he seems to have unlimited space around him. George Martin's steady harpsichord pulse actually provides most of the measured rhythmic momentum, freeing McCartney's bass and Ringo Starr's variety of percussion choices to show up in whatever spot best befits the narrator's solitary quest. Once an instrument finally does step forth, it's still in understated fashion, as George Harrison's guitar solo sticks to lower, unflashy notes yet perfectly captures the narrator's urgent need to not be urgent.

And therein lies the dichotomy at play in "Fixing a Hole." Much of the song is devoted to mind-numbing exercises, such as fixing holes and filling up cracks, exercises that serve the purpose of allowing the narrator to break from more serious responsibilities. His goal in these portions of the song is to imbue the unimportant with importance. The tune and the music that accompany dutifully play along, refusing to get caught up in the whirlwind rifling through the world outside the borders of his mind.

And it seems as though this is a realization that has only just dawned on him: "I'm taking the time for a number of things / That weren't important yesterday."

Yet that ease and patience is contrasted by the impassioned connecting sections of the song, which feature a sudden jolt in the tempo and some breezy backing vocals from John Lennon and Harrison. In these parts, the narrator seems to be lashing out at the unseen critics of his lifestyle: "And it really doesn't matter if I'm wrong, I'm right / Where I belong, I'm right / Where I belong." The way these phrases sit up against the bars of music lends them a double meaning, as McCartney finds a way to say both that it's okay to be wrong and that he's exactly where he should be.

The following lines tumble forth in a frenzy of lyrics, McCartney huffing and puffing to get them all in before he runs out of time: "See the people standing there / Who disagree and never win / And wonder why they don't get in my door." For a guy who seems to have a laissez-faire approach to life, he sure is adamant about keeping out those who might disturb his passion for procrastinating.

In the final moments of the song, McCartney's voice sounds distant and almost panicked as he repeats the lines "I'm fixing a hole where the rain gets in / To stop my mind from wandering / Where it will go." It's an almost unsettling finish, and it's up in the air whether McCartney is hinting at the consequences of drifting off too far into one's own subconscious, or if he fears that his efforts to drift away will be thwarted somehow.

This is just another of the engaging mysteries that "Fixing a Hole" throws at us. It's amazing to compare the complexities and subtleties of this song to the band that bashed away at full throttle on most of their tracks just four years earlier, but that just goes to show you what can happen when you do what the song advocates and occupy the body so that the mind may run free.

49. "Norwegian Wood (This Bird Has Flown)" (from *Rubber Soul*, 1965)

If there were any doubt about the Beatles' significant step toward musical maturity for the 1965 album *Rubber Soul*, the subject matter of the disc's first two songs should have settled any questions. "Drive My Car" is a thinly veiled account of a would-be starlet buying out the gigolo services of a humble innocent, while "Norwegian Wood (This Bird Has Flown)" tells of a one-night stand that ends in arson.

Or maybe it doesn't. One of the things that the Beatles were learning from Bob Dylan, whose influence on the group could be heard distinctly on the *Beatles for Sale* and *Help!* albums and may have reached its apex on *Rubber Soul*, was how to cloak their meanings with clever wordplay. As somewhat of a wordsmith himself, having authored two books by this time, John Lennon took to this subterfuge with ease with this subtly biting song. (Here is where we have to note that Lennon once gave credit to Paul McCartney for writing the middle eight, while McCartney himself stated that the two pretty much cowrote it after Lennon arrived with the opening line. McCartney also claims to have come up with the surprise ending.)

On the surface, the story of "Norwegian Wood (This Bird Has Flown)" goes like this: A girl brings a guy back to her house, where they make small talk until late in the evening before crashing in separate rooms. The guy wakes up alone and lights a fire to keep warm in the cold of the morning.

That's one way it could have happened. But the subtext allows for other interpretations. For example, there appears to be nothing that occurs besides a sitar solo (more on that later) from the moment the two principals decide it's time for bed to when the girl tells him she has to get up early for work. You can presume that the two scenes take place one right after another, or that something happened in the interim between the two, most likely the sexual encounter toward which the evening always seemed to be pointing.

And then there's that fiery ending. Again, it could just be the guy, a little groggy and chilly, lighting up the fireplace before he heads on his way. But considering that Lennon has already mentioned that her bedroom was made of Norwegian wood, the last lines ("So I lit a fire / Isn't it good / Norwegian wood") raise an interesting possibility: that he burned down the flat in a random act of destruction. It's somewhat akin to Chekhov's notion that a rifle introduced in the first act must go off later in the play. Why mention the wood if it wasn't going to come into play in some dramatic way down the road?

The beauty of the song is that it works either way. The innocent version plays like a droll satire on a possible rendezvous undone by miscommunication and lack of follow-through. In this interpretation, you can concentrate on the narrator's unaffected wittiness, like when she tells him to sit down and there's nothing on which to sit, or when he compares his own situation to hers: "She told me she worked in the morning and started to laugh / I told her I didn't and crawled off to sleep in the bath."

And then there's the more inflammatory, literally and figuratively, take on the song, which is that they messed around and he burned the house down for no good reason. If you choose this path, you have to admire how the group presented the anarchy of such a situation with matter-of-fact coolness.

No matter how you take the lyrics, it's impossible to consider "Norwegian Wood (This Bird Has Flown)" without noting the Indian feel lent by the sitar. George Harrison plays the rather simple riff that runs through the song, and it adds undeniable spice and mystery to what could have been your typical folky strum. While there were other artists who were just beginning to dabble in Eastern instruments around the time of the song's release in late 1965, the Beatles' stamp of approval turned a fleeting fad to a fully formed trend seemingly overnight, with all manner of Indian instruments suddenly adorning pop songs.

Bob Dylan never incorporated the sitar into any of his songs, but he did do an homage/parody to "Norwegian Wood (This Bird Has Flown)" with the song "4th Time Around" on 1966's *Blonde on Blonde*. Dylan has his fun with the episodic structure of the Beatles' track, but "4th Time Around" fails to achieve the kind of succinct (coming in at right about two minutes) impact that the Fab Four manages. Ironically, by utilizing the sitar in such memorable fashion, the Beatles ended up looking like innovators on a song that owed a great debt to Dylan. Now there's another twist ending that nobody saw coming.

48. "Back in the U.S.S.R." (from *The Beatles*, 1968)

After about three years of music that utilized studio technology, unique instrumentation, and exotic imagination to push the boundaries of rock and pop music to the point that those boundaries essentially ceased to exist, the Beatles kicked off their 1968 self-titled two-disc set, which would become known as the White Album, with a good old blast of American rock-and-roll music. But because they were still all about subverting expectations, the song cheekily paid tribute to the chief Cold War rival of the United States.

"Back in the U.S.S.R." was the brainchild of Paul McCartney, who wrote the American-sounding, Russia-praising song while he was in India, of course. The Beatles deserve some credit for having the open minds to see that there were young people in other countries who weren't necessarily defined by the beliefs of their respective powers that be and who deserved just as much glorification in song as anyone else. While it caused some problems in the United States with the anti-Russia set, the track eventually solidified the Beatles' status as worldwide youth ambassadors in song.

McCartney also cleverly adorned this controversial sentiment with the musical signposts of two artists whose music practically screamed Americana. From Chuck Berry's "Back in the USA" they borrowed the main structure of the song in terms of both the driving rhythm and the theme of homesickness. And, since the Beach Boys had themselves borrowed heavily from Berry at the start of their career, "Back in the U.S.S.R." also contains harmonies clearly modeled on those of the Wilson brothers, Mike Love, and Al Jardine, right down to the falsettos and Love-style bass vocals. (Love was actually in India with the Beatles and the Maharishi and claims to have advised McCartney on the lyrics.)

Although the song is as jovial as they come on the White Album thanks to its exuberant music and thrilling harmonies, it actually was recorded during a period of great discord within the band. Ringo Starr, frustrated by intraband tensions and criticism of his playing, left the sessions during the recording of this song and "Dear Prudence." McCartney took over the sticks on the song, and while at times he seems to be drumming on ice here, he manages to keep the furious pace well enough. (It's possible the other two Beatles at the session, George Harrison and John Lennon, pitched in on the skins, as the band appeared to do a lot of multitracking to atone for the fact that they were missing their percussive engine.)

All three present Beatles also contribute on electric guitar, giving the song a much grittier feel than what was the norm in their midsixties psychedelic period. The only major effect that they use here is the sound of the airplane taking off at the start of the song and landing at the end, mimicking the journey the narrator takes from Miami Beach back to his Russian home.

It's not the best flight the guy has ever had ("On the way the paper bag was on my knee"), but he's calmed by thoughts of his home. Starting in the bridge and continuing through the final verses, McCartney starts adding specific place names and other Russian touches to make the song sound as if it was indeed written by a Soviet citizen who just happened to speak great English.

The middle eight contains an homage to the Beach Boys' "California Girls," as McCartney drops Ukraine, Moscow, and Georgia into his girl-chasing itinerary. (And, by stating that "Georgia's always on my mind," he plays off the American standard "Georgia on My Mind," written by Hoagy Carmichael and immortalized by Ray Charles.) Instead of imagining guitars in the final verse, "balalaikas ringing out" are his soundtrack of choice as he implores his girl to "come and keep your comrade warm."

It's all very playful and cleverly done, but the music is so bold and brassy that the song easily rises above novelty song territory. The Beatles proved on "Back in the U.S.S.R." that they could still rock out with utter conviction, even when they were a man down and on figuratively foreign soil.

47. "The Long and Winding Road" (from Let It Be, 1970)

The camel's back was already broken by the time "The Long and Winding Road" was released, but let's just say it was the straw that added some serious insult to the dromedary's injury. As with most things Beatles, it became a success, hitting No. 1 in the United States for the band's twentieth and final chart topper, even as they had already gone their individual ways. And it somehow survived its tortured process from origination to finished product, perhaps the most tortured in the band's history (although you could make a case here for "Across the Universe" as well), thanks to the beauty and feeling of the song itself.

The fact that "The Long and Winding Road" landed on *Let It Be* should immediately send up red flags about the path it took. This was an album, released in 1970, that none of the Beatles could be bothered to finish, so it was essentially left in the hands of an outside party to put it all together. The work Phil Spector, the outsider in question, did on this song has caused consternation and debate for decades.

Even if he did go slightly astray, it's not entirely his fault, since the Beatles never truly finished the song on their own. Paul McCartney wrote "The Long and Winding Road" and worked on it with the band during the *Get Back/Let It Be* sessions in early 1969. What they managed was little more than a demo; while McCartney's piano and vocal performance was fully realized, his band seemed to be doing little more than feeling their way around the song. And John Lennon on bass played several wonky notes, when he could be bothered to play at all. You can hear the stripped-down version on *Anthology 3*.

The version on *Let It Be . . . Naked* is a little better instrumentally, if only for the inclusion of Billy Preston's brief keyboard solo, but McCartney's performance isn't quite as fine in that one. Spector took the sparse take found on *Anthology 3* and did what he thought needed to be done, adding copious strings and, most controversially, a female choral section, while pretty much drowning out the Beatles' instrumentation save for McCartney's piano.

Again, Spector deserves some slack because he didn't really have a finished product with which to work. And some of his choices work, especially the rising countermelody played by the violins in the break before the final verse. But the whole thing veers perilously close to middle-of-the-road territory. (George Martin's snarky take when he was told he wouldn't be receiving credit as the producer on the song: "I said, 'I produced the original and what you should do is have a credit saying: Produced by George Martin, over-produced by Phil Spector.' They didn't think that was a good idea.")[23]

McCartney flipped as well, sending to the group's late-period business manager Allen Klein what was essentially a cease-and-desist letter that gave step-by-step instructions on how the song should be fixed, ending with the threat, "Don't ever do it again."[24] His instructions went unheeded, and "The Long and Winding Road" was released in full Spectorama.

And yet, for all of that mess, the song still soars on the honesty of the emotions that McCartney evokes in his performance. You can hear the pain and regret in his voice as his narrator tries his find his way back to the person who can solve his mounting problems. His melody is both uplifting and bereft all at once, as the promise of the destination keeps driving him forth even as his resting place seems to lengthen away from him whenever he nears it. Any parallels to the struggles his band was enduring surely must have been intended.

When he sings, "You left me standing here a long, long time ago," you can almost hear the teardrops on the verge of falling. And when he closes it out with "Don't keep me waiting here, lead me to your door," you can picture this soul standing alone, pleading for the salvation that seems to be denied.

That's what should be remembered about the song. "The Long and Winding Road" should lead us ultimately to those moving moments, rather than to the dead ends of infighting and rancor.

46. "Glass Onion" (from *The Beatles*, 1968)

the Beatles have nobody but themselves to blame for the birth of rock-and-roll criticism. They wrote and performed songs that deserved to be picked apart and analyzed, and there was an audience clearly hungry for deep inspection into their words and music.

So John Lennon's frustration with overzealous interpretation of his work, while understandable, should have been directed inward, right? And if the professional critics and amateur musical detectives hadn't come to the fore, and he hadn't become exasperated with their occasional silliness and wrongheadedness about his work, the world might have missed out on the gloriously mysterious "Glass Onion."

Found on the White Album in 1968, "Glass Onion" flings clues left and right at fans looking for every possible scrap of information in their attempt to unravel a mystery that wasn't really ever there in the first place. And no, we're not referring to the "Paul Is Dead" insanity that gripped a few zealots back in the day (and, it must be mentioned, still burdens many a website today), although that is the most extreme manifestation of the phenomenon.

The nonexistent mystery in this case is the one that supposedly hid behind every morsel of the Beatles' lyrics, the one that, if properly solved, might either reveal the meaning of life or the preferred breakfast habits of Ringo Starr, depending on the aims and predilections of the sleuth in question. What those would-be Sherlocks tend to miss is that lyrics can often be interpreted in myriad ways, none of which is necessarily completely right or wrong. And sometimes lyrics hold no deeper meaning than the fact that the words sound real good when jumbled together.

Another problem is that somebody focusing solely on the lyrics of "Glass Onion" would miss out on one of the band's best grooves on record. Rarely have Ringo Starr's drums ever snapped with such force and precision, nor has Paul McCartney's bass often locked in quite so tightly with those drums as it does here. Lennon keeps a solid strum going on acoustic guitar underneath it all, while George Harrison chirps away at the margins with occasional stabs of electric guitar.

This rock-solid foundation seamlessly intertwines with the string section, which brings a little James Bond intrigue into the song. Meanwhile, Lennon's vocals strike conspiratorial tones, as if he's letting his listeners in on some profound secret, although he barely manages to hide the tongue lodged in his cheek.

Lennon name-drops several of the band's recent classics in the lyrics, including "Strawberry Fields Forever" and "I Am the Walrus." They make sense as choices for inclusion, since their nonlinear lyrical structure and dependence on imagery and stream of consciousness instead of a coherent storyline made them perfect fodder for fanciful interpretations. To these he adds some new red herrings, including "bent-backed tulips," "dovetail joints," and a "cast iron shore."

He even brings his bandmates into the strangeness, confessing that the walrus was not him but rather his buddy Paul. Had he known this throwaway line would have convinced many that McCartney was dead, Lennon might have thought twice about it. Or, knowing him, he might have taken perverse pleasure in it. Regardless, the effort and skill he puts into completely throwing people off course both amuses and stings all at once.

In the final verse, the "fool on the hill" makes an appearance, bringing his recorder theme along with him. But what sticks out is the way Lennon sings, "Listen to me." There is real urgency, even desperation in that part of the vocal. Perhaps he was again trying to pull one more over on his audience. Or maybe the intensity he brings to that line is the real Lennon trying to get through to the budding analysts out there, begging them to find another way to spend their time.

In the refrain, Lennon sings about "looking through a glass onion." The implication is that such a view would skew anything, making it look like whatever the viewer wanted or needed it to mean at that point in his or her life. Considering Lennon's point that you can make any song mean whatever you want if you twist it far enough, the metaphor is apt. Or maybe that's a misinterpretation of the misdirection, in which case this analysis of the analysis would prove his point even more.

It all gets a bit confusing. Just suffice it to say that "Glass Onion" confuses and fascinates, no matter what you think it means.

45. "Michelle" (from *Rubber Soul*, 1965)

There are many advantages to being a Beatles fan at a young age, with the obvious one being exposure to the very best of pop music in your formative years, thereby shaping your taste for the rest of your music-loving life. Additionally, having listened to "Michelle," young Beatles' fans have a leg up in their first French classes since they already know one phrase that fellow students who haven't yet fallen under the sway of the Fab Four don't.

Even beside its linguistic benefits, "Michelle" stands out as one of the most gorgeously longing Beatles' ballads ever recorded. It's also another excellent example of why 1965's *Rubber Soul* belongs right there in the discussion with *Revolver*, *Sgt. Pepper's Lonely Hearts Club Band*, the White Album, and *Abbey Road* for the all-time greatest Beatles' album, although you can't really go wrong with any of them.

Little did Paul McCartney know when he was playing an arty little guitar piece to impress girls at the parties of Austin Mitchell (John Lennon's art school acquaintance), long before the Beatles ever became famous, that the piece would turn into one of his most beloved compositions. But Lennon helped out in a big way, in terms of both reviving interest in the piece and completing it.

As McCartney explained to Barry Miles, the song's impact would not have extended beyond those parties had it not been for Lennon's recollection. "I remember sitting around there, and my recollection is of a black turtleneck sweater and sitting very enigmatically in the corner, playing this rather French tune," he said. "Years later, John said, 'D'you remember that French thing you used to do at Mitchell's parties?' I said yes. He said, 'Well, that's a good tune. You should do something with that.'"[25]

According to Lennon, he also helped McCartney out with the bridge. "I had been listening to Nina Simone—I think it was 'I Put a Spell on You,'" Lennon told David Sheff. "There was a line in it that went: 'I love you, I love you.' That's what made me think of the middle eight for Michelle: 'I love you, I love you, I l-o-ove you.'"[26]

With Lennon, McCartney, and George Harrison playing acoustic guitars and Ringo Starr playing the lightest of percussion to nudge the song along, the lonely prettiness of McCartney's tune stands out, while "ooh-ooh" harmonies from Lennon and Harrison provide a striking countermelody. In the song, it's the narrator who's trying to get through to a girl who speaks French. His knowledge of the language is minimal, but the earnest ardor in the vocal communicates far better than his rudimentary translation could ever possibly manage.

In those middle sections, McCartney gets to display the emotions that no language barrier could confuse. The bluesiness in his voice gets a boost from his underpinning bass notes in these portions of the song, and there's a great moment when his bellowing cry of "I love you" opens up into a Harrison solo.

The narrator's persistence in getting through to this mademoiselle is evident; he truly believes that he'll figure out how to make her understand even if he doesn't yet know the words. Until then, what words he does know he'll repeat over and over in an effort to get to her level and convey just how much she means to him.

Here again the Beatles find another way to sing a love song without saying the same thing that's been said a million times before. In this case, the language difference stands in for any trivial impediment to love, one that can be overcome easily enough if the feelings are strong enough. In the end, the music of "Michelle" and McCartney's vocal makes the case for love as well as any French poet ever could.

44. "You Never Give Me Your Money" (from *Abbey Road*, 1969)

Whether it was a subconscious things or a concerted effort to make sure that the waning days of his band were well documented, Paul McCartney spent a good portion of his final year with the Beatles writing about, well, the Beatles. Many people have attempted to uncover the exact causes and specific details that led the most successful and beloved band in rock-and-roll history to come apart at the seams; they could learn a lot simply by following the running commentary McCartney provided on *Abbey Road* and *Let It Be*.

Alas, even for a band who promoted peace and love to a grand degree, monetary issues did indeed play a role in their dissolution. McCartney's opening line in "You Never Give Me Your Money" complains, "You never give me your money / You only give me your funny paper." As George Harrison explained in *Anthology*, "'Funny paper'—that's what we get. We get bits of paper saying how much is earned and what this is and that is, but we never actually get it in pounds, shillings and pence.

We've all got a big house and a car and an office, but to actually get the money we've earned seems impossible."[27]

Yet McCartney's song, found on *Abbey Road*, goes beyond simply whining about financial issues, even if that's what may have inspired it. "You Never Give Me Your Money" ends up being a lament for lost innocence, for a time when four young men didn't have any money worries because they really didn't have any money. What the narrator seems to be profoundly lacking and actively seeking within the song isn't so much a clearer picture of his finances but rather the sense of freedom and possibility that existed in that long gone time.

"You Never Give Me Your Money" provided McCartney with a chance to do what John Lennon had done on the White Album with "Happiness Is a Warm Gun," which is take a bunch of smaller songs and meld them into a coherent whole. Whereas the thrill of Lennon's song was how he barreled from section to section and held the thing together through sheer will and attitude, McCartney's song amazes because of how seamlessly he intertwines the three distinct portions, a skill he would display again and again in his solo career.

The song also benefits from a brilliant band performance, as they capture the disparate moods of each section and provide flourishes along the way that really shine. In the opening portion McCartney is alone at his piano, somber chords betraying the hurt and disappointment he's about to express. The other instruments—bass, guitar, and drums—subtly show up one by one as if preparing for their bigger parts in the following sections. McCartney's vocal is spent of emotion, a meek cry at forces bigger than himself that he can no longer control; he has already broken down too many times to do it again.

Ringo Starr's drums jolt us out of the melancholy opening into the middle portion, and McCartney's voice shifts into a husky, bluesy tone not unlike the one he favored on R&B-flavored tunes like "Lady Madonna." He also adds the saloon piano while Starr lays heavy on the toms, giving this middle portion an undeniably jaunty feel.

The lyrics at first don't seem to jibe with the peppiness of the backing, with the narrator talking about getting canned from his job and not having the money to pay his rent, ultimately having "nowhere to go." That's when McCartney turns it around with the winning phrase "But oh that magic feeling, nowhere to go." The absence of money dovetails with the absence of responsibility.

George Harrison, whose guitar sounds like ringing bells in this section, then provides the connecting tissue with a solo that keeps ascending farther and farther skyward until it releases into the final portion. McCartney again has changed his tune, this time adopting an energetic and hopeful voice, and he begins describing his plans to get away from it all. He may not be able to definitively escape the quandaries surrounding him, but he can at least put them off for a bit with a little holiday. By that time, he was with his eventual wife Linda, and the excursions the two would take color this part of the song.

In the outro, McCartney joins Lennon and Harrison for a refrain of an old children's rhyme: "One, two, three, four, five, six, seven / All good children go to heaven." It's meant to reflect that youthful, vibrant feeling for which everyone longs once burdened with adult issues, but the three men sing it in a questioning kind of way, as if maybe that part of their lives was just a dream and the current headaches the reality. "You Never Give Me Your Money" identifies both the problems within the band and a temporary fix, but the permanent solution dangling well out of reach looms heavy over the whole affair.

43. "While My Guitar Gently Weeps" (from *The Beatles*, 1968)

One thing that's instantly noticeable about the White Album is the excess frivolity. The Beatles wrote a ton of music for the double album while on retreat in India early in 1968. Whether it was the meditation or the peaceful atmosphere, a lot of the songs they composed led with a playful sense of humor and didn't worry too much about making the kind of grand statements for a generation their 1967 music had sort of made, even when the group hadn't intended it.

And so side 1 of the first album seems almost like a reaction against that kind of import. "Back in the U.S.S.R." is a rocking satire; "Dear Prudence" is a gorgeous quasi–love song; "Glass Onion" takes aim at those who would take the group too seriously; "Ob-La-Di, Ob-La-Da" is a reggaefied romp; "Wild Honey Pie" is a weird instrumental; and "The Continuing Story of Bungalow Bill" is directed squarely at the funny bone.

Yet the moment that Paul McCartney's Morse code piano notes poke through the speakers, the band seems to be alerting us that something containing a little more gravitas is coming up. "While My Guitar Gently

Weeps" goes on to hold up its end of the bargain, delivering cosmic statements and warnings over dramatic sonics.

From McCartney's opening piano salvo to his stabbing staccato bass notes at the beginning of each bar of music, from Ringo Starr's stately drum beat to the whining organ in the middle eights, all the way down to McCartney's moaning harmonies and the strange cries at the end of the song, everything is pitched toward an intense musical experience. The Beatles then sealed the deal for that experience by having God himself come aboard and play lead guitar.

Those who have heard the quiet acoustic-and-organ version of the song (found on *Anthology 3*) can attest to the unadorned beauty of George Harrison's composition. But, like Jimi Hendrix brought out the apocalyptic portent in Bob Dylan's "All Along the Watchtower," so too did Eric Clapton's axe find the profound anguish in "While My Guitar Gently Weeps." And does he ever make that thing weep.

Some might say that the instrumental showcase was uncharacteristic for the group, but considering the title of the song, some kind of guitar pyrotechnics were necessary. And, according to Harrison, only Clapton's presence awakened his other band members to the possibility of the song. As he explained in *Anthology*, "We tried to record it, but John and Paul were so used to just cranking out their tunes that it was very difficult at times to get serious and record one of mine. It wasn't happening. They weren't taking it seriously and I don't think they were even all playing on it, and so I went home that night thinking, 'Well, that's a shame,' because I knew the song was pretty good."

A chance encounter the next day with Clapton gave Harrison the idea to invite him into the session. "I said, 'Eric's going to play on this one,' and it was good because that then made everyone act better," he said. "Paul got on the piano and played a nice intro and they all took it more seriously."[28]

On the lyrical side, "While My Guitar Gently Weeps" taps into the oracular point of view that Harrison had employed on songs like "Love You To" and "Within You Without You," as the narrator tries to enlighten someone, or maybe even a larger group, about the error of his or her ways. This fellow sees "love that is sleeping" and "every mistake we must surely be learning," and his only recourse is to play some sorrowful guitar since nobody seems to listen otherwise. One wonders how much of the song was a metaphor for Harrison's frustrations about struggling to have his voice heard among the intimidating talents and personalities of Lennon and McCartney within the Beatles.

In the middle section, he expresses confusion and regret at how this person he's addressing has gone so far astray. Harrison's lilting vocal does much to mask these rather tart accusations, considering he claims that the person in question has been "perverted" and "bought and sold."

It says something about Harrison's ability to deliver the song that it became one of his signature tunes even with Clapton's guitar so fore-grounded. And it was an important tune for him because it showed he could deliver a classic that wasn't either a sarcastic broadside or a medita-tive koan. You can find echoes of "While My Guitar Gently Weeps" and the heavy pall it casts all over Harrison's solo breakthrough *All Things Must Pass*. On the White Album, meanwhile, the song serves as an anti-dote to the zaniness all around it, demonstrating that the quiet Beatle had, at least at this time, the most serious things to say.

42. "Help!" (from *Help!*, 1965)

The Beatles wrote and recorded somewhere in the neighborhood of three hundred songs in their time together, many of which were released, while others went unheard until bootlegs and compilations unearthed them. "Help!" is the only one that included an exclamation point in its title.

The simple answer for the punctuation choice is that the song was also used as the title track for the Beatles' 1965 film, since that exclamation point certainly worked for marketing purposes. But its presence in the title of the song also gives a clue about just how heavy a funk the song's main writer, John Lennon, had fallen into, and also about how desperate he was to receive some assistance to find his way out.

In the middle of the maelstrom of fame and success, Lennon found himself a bit at sea with it all. He had gained weight, calling it, in typical-ly irreverent fashion, his "fat Elvis period,"[29] sublimating for whatever he was missing with food and drink. And although the writing of the song was necessitated by the timing of the movie, Lennon tapped into whatev-er subconscious pain he was feeling at the time when he composed it.

He recognized this when he mentioned to *Rolling Stone* in 1970 that it was one of his favorite efforts within the group. "I meant it—it's real," he said. "The lyric is as good now as it was then. It is no different, and it makes me feel secure to know that I was aware of myself then. It was just me singing 'help' and I meant it."[30]

Lennon also expressed dismay that the group had sped up the song to make it a hit single, which it turned out to be, yet another chart topper for the group in both England and the United States. While Lennon's point that the subtleties of the lyrics might get lost in the whoosh of the music, there is a case to be made that the quicker tempo also amplified the urgency of Lennon's message. Surely that opening scream of "Help!," which arrives before the music has even kicked in, couldn't be any more forceful and demonstrative.

Lennon's hustling acoustic guitar rhythm plays off Paul McCartney's bouncy bass and Ringo Starr's fast-stepping beat to create some impressive forward momentum; this was a band that could always blend speed and precision better than anybody else, especially in the early days when most of the numbers were up-tempo. George Harrison also chips in with speedy electric arpeggios while McCartney provides a clever countermelody on backing vocal in the verses, taking Lennon's lyrics and folding them into bluesy shapes behind the main tune. There's not even time enough for an instrumental break, just the opening blast, three verses, and two refrains before the final screams of "Help me, help me" run out the clock.

In the final verse, the heavier portions of the music back out to give a glimpse of what the ballad version might have sounded like, as Lennon muses, "When I was younger, so much younger than today / I never needed anybody's help in any way." He contrasts that with his current life of insecurity and loss of independence, which "seems to vanish in the haze."

The refrains have Lennon pleading to an unknown person in the hopes that he'll receive the help he requires. Whether a lover, a friend, or divine intervention was the target of these pleas is really irrelevant. What matters is the admission of vulnerability, and that's what comes through clear as a bell, even when the music is loud and fast all around him.

That brief acoustic section also serves to maximize the impact when the other instruments and backing vocals return, another way in which this cry for aid becomes vibrant rock and roll. "Help!" delves into some pretty deep psychological realms, and although its creator may not have thought so, the fact that it does so in such a punchy, catchy way makes it a true rarity among your typical two-minute pop songs. In the end, that exclamation point not only serves to emphasize the import of the message but also signifies the powerful way in which it is delivered.

41. "Two of Us" (from *Let It Be*, 1970)

Although the actual breakup had been known to group members for several months previous, the Beatles' fracture wasn't announced to the world until a press release by Paul McCartney confirming his first solo album included the news on April 10, 1970. *Let It Be*, the group's final album, arrived in the United Kingdom on May 8, 1970, and in the United States ten days later.

The time line means that fans who put *Let It Be* on the record player and heard the opening track, "Two of Us," with its sweet harmonies sung by John Lennon and Paul McCartney, likely felt deep sadness instead of the warm fuzzies the song was intended to engender. Those folks also might have assumed that the song was intended as a requiem for the relationship between the group's two chief songwriters, a way to send the group's fans out on a positive note (which was actually the intention of much of *Abbey Road*, recorded after but released before *Let It Be*).

Little did the fans know that McCartney, who wrote the song, was actually referencing the trips he liked to take with Linda Eastman, whom he had married by the time the song was released. And little did they know that the recording of this song started a row between McCartney and George Harrison, causing Harrison to briefly walk out of the band and further intensifying a rift between the two men that would linger for years.

Upon listening to the song, it's hard to hear anything but a tender ode to the band's good old days, when things were simpler and the complicating factors that were tearing the band apart weren't even yet in existence. It's a testament to the professionalism, chemistry, and talent of the group that they were able to pull it together just enough to create the illusion of cohesion for at least the duration of the song.

It doesn't hurt either that "Two of Us" also features the best songwriting on the album. You could also make a case for both "Across the Universe" and "The Long and Winding Road" in this respect, but both of those songs suffered from both the band's negligence in recording them and the choices made after the dissolution by producer Phil Spector. In the case of "Two of Us," Spector pretty much kept his hands off because he had a pretty solid product already in the can.

The interlocked acoustic guitars are pushed along by Ringo Starr's thumping shuffle of a beat. McCartney may have given Harrison grief about how to play the song, but the recorded evidence shows a subtle and affecting lead guitar effort played low to act almost like a bass. The song keeps coming to false stops, only to be revved back up each time by that twanging acoustic riff, as if the band doesn't want the good feelings to end.

McCartney's song details the kind of trivial activities that can be endlessly meaningful when completed in the presence of someone you love. What does it matter if you're "getting nowhere" or "not arriving" when you're enjoying the time so much? Burning matches, chasing paper, and wearing raincoats on sunny days: as another McCartney song queries, "Who could ask for more?"

In the middle section, McCartney takes a solo vocal for this bit of moving testimony: "You and I have memories / Longer than the road that stretches on ahead." If you read the line closely, and if you believe that he had segued in this portion of the song from talking about Linda to commenting on Lennon, you'll see beyond the affection to the admission that the relationship may be running its course, hence the idea that looking back provides the better view. It's the line that lends the song its bittersweet hue, although the context in which it was released needed no help for that.

McCartney and Lennon come together time and again to sing the lines, "We're on our way home / We're going home." The sentiment there can be compared to the opening lines of "Golden Slumbers," when McCartney sang, "Once there was a way to get back home." Had his view changed that much in the short period of time between when the two songs were written?

You could write it off and say that the song wasn't entirely about his relationship with Lennon and the band; it may have only barely been about it, as a matter of fact. But, considering all that was going down at the time the song was recorded, you can't help but wonder if Paul McCartney was himself indulging in a bit of wish fulfillment about the Beatles, imagining some sort of return to a time and place when the four men could be bandmates and good friends all over again like they had been in the beginning. That's certainly what millions of fans were doing when they heard "Two of Us," knowing that it would have to serve as touching nostalgia instead of a refreshing new start for the band they loved so dearly.

40. "Yes It Is" (from *Past Masters, Volume 1*, released as a B-side in 1965)

It is difficult for any Beatles' song to be considered unheralded. As the most celebrated band in the history of music, they can lay claim to a fan base with members who are generally as comprehensive in their dissection of the band's musical output as they are passionate about it. Consider also that the Beatles released a relatively finite amount of music, contained within a dozen (British) albums and a handful of singles and EPs over about an eight-year period. When you compare that to the seemingly bottomless output of equally lauded contemporaries like Bob Dylan and the Rolling Stones, it's hard to imagine how any release by the Fab Four could ever hide under the radar.

This can happen to some extent though. Songs that were B-sides tend to be among those that receive the least attention. Most weren't included on studio albums, and they didn't receive the airplay of the A-sides, which were often giant hits. So the B-side songs are kind of unmoored within the Beatles' catalog, drifting apart from the recognition the band's other songs usually receive.

In addition, songs can be underheard when they are first underrated. Again, how can the band generally regarded as the best ever have songs that are considered subpar? Well, that can occur when the members of that band were the ones doing the bad-mouthing. John Lennon was the most notorious of these offenders, ripping apart not just songs written by his cohorts but also several of his own compositions when asked about them in his post-Beatles life.

Hopefully fans realize that in many of these interviews Lennon had an agenda of sorts to leave his former band behind and that sometimes the most unreliable judge of art is the person who creates it. Nonetheless, it's not out of the question that people might ask of these besmirched songs, "Well, if the band didn't like it, how good can it be?"

All of which leads us to "Yes It Is," which falls into both of the aforementioned categories. It was the B-side of the immensely successful single "Ticket to Ride" in 1965 and never appeared on a studio album, only being collected on the (equally unheralded) *Love Songs* compilation released in 1977 before finally being included on the *Past Masters* CD release along with all of its B-side brethren.

And John Lennon took direct aim at the song when discussing it with interviewers. In 1980 he told David Sheff, "That's me trying a rewrite of 'This Boy,' but it didn't work."[31] He not only dismissed the track but also didn't even feel it was worthy of providing reasons for why it failed.

So maybe there are some people out there who either haven't yet been exposed to "Yes It Is" or have dismissed it out of hand. Those people should immediately look it up and play it, because they're going to discover a song that rips your heart out in the best possible way.

Lennon may indeed have modeled the song on "This Boy," also a B-side but one that became famous nonetheless through live performance. But "Yes It Is" bests the earlier song, which, as great as it is, is a pretty clear homage to Smokey Robinson and other Motown balladeers. "Yes It Is" manages its own distinct musical mood, something that's not quite folk, not quite soul, but absolutely gut-wrenching.

"Yes It Is" also follows the "This Boy" template of restrained verses followed by impassioned middle eights. But there is more versatility in the melody, both in the verses, where Lennon seems to climb deeper down into despair with each succeeding line, and in the bridges, where he briefly feigns hope only to let out the kind of feral cries of pain that accompany wounds too deeply ingrained to be treated. (The fact that he's singing the positive words "Yes it is" at this point in the song makes the pain seem that much more devastating.)

The lyrics tell of a man who has lost someone he loves but is trying to bravely move on with someone new. The operative word there is "trying," because he can only see this new girl if she promises not to wear the color that his ex preferred. Obviously this new relationship seems to have little hope of succeeding, because he's clearly still hung up on what's gone instead of concentrating on what's in front of him. So he's about to continue a tortuous cycle, for he's about to break a hopeful heart in a futile effort to heal his own.

On top of all this, "Yes It Is" features the Beatles' three-part harmonies at their most luscious, an indelible vocal by Lennon, and some guitar effects from George Harrison that sound suspiciously like teardrops. Maybe Lennon didn't like the song because it was an imagined situation and not the kind of confessional material he favored. Or maybe it's just a song that got lost in the shuffle amid touring and recording and the wild schedule the band had to keep. But only the most stubborn soul would argue that the band failed to create melancholy magic with "Yes It Is," which coincidentally should be the answer when someone asks whether this is the most undeservedly unheralded song in Beatles history.

39. "Here Comes the Sun" (from *Abbey Road*, 1969)

Paul McCartney receives much of the credit for keeping the Beatles afloat long enough so that they could give their fans a proper good-bye album with *Abbey Road*. While that credit is certainly deserved, especially for his genius in assembling the side 2 medley, the first side of the album soars largely thanks to the contributions of George Harrison.

The upward trend in the quality of Harrison's songwriting by that point had pushed him onto the same level with McCartney and John Lennon, so much so that you could argue that his two songs on *Abbey Road* are the finest two complete songs on the album. (The counterargument for John Lennon's "Come Together" muscling in just ahead of the song we're about to discuss is coming up as you read a little further.) Whether it was a case of simple improvement or a backlog of songs that weren't being recorded due to his usual one- or two-song allotment on each album, Harrison was really coming into his own. (The full flowering of this phenomenon came on his 1970 triple album *All Things Must Pass*, which dwarfed the first solo efforts of Lennon and McCartney in terms of both sheer ambition and the music's realization of those ambitions.)

Harrison wrote "Here Comes the Sun" as he played hooky one day from the craziness in the Beatles' world circa 1969. "'Here Comes the Sun' was written at the time when Apple was getting like school, where we had to go and be businessmen: 'Sign this' and 'Sign that,'" he remembered for *Anthology*. "Anyway, it seems as if winter in England goes on forever; by the time spring comes you really deserve it. So one day I decided I was going to sag off Apple and I went over to Eric Clapton's house. The relief of not having to go and see all those dopey accountants was wonderful, and I walked around the garden with one of Eric's acoustic guitars and wrote 'Here Comes the Sun.'"[32]

It's a good thing it hadn't rained that day, because the fair weather yielded the Beatles' best song about the sun. McCartney had made his effort on this front years before with "Good Day Sunshine," which sounded too much like the advertising jingle it eventually became. Lennon contributed the *Abbey Road* fragment "Sun King," which lolled about in a haze before devolving into gibberish lyrics. Only Harrison's song can actually make you feel warm even when Mother Nature hasn't yet cooperated.

His acoustic guitar work certainly helps in that cause, as arpeggios keep unfurling like rays of sunlight hugging around the listener. The rhythm section of McCartney and Ringo Starr keeps things chugging along at a solid pace lest we be tempted into napping this gorgeous day away. Harrison's utilization of an early-model Moog synthesizer brightens the colors of the song, as do the effectively rendered strings and horns. This is a recording on which everything fits snugly into place and adeptly supports the winning melody.

Harrison also realizes that the enjoyment of the sunshine increases by comparing it to the harsher weather. So it is that he mentions the ice and the cold, detailing just how long it's been since the sun arrived: "It seems like years since it's been here." Anyone stuck in the middle of a cold snap can relate. And by mentioning that it's been a "long cold lonely winter," he is also intimating that the return of the warm weather can alleviate the isolation that the cold often forces on us.

"The smiles returning to their faces," he sings, and the stirring music coaxes grins as if on cue. The "doot-in-doo-doo" refrain is just the kind of thing that someone would sing walking around a garden on a lovely summer day. The music keeps hitting high points, like the thrilling modulation into the final verse and Harrison's guitar breakdown preceding that, but there's also just the slightest bit of darkness looming at the edge of the music to make the eventual triumph of the brightness that much sweeter. Harrison keeps reassuring us, "It's all right," but the music has already proven that many times over.

"Here Comes The Sun" is more than just all right, of course. Not only did it help *Abbey Road* on its way to greatness, but its outstanding quality also proved that Harrison's looming post-Beatles musical life would be quite sunny in its own regard.

38. "I Feel Fine" (from *Past Masters, Volume I*, released as a single in 1964)

Trying to put a finger on exactly what made the Beatles so special is impossible, of course; otherwise others would be able to replicate their magic to some extent. Yes, they were great songwriters, but there have been many great songwriters before and since. They played their instruments really well but on the whole not much better than other bands of their day. Talking about chemistry between members also doesn't quite cover it, although there was something indefinable and explosive about the way their personalities and talents intertwined.

No one thing would ever cover it. But their ability to transmit joy via their music is something that should be very high on any list of reasons for their greatness. Certainly it's something that they did better than anybody else, and it's really not even that close. You'll hear songwriters all the time complain about how it's difficult to write a happy song. The Beatles not only wrote a bunch of great ones but were also able to record them in such a manner that the good feelings within the song have a way of latching onto the listener like a benevolent parasite, infusing the whole person with positivity and gladness.

The apotheosis of this ability may have come when the Beatles released "I Feel Fine" as a single in late 1964. As the group progressed, their songwriting began to tackle more complicated emotions, so the early period of 1963 and '64 was the real apex for them in terms of their ebullient songs. "I Feel Fine" hit a sweet spot when the band was still happy to beam in their songs and had reached a point when their facility in the studio allowed them to maximize the impact of the song as well as the intended emotional charge it would give the listener.

Yet, ironically, the song begins with a sound that is often an unpleasant one. When John Lennon accidentally leaned his guitar on one of Paul McCartney's amplifiers, it produced the squalling sound known as feedback. For whatever reason, the sound appealed to them in that moment, and, with the help of producer George Martin, they recreated it for the beginning of "I Feel Fine." Instead of sounding off-putting, the bass note (played by McCartney) that feeds back on itself gives the impression of a light being turned on in the midst of pitch darkness. When that feedback then bends into Lennon's countrified opening riff and Ringo Starr whacks the snare as a kind of countdown to pull the band into the main rhythm, well, let's just say that the rest of the song could have been lousy, and the perfection of that opening still would have carried it a long way. But it just gets better from there.

That opening riff drives the song, although it keeps coming back in different permutations from Lennon on acoustic and George Harrison on electric. Ringo Starr carries the rest of the load with an R&B-styled rumble that could have sounded fussy in lesser hands; he turns it into a beat that's bursting with energy.

The funny thing about "I Feel Fine" is that it maintains a bluesy edge for much of the way even as Lennon's narrator beams about being in love with a girl and her reciprocation of those feelings. Once the group hits the middle section, however, they cut loose those three-part harmonies on the line "I'm so glad" and the sound simply overwhelms. We've talked throughout the list about the ability of the blended voices of Lennon, McCartney, and Harrison to invoke sorrow, wonder, or camaraderie; here they deliver unparalleled, unfathomable joy with just those three words, before McCartney and Harrison hit the "oohs" and Lennon goes back at it alone.

If you can't tell from listening to "I Feel Fine" that it was a runaway No. 1 hit in both the United States and the United Kingdom, perhaps you also need to be informed about the blueness of the sky. When Lennon sings the song, he seems to be doing it with a smile on his face. It makes sense, because everyone listening is likely smiling right back, at both the wonder of the song and the magical ability of the Beatles, by merely singing and playing musical instruments, to bring such joy to the world.

37. "Revolution" (from *Past Masters, Volume 2*, released as a B-side in 1968)

The Beatles largely stayed away from pointed commentary on the hot-button issues of the day in their music. It was a strategy group manager Brian Epstein devised early on; if they were going to court the largest possible audience, they couldn't afford to alienate even the smallest section of it by making a statement on one side of the political spectrum or the other.

Other than the occasional diatribe against universally loathed phenomena like taxation, the group pretty much kept their heads out of the political arena. And yet they still were able to capture the times; no album quite summed up 1967's Summer of Love and a younger generation's efforts to leave behind the old routine than *Sgt. Pepper's Lonely Hearts Club Band*. One could also argue that their music performed a valuable service by distracting folks from the bad headlines and thorny issues spread throughout the world, so their avoidance of those downers was actually a relief.

By 1968, one of the most tumultuous years of human existence, they could clam up no more. John Lennon, who would go on to be a fearless critic of hypocrisy and injustice both in his songs and with his publicity stunts, wrote "Revolution." The tricky thing became convincing the other members of his band that it deserved a wider audience.

When he first recorded the song, Lennon rendered it in a leisurely pace with lazy horns. When Paul McCartney and George Harrison balked at using the song as a single, because of the tempo, Lennon decided to turn up the heat with a searing electric version highlighted by fuzzed-out guitars. Yet even that wasn't enough to get to the A-side; the Beatles went with "Hey Jude" as their summer '68 single, and you can't argue with the choice, as it would go on to be their all-time top-selling single.

McCartney and Harrison were also right to push Lennon into super-charging the song, as the slowed-down version, which made it onto the White Album as "Revolution 1" (where it was joined by a grotesque mutation called "Revolution 9"), doesn't have enough juice to make people stand up and take notice. Where McCartney and Harrison were wrong was in their decision to relegate "Revolution," in its faster form, to a B-side; certainly "Hey Jude" deserved the A-side, but "Revolution" could have been held back or even released as a simultaneous A-side so that it could receive full attention from the masses, because that's what this rip-snorting track that can still make you think deserved.

Rarely have the Beatles, known for the precision and pristineness of their playing, ever sounded so raw. The guitars of Lennon and Harrison churn with relentless intensity throughout, the distortion a visceral manifestation of that intensity. As always, the rhythm section keeps things from spinning too far out of control, while special guest Nicky Hopkins plays a piano solo that boogies away even as those crazed guitars rain fire all around it. The group even reaches back into the past for the section when all instruments drop away except for the vocal and the percussion; on "Eight Days a Week," the group had utilized that tactic with hand claps, while here Lennon's bleats are surrounded by Ringo Starr's drum wallops.

While the music was rough and ready for a fight, Lennon's lyrics actually take a much more measured tone. His message throughout is one of patience and forethought, as he refuses to be pulled into the battle without some sort of sound reasoning behind it all. "You say you got a real solution," he says. "Well, you know / We'd all love to see the plan."

"But when you talk about destruction / Don't you know that you can count me out," he sings, refusing to get caught up in violence. That he equivocated on "Revolution 1" by adding the word "in" after that line seems to be little more than typical Lennon gamesmanship; his actions after the song's release were always aimed toward peace first and foremost. But the lesson that he seems to be teaching here is that those inflamed by passion tend to act without thinking, leading to even worse problems. And those who are angry can also be led astray by those with bad intentions: "If you want money for people with minds that hate / All I can tell you is, brother, you have to wait."

Lennon's clear thinking on the subject shines through even in the midst of the thunderous music struck up by him and his band. In many ways, the song mirrors the Rolling Stones' "Street Fighting Man," released around the same time and featuring Mick Jagger taking a similar wait-and-see approach before diving into the breach. The Beatles' first-ever overt political statement in song, "Revolution" turned out to be a wise and insightful one that demonstrated it was okay to speak out. The consequences of acting out are where it gets tricky.

36. "You Won't See Me" (from *Rubber Soul*, 1965)

Once again we're back on *Rubber Soul* and hearing Paul McCartney lament his roller coaster relationship with former girlfriend Jane Asher. (The year 1965 must have been difficult for them, since songs on both *Help!* and *Rubber Soul* seem to hint at some rough patches, although things must have improved by the time '66 rolled around and he was writing "Here, There and Everywhere" about her.) We've also got another song on which the Beatles started based on a clear musical influence that, when filtered through their style of writing and playing, ended up producing one of the more Beatles-y tracks not just on the album but throughout their whole catalog.

McCartney started writing the song based on the bass techniques of another player, the Liverpudlian giving a nod to Detroit. "To me it was very Motown-flavoured. It's got a James Jamerson feel," he told Barry Miles. "He was the Motown bass player, he was fabulous, the guy who did all those great melodic bass lines."[33]

When the Beatles took off and ran with "You Won't See Me," they clearly had Motown in mind, what with the constant presence of the backing vocalists and that wandering bass line. But somewhere along the line it took on a more pop-oriented sound, partly due to the brightness of McCartney's playing, even as he sang about romantic frustration, and also owing to the clarity of George Martin's production, which snaps and pops in all the right places.

There also isn't much of a guitar presence in the song, as McCartney's piano carries most of the melodic load. Ringo Starr's drumming, however, is involved in practically every twist and turn of the music, as he utilizes every part of the kit to provide pointed percussive commentary. As for the backing vocals, they're just idiosyncratic enough to break out of the Motown mold as well, whether John Lennon is seconding McCartney's exhortations on the bridge with a little countermelody or he and George Harrison are soaring up into falsetto range for the "ooh-la-la" parts at the end.

As the music keeps you on your toes with these little unexpected flourishes, McCartney plows ahead with his relationship issues. He frames the story as a direct address to his girlfriend; you can picture him sitting on the bed making his case to her as she tries to interrupt. He plays to her sympathy ("I just can't go on") but also gets so prickly ("I have had enough / So act your age") that we can maybe understand why she gets out of town every once in a while.

McCartney also slips in heartbreak humor to ease his attack: "Time after time you refuse to even listen / I wouldn't mind if I knew what I was missing." As the song progresses, all the anger and wisecracking turn to flat-out sorrow: "Though the days are few they're filled with tears."

Then again, you don't really need to hear any words to follow the arc of the narrator's feelings. Like that slick little bass line and the ingratiating tune, it bounds up hopefully only to be knocked back down when she disappears again. This is McCartney at his melodic best, tying the angsty lyrics to music that touches on the hard times but never wallows.

Rubber Soul is practically teeming with picture-perfect pop songs like this, so much so that a nonsingle like "You Won't See Me" can get lost in the shuffle. In a little over three minutes, it drops us into a colorful musical world and depicts, comprehensively and convincingly, a strained relationship, to the point that we're unsure it will survive by the time the song ends. That's a pretty good day's work for one song, so reshuffle and check this one out whenever you have the opportunity.

35. "Come Together" (from *Abbey Road*, 1969)

What drove the Beatles toward the *Let It Be* project in the beginning of 1969 was a desire to rid their music of some of the overdubs and instrumental excess that had characterized much of their mind-bendingly brilliant work from 1965 to 1967. They had stepped tentatively toward that kind of feeling on 1968's the White Album, but the wide variety of songs they wrote for the double disc made any kind of unified sonic statement impossible

Let It Be moved more decisively in that direction as the Beatles vied for the title of the world's most overqualified garage band. But the album suffered for a couple reasons. First, the idea of playing the music live meant that the participants had to be in the same room together, which wasn't the best idea for the band at the time; the resulting infighting meant that the album went unfinished and ultimately untended by the band.

There was also the problem of the material on the album. With some notable exceptions, a few of which we've seen on this list, the Beatles tried to push the music in a looser, bluesier direction. That might have been fine had they written enough songs that rose to the occasion. Tracks like "Dig a Pony" and "For You Blue," meant to feel loose and playful, instead sounded slight. Add in the chaos attached to some of the better-written songs, and you can understand why the album was so star-crossed.

That's not to say that the Beatles couldn't succeed with material that had somewhat of a bluesy vibe to it. Oddly enough, *Abbey Road*, the album for which they abandoned the *Let It Be* project, starts with just such a song, the smoky, swampy John Lennon number "Come Together." It certainly gave the impression of the four men in a room together bashing away, even if that probably wasn't the case. It also was an affectingly idiosyncratic bit of songwriting before it ever reached the studios for the group to work it into its finished form.

"Come Together" emanated from an aborted attempt by Lennon to write a kind of campaign slogan for LSD guru Timothy Leary, who briefly considered running for governor of California. Although that campaign never happened, Lennon stuck with the song and ended up with a No. 1 hit in the United States in the process. (It was a double A-side release with "Something.")

Lennon begins "Come Together" with the line "Here come old flat top," which he borrowed from Chuck Berry's "You Can't Catch Me." The appropriation would dog Lennon even into his solo career. He finally had to fend off a lawsuit by doing some cover versions of songs from the same publishing company as the Berry song, even though there are really no similarities between "Come Together" and "You Can't Catch Me" except maybe the lyrical meter and the opening line.

"Come Together" quickly deviates into bizarre territory as Lennon paints a portrait of a kind of deranged cult leader whose grotesqueries only seem to win him more popularity. Whatever self-styled guru he may have been targeting with the lyrics, it's clear that he taps into the strange charisma that draws in the naïve and rudderless. Hence no amount of diseased armchairs, "toe-jam football," or "ju-ju eyeballs" distract the true believers from this dude.

As you may have been able to tell by those quoted lyrics, "Come Together" was also an opportunity for Lennon to flash the free-associative phrasing he had come to favor in the previous few years. He also indulged in some wordplay that melded Lewis Carroll with Groucho Marx on lines like "One and one and one is three / Got to be good-looking 'cause he's so hard to see." In this way he expertly parodies a messiah who talks real fancy but doesn't really say anything.

Lennon can play these kinds of games with the lyrics because he has a powerful musical foundation below him. Driven by Paul McCartney's slyly sinister bass riff and Ringo Starr's battering drums, "Come Together" wallows in the muck and loves it. McCartney adds a piano solo that plows its way into the dense groove and comes out the other side amid some heavy breathing. The outro finally dares to scrape the rafters via George Harrison's soaring lead guitar and Lennon's ever-rising wails. After maintaining a coiled intensity throughout, the music releases all the tension in those exhilarating final moments.

"Come Together" would be Lennon's chief contribution to *Abbey Road*, an album from which he was occasionally absent, either physically or mentally. At least he provided the bluesy edge the album otherwise would have been lacking, the same edge the group had valiantly tried to apply to *Let It Be*. Better late than never.

34. "I Want to Hold You Hand" (from *Past Masters, Volume 1*, released as a single in 1963)

This is a list of the Beatles' best songs ranked purely in terms of their quality. Were we ranking their songs by importance, it's very possible that "I Want to Hold Your Hand" would top the list. Surely it would be in the top five.

As Beatlemania raged through Great Britain in 1963, the group members themselves were well aware of the difficulties other British success stories had in breaking big in America. It had certainly not yet occurred for any artist playing music similar to the Beatles'. Raising their consternation about this prospect was the fact that several songs that had already been monster hits in England had been picked up by smaller labels in the States for distribution, only to sink without a trace on American release.

For "I Want to Hold Your Hand," the group's fourth UK single, the Beatles received distribution from Capitol Records, the American counterpart of EMI, their British label. Whether or not Capitol made a difference in the song's American success is debatable, because news reports about the group's British success that played in the United States inspired intrepid fans and disc jockeys to seek out the single before its official stateside release, and the sweeping response forced Capitol's hand to rush that release by a few weeks.

To seal the deal, "I Want to Hold Your Hand" hit No. 1 on the US charts just a week ahead of the group's historic appearance on *The Ed Sullivan Show*. The serendipity of it all was something that couldn't ever have been planned, and sometimes it seems like the crazed sequence of events actually overshadows the merits of the song itself, as if any one of the Beatles' many songs would have enjoyed the same success at the same time.

Yet that shortchanges just how explosive and exciting "I Want to Hold Your Hand" remains to this day. Maybe the sentiment is chaste compared to the more overt declarations of passion that rock and roll would soon produce. But another way of looking at it is that the Beatles legitimized the kind of tentative yet heartfelt displays of affection that were common among teenagers, who, as their main audience, could certainly relate.

If you can listen to the music, you can hear the passion roiling unspoken underneath the innocence of the words. Maybe the lyrics only get as far as hand holding and touching, but the thrust of the rhythm section and the exultation of the vocals of John Lennon and Paul McCartney say something else entirely. Notice that the guitars of Lennon and George Harrison largely stay on the fringes, allowing for the full impact of the voices to shine through when they sprint into those high harmonies.

This song is deceptively simple; when you take a closer listen, you start to hear the ingenious ways in which the group makes it stand out. McCartney's squirrely little bass run in the verses toward that surprising, somewhat somber chord change provides just enough misdirection so that the charge into the chorus is magnified. And the quiet middle eights, rendered so tenderly, steady the boat for a moment before the soaring, "Twist and Shout"–like repetition of "I can't hide," the words and the music clearly stating that the narrator doesn't care if the whole world hears his intentions.

Needless to say, "I Want to Hold Your Hand" made for the perfect live vehicle for these very reasons. The quiet parts allowed the girls to swoon, while the loud ones allowed them to lose their minds. Even listening to the studio version, your mind tends to imagine the screams that aren't really there. That's a testament to the immediacy of the recording.

We'll never know if or when the Beatles would have conquered America had it not been for "I Want to Hold Your Hand." But it's important to remember that it is in the trivia books not just because it was released at the right time and in the right place but also because it was the right song for the job.

33. "The Fool on the Hill" (from *Magical Mystery Tour*, 1967)

Are you looking for a surprise contender for the Beatles' best album? How about one that wasn't really an album at all? In late 1967, still riding high off the massive success of *Sgt. Pepper's Lonely Hearts Club Band*, the Beatles churned out a sextet of songs for their new television film titled *Magical Mystery Tour*, which was released at the end of 1967.

In the United Kingdom, those six songs were released as an EP (extended play) disc. But in America, Capitol Records, which had long taken a cleaver to the British Beatles' albums and rearranged them at their own will without any thought given to thematic soundness or unity, finally got one right. They added to the aforementioned six songs five more tracks that had been released as singles in the past year, a group that included heavyweights like "Strawberry Fields Forever," "Penny Lane," and "All You Need Is Love." All of a sudden *Magical Mystery Tour*, instead of a tasty sampler, was a powerhouse of a full meal.

The only minor detriment to this approach by Capitol was that it may have backgrounded some of those original six songs, especially since the film that contained them was poorly received. But "The Fool on the Hill" was just too good to be silenced for too long; it made enough of an impact on fans that its inclusion on the greatest hits collection *1967–1970*, which sold massively on its release in 1973, made perfect sense and furthered its exposure.

The odd thing about the song's trajectory toward popularity is that it profiles a character who would much rather be left to his solitude. "The Fool on the Hill" is one of Paul McCartney's keenly observed character sketches, in this case detailing a dreamer who is misunderstood by those who encounter him.

It might be a bit of overanalysis to look into this character and perhaps find hints of its author's own personality in there, but those seeking for McCartney to reveal his true self in his lyrics, which isn't something he was ever too eager to do, might want to check out "The Fool on the Hill." After all, at the time of the song's release, McCartney was already seen by many fans and critics as a musical genius who lacked the lyrical bite and insight of his cohort John Lennon. If you read that kind of underestimating into the lyrics here, you can certainly hear it as a bit of veiled autobiography.

If nothing else, McCartney, who, it must be noted, has never claimed the song was in any way confessional, instead stating that it was about a Maharishi-like character and his response to the naysayers who doubted him, certainly has respect and empathy for this character whom other people seem to view as a bit of a nut. The narrator suggests that this is because nobody takes time or makes the effort to listen and truly understand what it is the character is trying to say.

Hence you have this "fool" speaking loudly, yet nobody hears. He is disliked and unknown, but the chorus insists on his wisdom: "But the fool on the hill sees the sun going down / And the eyes in his head see the world spinning round."

McCartney's melody is dreamy and sad, and the music surrounding it floats about weightlessly, toggling between waves of boundless joy and an undertow of loneliness. The flutes flutter about brightly in the verses, only to darken noticeably at the beginning of the chorus. That in turn sets the listener up for the drastic transformation in the instrumental break, as McCartney toots away on a recorder while Lennon's mouth harp provides a rhythm worthy of a jug band.

In the final verse, McCartney's voice takes on a hint of desperation as he finally shows the fool's take on all of this: "He never listens to them / He knows that they're the fool." In the outro, he joins in the celebration with wordless vocals pitched high into the heavens. That ebullient ending suggests that "The Fool on the Hill" walks away triumphant in the end, even if nobody bothers to notice.

32. "Penny Lane" (from *Magical Mystery Tour*, 1967)

Before the Beatles unleashed *Sgt. Pepper's Lonely Hearts Club Band* on the world in 1967, they prepared listeners for the changes to come with the double-A-sided single "Strawberry Fields Forever"/"Penny Lane." In the *Anthology* documentary, there's a great scene of Dick Clark interviewing teenage fans about the songs after their psychedelic videos premiered on his show. The kids were skeptical if not downright dismissive of the direction the band had chosen to take their music.

It's a pretty good illustration of the risk the band was taking with their decision to go off the road and follow their muses down the studio rabbit hole, wherever they might lead. Both songs are masterpieces of course, paving the way for *Sgt. Pepper's* and signaling an era when the group's music left behind most of the vestiges of their youthful moptop days in favor of a sophisticated yet progressive sound. And, ironically enough, they did it with a pair of songs looking back to their younger days.

In the case of "Penny Lane," the titular road was a junction where John Lennon and Paul McCartney often met to catch a bus elsewhere. McCartney, his natural tendency toward being observant aiding his songwriting yet again, was able to recreate the sights and sounds of the place, taking a little poetic license here and there to create a slew of memorable characters that populate it. And, as a perfect preview for what was to come on *Sgt. Pepper's*, the song featured the kind of music that made this seemingly average location appear to be the hub of everything wondrous and magical in the world.

Like much of the music that the band would produce in the next year, "Penny Lane" strays from typical rock instrumentation. There are guitars in there, but they're not ever at the forefront; McCartney's piano pushes the song forward with his minimalist bass while Ringo Starr bangs out a workmanlike beat. Nobody did this kind of bouncy-tempo song better than McCartney, in part because he always seemed to have a melody in his hip pocket that could bounce right alongside.

Woodwinds sneak in to add a little mystery at the end of each verse, while brass shows up in the refrains to warm up the summer day described in the song. Starr rings a handbell to add some natural sound to the proceedings, but there's nothing quite as striking within the song as the piccolo trumpet played by session man David Mason. It streaks through the blue skies so piercingly that there's no way for night to invade until the trumpet steps back and gives its permission.

McCartney's lyrics read like the stage directions at the beginning of a play; it's no coincidence that the poppy-pushing nurse "feels as if she's in a play" and a line in the last verse reads, "We see the banker sitting waiting for a trim." His aim here is to efficiently provide us with as much visual imagery as possible so that this avenue can be seen as well as heard. After all, the key line of the refrain is "Penny Lane is in my ears and in my eyes," so it makes sense that he wants to provide the full sensory experience for us in turn.

McCartney does a wonderful job of giving all of the characters in this little production some kind of quirk or peccadillo. Thus they have distinct personalities beyond just being moving parts in the machinery of the street. So you have the barber proudly displaying his handiwork on the walls of his shop, the frazzled banker getting drenched in the rain and targeted for jokes by the kids, the fireman devoted to cleanliness and the queen, and the nurse aware more than the others that she's a part of something bigger than herself.

In the final verse, McCartney brings them all together in the barber shop (except for the nurse, who's probably daydreaming too much to leave her spot), these humble denizens who were going about their merry ways suddenly forming a community. And yet it all seems "very strange" to the narrator.

Some might see that line as McCartney's admission that you can't go home again, that his life as a superstar rendered the sights and sounds of his former life odd and unfamiliar. But the truer assessment is that it's his way of saying that even an unassuming neighborhood contains surprising amounts of profundity and grace if you can see below the surface. "Penny Lane" found the Beatles boldly going forward even as they looked back, as they began the greatest year of music any band has ever produced, even if those kids on *American Bandstand* were slow to realize it.

31. "Lady Madonna" (from *Past Masters, Volume 2*, released as a single in 1968)

We're closing in on a half century since the Beatles released "Lady Madonna" as their first single in 1968. Technological advances in the recording industry in that time span make the techniques used in the former time seem practically archaic. So why is it that "Lady Madonna" pops out of the speakers and, regardless of its artistic quality, which is extremely high, just generally sounds better than so much of what's recorded today?

That's a question with answers too myriad and complicated to be inspected here, but rest assured the electrifying sound of "Lady Madonna" is just one of its many redeeming qualities. Bringing a bluesy throwback vibe to the band's sound after a year (1967) when experimentation and boundary-pushing was the name of the game, the song shows that the band's ability to lock into a groove and ride it straight to glory was still very much intact.

Paul McCartney does his best Fats Domino impression on the song, both in terms of the barreling piano style he uses and the husky timbre he lends to his voice. Most of the musical contributions come on the low end, from McCartney's rumbling bass to Ringo Starr's thumping bass drum to the churning guitars of John Lennon and George Harrison. The saxophones that enter the picture about halfway through the song provide more gritty flavor. None of the players are doing anything too showy; instead they all focus on contributing to the song's relentless forward surge.

"Lady Madonna" acts as McCartney's tribute to mothers, contrasting all of the sacrifices they make and hardships they endure with what he clearly perceives as too little recognition they receive in return. The use of the word "Madonna" cleverly makes a connection between the drudgery of the daily work that moms do and the divine.

This was a topic that clearly appealed to McCartney. A few months earlier, "Your Mother Should Know" played off the seemingly infinite wisdom mothers possess, albeit in a playful manner. Later on McCartney would once again intermingle the secular and religious in his praise of motherhood on "Let It Be," in which his own mother, who had passed away when he was still in his teens, appears in a dream to offer advice.

"Lady Madonna" falls somewhere in between those two extremes in terms of its tone; while the travails of a typical mother as described in the song are no laughing matter, there's just a little bit of lightness in the musical approach, mostly coming through in the vocalized imitation of brass sung by McCartney, Lennon, and Harrison in the "instrumental" break. That offbeat section seems to mimic the children forever orbiting the mother at the center of their universe.

The narrator views this everywoman at the heart of the story with nothing short of awe, as he wonders how she manages to feed, clothe, and take care of the kids on a seemingly miniscule budget. These sections also indirectly comment on the cluelessness of males in terms of these tasks.

In the connecting parts, McCartney runs through a whole week (sans Saturday, which would have troubled the meter) of activities and crises. Before one of these problems can be tackled, the next one arises. These lyrics are cleverly rendered ("Sunday morning creeping like a nun") and lead to the line "See how they run," which briefly separates from the rugged instrumentation for a dreamy moment. This line is crucial, because it demonstrates that no chore is so frustrating that it overcomes the genuine joy a mother reaps from seeing her children at play.

McCartney also tries to get this woman to enjoy herself a little bit, asking her to "listen to the music playing in your head" as she takes a brief rest. But soon it's back to the pummeling groove and the relentless pull of cooking and cleaning and the like, with McCartney ending once again on a note of wonder as Starr funkily kicks the beat to a halt.

"Lady Madonna" earned No. 1 status in the United Kingdom, while, surprisingly, it only hit No. 4 in America, especially considering how assured and adept it is at bringing domestic doldrums to thrilling life. No Mother's Day card could ever make its case as well as "Lady Madonna"—not that it's a fair fight, with McCartney combining such punchy music to his pure affection for Moms everywhere.

30. "Rain" (from *Past Masters, Volume 2*, released as a B-side in 1966)

Because it was the year of the Summer of Love and because *Sgt. Pepper's Lonely Hearts Club Band* was released in the midst of that cultural phenomenon and served as its unofficial soundtrack, 1967 is often considered the height of the Beatles' psychedelic period. In actuality, they had moved on from that kind of sound somewhat; although songs like "Strawberry Fields Forever" and "Lucy in the Sky with Diamonds" would still cling to the backward sound effects, jangly guitars, and ethereal vocals, most of the music the group released in that magical year, while experimental and forward-looking, relied on sounds a bit more traditional, even antiquated on songs like "When I'm Sixty-Four" or "Your Mother Should Know," to get their point across.

In fact, 1966 was when the Beatles really adopted psychedelia most fearlessly. It was all over their landmark 1966 album *Revolver*, and it even made its way to the B-side of their single that preceded the album. Backing up "Paperback Writer," "Rain" featured the group creating surreal sounds via their usual rock instrumentation and some studio affectation. John Lennon assists with one of his most blissed-out vocals, singing as if he's floating on a cloud, directing the rain celebrated in the song to fall.

The lyrics are all about perception trumping reality. "Can you hear me that when it rains and shines / It's just a state of mind?" Lennon asks, his voice sounding as if he's on another, more peaceful plane of existence. "I can show you," he promises, and you can't help but believe him, so striking is the wisdom in his voice as he drags out the words.

"Rain" would have been an interesting little acoustic ditty if the Beatles had taken it in that direction. But there's no doubt that the track they constructed elevated the song considerably, another example of their wizardry in the studio paying huge dividends. The group played the song at a faster tempo than what you hear on the record, then slowed it down after the fact. This effect plays a great deal into the slightly off-kilter feel of the entire affair. (Lennon's backward vocals in the outro don't hurt either.)

Everything seems just a little stretched out, creating a wide canvas for the rhythm section to do its fantastic work. Paul McCartney's bass work is a marvel here. It essentially serves as the lead instrument; while the electric guitars unwind at the flanks of the song, the bass is front and center, pushing and pulling, rising and falling, as McCartney contrasts droning longer notes with flickering runs to keep the song light and heavy all at once.

Ringo Starr has spoken often in interviews about how "Rain" featured his favorite bit of drumming while with the group, and that's an understandable judgment. Those drums are miked in such a way that they both snap and linger somehow, especially the snares, to which he goes heavily here. Think about some of the more aggressive rock drummers in history, guys like Keith Moon and John Bonham, who somehow pushed their way to the forefront even as they laid down the bedrock, and you can hear the template for their exploits in Starr's work on "Rain."

The elongated vocals from Lennon, McCartney, and George Harrison on the words "rain" and "shine" have a hypnotic effect, imbuing those words with greater meaning somehow beyond their physical manifestation as weather events. Every production choice seems to have been done with forethought as to how the sound would contribute to the overall effect rather than at random. That may not seem like much, but in an era when the bands could overbake songs with special effects like kids annoying their elders with a loud whistle, it's high praise indeed.

It's amazing to think of this daring, boundary-pushing song as a nonalbum B-side, but it just demonstrates exactly how prolific the group was in that period. It certainly paved the way for out-there recordings on *Revolver* like "Love You To" and "Tomorrow Never Knows." "Rain" captures the Beatles at their psychedelic peak, as they propel listeners nearer that apex with every beautiful drop that falls.

29. "Things We Said Today" (from *A Hard Day's Night*, 1964)

In addition to being one of the great rock-and-roll movies of all time, 1964's *A Hard Day's Night* was also important in the Beatles' career because it represented a huge leap forward in the quality of John Lennon and Paul McCartney's songwriting. This was evident in the hits, like the title track and "Can't Buy Me Love," which added a bit more nuance to the formula that drove 1963 singles like "She Loves You" and "I Want to Hold Your Hand."

But Beatles fans who go beyond the hits also know that the album featured a mix of offbeat and heartfelt songs about romance. It was the first time that shades of gray began to filter into the band's work, and, as with everything else, they thrived with this kind of material. There were hushed assertions like "I'll Be Back" mixed with playfully woeful admissions like "I'll Cry Instead." The desperately earnest "And I Love Her" contrasted with the tenderly ambivalent "If I Fell."

McCartney, like Lennon, was just getting his feet wet with balladry, but was he ever learning fast. "And I Love Her," his first real slow one in terms of an original composition, featured a nice melody but felt a bit too consciously arty, both in terms of the exotic feel of the music and the poetic ambitions of the lyric.

"Things We Said Today," on the other hand, doesn't really slow the tempo down much. Ringo Starr keeps his metronomic beat at a brisk jog before charging into a full gallop in the middle eight. Yet the emotions displayed in the song and the hushed quality of the instrumental backing allows this one to certainly pass as a ballad, and, as such, it's McCartney's first real triumph in that department.

There's an old songwriting adage that says you should mix sad sentiments with upbeat music and vice versa. McCartney chooses vice versa here. The lyrics tell a tale of romantic commitment and steadfastness even when faced with the separation of time and distance. By contrast, the music relates quite a different story, a minor-key saga of doubt and concern.

John Lennon's rapidly strummed acoustic guitar immediately gets our attention and clears the air for McCartney to begin; the little hook it creates is as much of an instrumental flourish as the group allow themselves here, preferring instead to let McCartney's mostly pensive melody unfold unhindered. The music does take a major turn when it suddenly modulates into the bounding middle sections; that they make the switch and then the switch back again so seamlessly is a testament both to the band's dexterity and the clever construction of McCartney's song.

The narrator in the song is the type who can't seem to enjoy the good thing he's found, instead projecting his relationship into a future time when the pair might not be together. Although there's never any indication that this separation would be anything but temporary, the unspoken tug of the music pulls us into thinking the worst and that his ruminations are based on his belief that maybe they won't be able to sustain the love they currently enjoy.

Meanwhile, the lyrics, which, on the page, seem like a testament to certainty in love, are colored by the music to sound suspicious and questioning. "You say you will love me, if I have to go," McCartney sings. "You'll be thinking of me, somehow I will know." Within the context of the downcast music, you can almost anticipate him asking how she's going to do that. In the same manner, the lines "You say you'll be mine, girl, till the end of time / These days such a kind, girl, is so hard to find" make it seem like he's doubting if such a steadfast person is even a possibility, rather than celebrating that she happens to be one.

Perhaps McCartney worried that the song was pulling too far in that direction, hence the more energetically sung declarations about the constancy and durability of love in the middle eights. But they don't last, which might be the point, instead twisting back into the somewhat mournful shape of the verses.

Leading up to the refrain, the narrator pulls himself out of the present to look ahead to times when he's away from her, lonely and dreaming of their former time together. "Then we will remember things we said today." Is this a positive outlook, one that promises him comfort and succor when their paths deviate down the road? Or is it the glass-half-empty take that prevails, the one that seems to be saying they should hold on to the moment with everything they've got because it's soon to pass into much more sorrowful territory?

The beauty of "Things We Said Today" is that it works either way. No matter how you read it though, you can't help but notice the burgeoning songwriting prowess of McCartney and the rising confidence in the band at handling such delicate material.

28. "No Reply" (from *Beatles for Sale*, 1964)

Bands often use the opening song of an album to set the tone. On the Beatles' first two albums, *Please Please Me* and *With the Beatles*, they began with "I Saw Her Standing There" and "It Won't Be Long," respectively—two songs that immediately clued listeners into the frenetic charm of those two LPs. The title track that kicked off their third album, 1964's *A Hard Day's Night*, let people know they were still keeping a rapid pace even though they were starting to think about the toll it was taking.

Perhaps no opening song up to that point made a clearer statement about what fans could expect than the kickoff for 1964's *Beatles for Sale*. "No Reply" strikes an ominous tone, one that doesn't even feel resolved after the song comes to a close. As if the somber faces on the album cover and the double-meaning wordplay of the title hadn't clued them in about what to expect, "No Reply" certainly informed fans that *Beatles for Sale* would be the first album by the Fab Four on which cloudy skies interrupted the unremitting sunshine of their earlier efforts.

Certainly the Beatles had been trending in a more versatile direction on *A Hard Day's Night*, which featured nuanced love, and anti-love, songs like "If I Fell" and "Things We Said Today." "No Reply" commits to the darker aspects of a relationship more forcefully, and it accentuates this darkness by coming off so counterintuitively sunny in certain places.

The song begins quite benignly, with John Lennon singing, "This happened once before," even before the band can even kick in with their trademark acoustic lilt. He goes on to talk about having come to someone's door, only to be told that this person isn't home, although he is suspicious about this. Seems innocent enough.

Out of nowhere, the cymbals clash, the bass and acoustic guitars are struck with intensity, and Lennon, with Paul McCartney yelping in high harmony, screams out "I saw the light, I saw the light." This line represents his actual experience and the figurative realization that dawns on him that he's being duped. After that, the music calms again as he matter-of-factly recounts how he catches a glimpse through the window of the person he's seeking, thereby proving his side of the story.

In this manic way, the song continues to seesaw back and forth between what seems like casual acceptance of the girl's deceptions and wild bursts of anguish. In the second verse, the music again coasts along gently as the narrator goes on to talk about his attempts to connect via telephone. "That's a lie" is his cold response, albeit sung very genially, when he's told the girl isn't home. And then, again, the sudden shift on the line "I nearly died," as the intensified music and vocals make you believe it. The reason he nearly died: "'Cause you walked hand in hand / With another place / In my place," again, sung in a kind of "tra-la-la" way, as if the narrator couldn't be happier about this turn of events.

That leads to yet another shift, both in the persona of the narrator and the tenor of the music. Hand claps kick the rhythm into another gear as Lennon and McCartney harmonize on lines that veer from threatening to conciliatory in a heartbeat. First the narrator says that she better watch out for the consequences of neglecting him, and then he says that he can forgive it all.

The inconsistency in his response actually turns out to be a pretty accurate representation of the kind of behavior someone overwhelmed by suspicion leaning almost toward paranoia would put forth. Meanwhile, the music contains that same kind of roller coaster of emotions within it, and Lennon perfectly gets into character with his mild-to-mad performance.

With the final refrain of "No Reply," this time rendered in dramatic, portentous fashion, the meaning has transformed; it now refers to the girl's inability to answer these charges he's made. The Beatles made the right choice to begin their most introspective album to that point with a bleak tale of mistrust, because when fans bought *Beatles for Sale*, they were getting something far more complicated for their buck than teenage wish fulfillment.

27. "I Saw Her Standing There" (from *Please Please Me*, 1963)

"Love Me Do" was the first single. "Please Please Me" followed that. Plus there were the two B-sides to those two As. So there were technically four songs that preceded "I Saw Her Standing There" in giving people a chance to hear a song by those four young men from Liverpool, England, who somehow beat the odds and secured themselves a recording contract.

But "I Saw Her Standing There" was the first song on the Beatles' first album, 1963's *Please Please Me*, so in many ways, the story starts there. After all, rock and roll is an album-oriented genre. It wasn't, of course, at the time of the release of *Please Please Me*, but that collection of songs definitely started to nudge the album as art form forward in prominence.

The Beatles hadn't really intended *Please Please Me to* do this. They were just making an album like so many other pop and rock artists had. With a few hit singles in tow and a record company wanting to milk a bit more money from those songs, they hustled into the studio and in one evening polished off enough songs to fill out both sides of a long-player, which they achieved by collecting a bunch of cover songs and originals that weren't considered good enough to be singles.

But a funny thing happened. The cover songs were rendered with such pep and personality that they often sounded better than the original versions. And the Beatles' originals that weren't thought up to snuff for a single release were, thanks to the rising songwriting prowess of John Lennon and Paul McCartney, often better than the A-sides of competing acts. So *Please Please Me* is an album generally devoid of filler, one of the first complete rock-and-roll listening experiences, even though it was essentially just the Beatles going through the motions.

Like all great albums, *Please Please Me* has a great opener. The decision to include the count-in from Paul McCartney ("One, two, three, faw!") was the first excellent one made on that debut album. In a way, it put the Beatles in the same league as every band that ever assembled in a garage to bang on some instruments and dream of glory. That they would become the standard to which those bands would eventually aspire somehow makes the opening to "I Saw Her Standing There" even more apt.

From there, the Beatles hurtle headlong into a tale of teenage romance that, again, wasn't all that dissimilar from the songs that populated the charts in the years just before the song's release. But rarely did the music of those earlier songs have the combination of abandon and precision that enlivens "I Saw Her Standing There."

Paul McCartney's bopping bass line is the main agent of momentum, while Ringo Starr performs one of his first bits of flawless time keeping and connects the song's different dots with peppery snares. Meanwhile, John Lennon's rhythm guitar, always an underrated part of the group's chemistry, chimes in just when you need it. Given the chance in the break, George Harrison cuts loose with one of his first solos with the band, a high-stepping one that would hold up through the years to be one of his finest.

McCartney doesn't get enough credit for the lyrics, especially the way they follow the rituals of a teenage dance, from first sight to nervous meeting to potential romance. All he needs to say to convince us of this girl's irresistibility? "Well, she was just seventeen / You know what I mean." Anybody who's ever been in that situation, palms sweating, heart palpitating, every nerve tingling, ready to explode, knows exactly what he means, which is why he didn't need to elaborate any further.

Lennon's low harmonies are perfectly pitched, the calming voice of reason to McCartney's wild exuberance. That exuberance finally spills over in the screams right before the break. The excitement is simply off the charts throughout the song, as we get a great example of how a piece of music can explode from silence and drive us from zero to frenzy in two minutes.

Somehow "I Saw Her Standing There" comes to a full stop with one last guitar chord; one would have thought it would need to slow down or at least skid a little bit. It's the song that started to put the notion of album filler to bed. And it will forever be the first impression the Beatles make on fans going through their albums in chronological order. The Fab Four couldn't have chosen a better way to introduce themselves.

26. "Here, There and Everywhere" (from *Revolver*, 1966)

When comparing the Beatles to other artists of the 1960s, many people turn first to the Rolling Stones, fellow Brits whose bad-boy image contrasted with the polish of the Fab Four. Then there's Bob Dylan, whose influence gently nudged the group to more sophisticated lyrical territory, even as they reciprocated by helping open Dylan's ears to the power of electric music.

Yet there's an argument to be made that no artist made more of an impression on the musical direction of the group than the Beach Boys, in particular their mastermind songwriter/producer Brian Wilson. Paul McCartney certainly felt a kinship to Wilson, as both were bass players who saw the instrument in melodic terms and both had a knack for complicated yet accessible tunes.

For a good portion of the middle of the decade, there emerged a kind of back-and-forth, escalating (albeit friendly) rivalry between the two groups. When Wilson heard *Rubber Soul*, the Beatles' stunning 1965 album, he was floored that every song, not just a couple of them, seemed ambitious and brilliant. It inspired Wilson to compose the songs that would make up *Pet Sounds*, the Beach Boys' 1966 album that didn't sell as well as their teenage epics about fast cars and surfboards from the early part of the decade but soon came to be recognized as a masterpiece, especially by other musical artists.

McCartney certainly heard the genius in *Pet Sounds*. Now the time line gets a little tight, because *Pet Sounds* was released in May 1966 and principal recording on the song in question occurred just a month later, but it's impossible to hear "Here, There and Everywhere" as anything but a direct homage to the Wilson sound. However it was intended, and as high as it ranks on this imposing list, the song may top the list of the most beautiful songs the Beatles ever recorded.

Though it may have tipped its cap to the Beach Boys, McCartney also casts a glance toward the Great American Songbook with "Here, There and Everywhere." From the intro separate from the rest of the song ("To lead a better life / I need my love to be here") to the soundness of the structure to the lyrical deftness, which would have made Cole Porter proud, this could easily have been a standard had it been written twenty or thirty years before.

Speaking of the lyrics, they are an area in which McCartney always had an edge on Wilson. Wilson often used outside collaborators to pen the words on some of his most ambitious works; McCartney had John Lennon to help out, although many of his most famous songs were essentially solo compositions, including this one. The gentle beauty of "Here, There and Everywhere" comes not just from the music but also from the sentiment about the omnipresence of true love.

The two clear areas the song shares with a typical Beach Boys' ballad are McCartney's just-shy-of-falsetto vocals and the harmonies he and Beatle buddies John Lennon and George Harrison dole out generously, essentially forming the chordal backing for the main melody. Those jaw-dropping backing vocals, rising through the verses and sighing as they approach the bridge, show that the group's trio of singers could hang with the Wilson brothers and company when called on to do so. And McCartney caresses his lead vocal with the same kind of tenderness that the narrator uses to run his hands through the hair of his beloved.

In the bridge, McCartney goes solo on lead, although Harrison trips alongside him with some trembling guitar notes. When the final verse arrives, the harmonies are back to buffer him, as he testifies to the way the right relationship can reaffirm one's faith in the intangible: "Each one believing that love never dies."

Revolver is a fascinating album for many reasons, not the least of which is how it incorporates so seamlessly all kinds of sounds, from psychedelic rock to Eastern drone to children's music. McCartney consistently provides the tunefulness that keeps things from spiraling too far out into the ether, with "For No One" and "Eleanor Rigby" being other wonderful examples of his melodic gifts.

"Here, There and Everywhere" is, in many ways, the heart of this beloved album. It may have begun as an attempt to hang with Brian Wilson, but it ends with the Beatles singing convincingly and beautifully about love, and for that, they never needed any influence besides their own.

25. "You've Got to Hide Your Love Away" (from *Help!*, 1965)

In much the same way that "Here, There and Everywhere" could be heard as a kind of tribute to the sound of Brian Wilson and the Beach Boys, the direct antecedent of "You've Got to Hide Your Love Away" is the early 1960s acoustic music of Bob Dylan. Most people think of Dylan with his acoustic guitar and harmonica churning out protest songs, and that was a big part of it. But he also wrote and recorded many songs in that time period about relationship travails, especially on 1964's *Another Side of Bob Dylan* album. It's likely that album was playing often on John Lennon's turntable around the time that he wrote "You've Got to Hide Your Love Away," which appeared on *Help!* in 1965.

Lennon wasn't shy about acknowledging that debt. In a quote from *Anthology*, he said, "Instead of projecting myself into a situation, I would try to express what I felt about myself, which I'd done in my books. I think it was Dylan who helped me realize that—not by any discussion or anything, but by hearing his work."[34]

Throughout this list, it's been documented how the Beatles were influenced by many artists, especially in their first three years of recording. And yet in each case they were able to either veer away from or simply transcend those influences so that the end result was pure Fab Four. "You've Got to Hide Your Love Away" provides a pretty good example of this process.

Lennon may have heard Dylan's confessional material and been inspired to dig deep into his own emotions and psyche to write the song. But what he found there, naturally, was pure John Lennon. As a result, "You've Got to Hide Your Love Away" comes from his unique personal perspective, full of insecurity, naked emotion, and sly humor, on a relationship that has either faded or has run its course completely.

The narrator in the song quickly lets us in on his misery as he reclines in the classic stance of the heartbroken: "Here I stand, head in hand / Turn my face to the wall." The humor shows up in the next line, when he admits to feeling two foot "small" instead of two foot "tall," as you might have expected. The word change not only causes a chuckle but also demonstrates just how woeful he feels.

The next lines depict a crowd of onlookers staring and laughing at the narrator, presumably mocking him for his misery. And here seems to be the main theme of the song: the narrator seems to be rebuked for his sensitivity and feeling, the rest of the world telling him to buck up when all he wants to do is wallow. It's right there in the chorus as they chant out, "Hey, you've got to hide your love away."

In this way, you can almost read the song as a kind of rebuke to the songs that Dylan was writing around that time. Taking a look at the songs on *Another Side*, there are several that reference relationship squabbles. But Dylan rarely plays the role of victim and often comes at the issues by turning his gaze to the girl instead of looking inward. He's alternately sarcastic ("I Don't Believe You") and self-aware ("It Ain't Me Babe") but rarely seems to be on the verge of tears.

There's even a song ("To Ramona") on which he advises a heartbroken girl to get over it, albeit in a more benevolent and eloquent manner; while he's not as nasty about it as the "clowns" in Lennon's song jeering him, the message is essentially the same. But Lennon defends his right to self-pity: "How can I even try, I can never win / Hearing them, seeing them, in the state I'm in." The only thing about which he's derisive is the notion that "love will find a way." Clearly the evidence suggests otherwise.

Thus Lennon, although he might have started off strumming and singing à la Dylan, treads his own path. Meanwhile, he gets help from his band and an outside source to add the kind of flavor to the recording that Dylan rarely even attempted in the early days. While Lennon strums the twelve-string, George Harrison and Paul McCartney pick away beneath him on acoustic and bass, respectively, to add subtle shadings. Ringo Starr's tambourine and maracas, held back early in the song, each make an impact once they arrive. And the flute work of session player John Scott provides one of the earliest examples of the Beatles including a surprising element that turns out to be an ideal fit for a song.

In the end, all that is subordinate to the intimacy of Lennon's vocal; his shouts of "Hey" can still produce chills. Listen closely enough and you might find that "You've Got to Hide Your Love Away" seems to be far more Lennonish than Dylanesque.

24. "Taxman" (from *Revolver*, 1966)

Although he hadn't yet been awarded an A-side (that wouldn't occur for another three years), George Harrison's bandmates granted him the honor of opening the 1966 Beatles' album *Revolver* with his composition "Taxman." It was a testament to just how far he had progressed in the songwriting department in a relatively short time.

Recall that Harrison had written just one song on the Beatles' first four albums, the rather sour, if intriguing, 1963 ditty "Don't Bother Me" from *With the Beatles*. *Help!* in 1965 contained "I Need You," his first really great track, although that had been more a triumph of mood and performance than an example of complex songcraft. But it was a way forward, and he solidified his standing with his work on *Rubber Soul* later that year, including the droning "Think for Yourself" and the chiming "If I Needed Someone."

Revolver contained three of Harrison's songs, which was a new high for him. In addition to "Taxman," there was "Love You To," his full dive into the Indian music in which he had previously only dipped his toes, and "I Want to Tell You," featuring typically askew Harrison chords and harmonies and just odd enough to work. But "Taxman" is an ace, as Harrison became the first Beatle to question the status quo, doing so in biting, thrilling fashion.

Harrison's reasons for writing the song were pretty straightforward: "I had discovered I was paying a huge amount of money to the taxman," he remembered in *Anthology*. "You are so happy that you've finally started earning money—and then you find out about tax."

"In those days we paid 19 shillings and sixpence (96p) out of every pound, and with supertax and surtax and tax-tax it was ridiculous—a heavy penalty to pay for making money."[35]

John Lennon also helped out with the lyrics at Harrison's request; having the two most acerbic members of the group penning the punch lines certainly worked in the song's favor. Harrison tells the story from the perspective of the "Taxman," who in this case stands in for the entire machinery of the taxation system. It's a clever gambit, as it makes the effrontery and audacity of the demands seem even more outrageous.

The way he phrases the amount of the taxation is brilliant as well: "Let me tell you how it will be / There's one for you, nineteen for me." Doesn't seem very fair when you sum it up that way, does it? But this formless entity isn't afraid to threaten even worse: "Should five percent appear too small / Be thankful I don't take it all."

In the middle section, Harrison does some memorable call-and-response with Lennon and Paul McCartney; they set up the hypotheticals, and he explains the penalty, each one more absurd and egregious than the next, culminating with "If you take a walk, I'll tax your feet." Later, while Lennon and McCartney name-drop a couple then current tax officials in their backing vocals, Harrison delivers a chilling couplet: "Now my advice for those who die / Declare the pennies on your eyes." The final verdict: "And you're working for no one but me." All that's left out is some maniacal laughter and a twirl of the handlebar mustache to complete the portrait of utter villainy.

It's a cutting piece of writing, made all the more incisive by the ferocity of the music. After a woozy count-in from Harrison, the basic structure of McCartney's head-bobbing bass, Harrison's stabbing staccato chords, and Ringo Starr's rapid heartbeat of a kick drum establishes itself. McCartney steps forward with a crazed electric solo in the break before the relentless pursuit of the groove continues. The high-pitched refrain of "Taxman" from Lennon and McCartney seems almost like a plea for mercy in this context. (And, it must be noted, they bear more than a passing resemblance to the musical theme of the then popular American television iteration of *Batman*; maybe it was an in-joke by Harrison or maybe he was a secret Caped Crusader acolyte.)

While the Beatles weren't exactly going out on a limb with the song, as you won't find too many citizens happy about getting their money taken even if they believe the practice of taxation is valid, it was notable that they stepped up to the plate and made this kind of statement. George Harrison might have been a bit late to develop his songwriting voice compared to Lennon and McCartney, but he proved on "Taxman" that he was ahead of the other two in terms of being ready, willing, and able to use that voice to needle the powers that be.

23. "Blackbird" (from *The Beatles*, 1968)

For those of you who have checked out or lost track of Paul McCartney's musical career lately (and you're missing out on some of his finest solo work if you have), you might not have heard a gem off 2005's *Chaos and Creation in the Backyard* titled "Jenny Wren." When you do check it out, get set for a little déjà vu, because you'll hear him singing a song with a bird in the title set to his acoustic guitar and simple percussion.

Of course, the guy had done this kind of thing before when he was a member of the Beatles, and quite well at that. "Blackbird" was the song, and it is indubitably one of the highlights of the White Album. In the midst of a whole lot of genial weirdness (it's sequenced on side 1 of the first disc between John Lennon's insomniac's lament "I'm So Tired" and George Harrison's satire "Piggies"), the song's intent is genuinely heartfelt and unapologetically earnest. Songs like those can be a slog, quite frankly, if executed poorly; McCartney soars over those concerns much as he wishes the title creature will fly to heights she couldn't possibly imagine.

McCartney has stated recently that his inspiration for the song came from racial strife in the United States, which, in 1968, when the song was written, was manifesting itself in race riots in major cities, particularly following the assassination of Dr. Martin Luther King Jr. Some have questioned this, pointing to contradictory statements McCartney made throughout the years about the song. One interesting quote from his talks with Barry Miles collected in the book *Many Years from Now* shows how his efforts to make the song more universal may have indirectly led to these doubts.

"I had in mind a black woman, rather than a bird," he remembered. "Those were the days of the civil rights movement, which all of us cared passionately about, so this was really a song from me to a black woman, experiencing these problems in the States: 'Let me encourage you to keep trying, to keep your faith, there is hope.' As is often the case with my things, a veiling took place so, rather than say 'Black woman living in Little Rock' and be very specific, she became a bird, became symbolic, so you could apply it to your particular problem."[36]

Whether you feel that McCartney really wrote the song as a commentary on current events or that it was just a vague notion to which those events attached themselves, his statement about the song says a lot about his songwriting approach. Some critics get frustrated with him for his unwillingness to confess and navel-gaze in his songs. Yet when a song like "Blackbird" becomes a universal anthem that's somehow bigger than the words and music that comprise it, that kind of strategy comes in handy.

So it is that "Blackbird" works with any interpretation. You can make it a civil rights anthem if you want, or you can hear it as a simple song of compassion. The composition and execution are what matter, and both of those are flawless.

The mistake in a song like this would have been to make it too rah-rah. McCartney avoids this with his melancholy acoustic guitar chords and the quiver in his vocals, neither of which skimp on the pain of the title character's struggle. That makes the uplift, when it arrives, all the more powerful. And although this was one of those McCartney "solo" Beatles' tracks that aggravated his cohorts in the band, the intimacy of him performing with just his guitar and tapping foot is the right call here, making the song seem like a one-on-one conversation with this girl, or bird, or whatever you think the case may be.

McCartney's message is one of perseverance in the face of unimaginable hardship. The bird's wings are broken, yet he urges it to fly; its "sunken eyes" (a particularly evocative image), the narrator suggests, shouldn't prevent sight. In this way, the bird can reach its destination and attain freedom that otherwise would have been denied it.

Maybe that kind of advice might seem naïve and unrealistic, especially if the song was pointed toward black Americans, but the song is meant to be a straightforward pick-me-up, not a deep treatise on anything. It's supposed to give a glimmer of hope to someone in despair, and that someone need not be in any particular lot in life to feel that glimmer warm them.

Getting back to "Jenny Wren," it tells of a girl who wishes to sing only to have her voice stolen by the problems in the world. Yet she gains a measure of triumph at least for not being a part of those problems. A sequel to "Blackbird" in a way? Perhaps. What's for certain is that even the bird with the prettiest song has a real rival in terms of sonic beauty when Paul McCartney gets to singing about its feathered friends.

22. "Ticket to Ride" (from *Help!*, 1965)

You might have been able to tell from the writing in this book to this point, but in case you couldn't, suffice it to say that we're big John Lennon fans around these parts. That said, it must be acknowledged that the guy could say some flat-out crazy things in interviews. Sometimes it was because he had an agenda, other times it was because he liked to stir things up, and there were undoubtedly some instances when he was just being a little kooky.

In any case, one of his biggest whoppers was in 1980 when *Playboy* interviewer David Sheff asked him about the Beatles' No. 1 hit from 1965 called "Ticket to Ride." "That was one of the earliest heavy metal records made," Lennon said.[37]

It's hard to listen to "Ticket to Ride" and do the kind of mental gymnastics necessary to turn it into a proto-metal track. There is never any point in the song where you feel like devils horns should be raised or heads should be banged. Even when the tempo picks up in the coda, it sounds a little more like a hoedown than a metal mash.

What is certain is that the song marked a vast departure in the sound of the band from their previous singles. When you think of the songs that were released as A-sides in the first two years or so of the Beatles' recording career, they were for the most part full-speed-ahead, look-out-below kinds of numbers. If they paused to catch their breath, it was only to gather momentum again for the final rush.

"Ticket to Ride" is more measured in the way it gets where it needs to go. Much of that is due to Ringo Starr's novel drum rhythm (apparently devised by Paul McCartney). Instead of the rushing boom-boom-bap beat that was common in so many of the group's songs and those of many others, Starr plays a kind of hesitation thump, which opens a lot of space up in the middle of the song and makes each drum strike that much more impactful when it comes. It's a pattern that's since been mimicked often in other rock songs. ("Go Your Own Way" by Fleetwood Mac and "This Year's Girl" by Elvis Costello are just two of the more popular of these.)

Starr's beat is rendered even more distinctive by the way it's introduced. After George Harrison's arching opening guitar riff, Starr plays a quick roll on the toms and gets to it. Meanwhile, Paul McCartney's one-note bass drone is seconded by an electric guitar also playing low notes, giving the song a resounding, insistent bottom end. Lennon's main vocal line, on which he's occasionally helped on harmony by McCartney, picks up from where Harrison left off and fills up the higher altitudes of the song.

In the choruses, there's a similar sense of space maintained by each of the instruments, so much so that Lennon occasionally has the room to let out an anguished little shout before each repeat of the refrain "She's got a ticket to ride." That refrain is repeated three times, with one false stop and another Starr drum roll interceding before the kicker: "And she don't care."

Again, it's fascinating to compare the crisp, clean sound and the separation between instruments and vocals to the dense, forward propulsion of the earlier hits. It's as if the Beatles were demanding that audiences listen a bit closer to the individual sounds they were making, perhaps knowing that those sounds were about to get exponentially wilder and weirder. "Ticket to Ride" was just the beginning.

There's not too much going on lyrically with "Ticket to Ride," just a simple tale of a guy who knows that his girl is about to leave and is helpless to stop her. It doesn't really matter, because the music leaves enough of a mark. If Lennon had wanted to make a more apt comparison, he would have named the song as a precursor to power pop, as the crisp, everything-in-its-right-place songs from '70s bands like Big Star and Cheap Trick, as well as Badfinger—who the Beatles signed to Apple—certainly follow a similar template to "Ticket to Ride."

In the song's coda, the Beatles kick into a double-time romp to the finish, almost as if they were reminding people of what they could do when they switched into a higher gear. It may not have been as heavy as Lennon intimated, but "Ticket to Ride" certainly displayed the band throwing the weight of their talent around in novel and equally captivating ways.

21. "A Hard Day's Night" (from *A Hard Day's Night*, 1964)

The Beatles made conquering the music world look so easy that it was almost unfair when they knocked their first motion picture out of the park as well. *A Hard Day's Night* proved that the individual personalities within the group were as winning and charismatic as their music. Buoyed by the innovative direction of Richard Lester, the film definitively captured the hustle and bustle of Beatlemania, as well as the thrilling absurdity of being in the middle of it all.

In the film, the title track is heard in the opening scenes as the on-screen Beatles are chased by a mob of screaming fans through the streets. So precisely is the film married to the music that it seems as though the band surely worked tirelessly to come up with a song so apt. In fact, John Lennon dashed the thing off in one night after the band agreed on the title for the film, based on one of Ringo Starr's offhand comments.

That the band was able to churn out such an apropos approximation of weariness was understandable. They were living through a ridiculously brutal schedule as they attempted to cash in on their first flush of international success by keeping an itinerary filled with recording sessions, television appearances, concert dates, and the filming of a major motion picture. And yet the product only seemed to improve: Lennon and Paul McCartney wrote the entire *A Hard Day's Night* album, the first time one of the group's LPs was filled with entirely original material, and they did it in a matter of weeks with the deadline for completion fast approaching.

Since they were writing so many songs, it stood to reason that the chief songwriters would have to do more than regurgitate the same kind of teen-oriented odes to love they had churned out with regularity the previous year, lest they run the risk of sinking into a rut. "A Hard Day's Night" solves that problem by touching on the relentless working schedule that Lennon and the band were actually facing. And, when it dabbles in romance, it suggests the kind of adult pleasures at which the songs of 1962 and '63 might have blushed.

"A Hard Day's Night" immediately announces its presence with its iconic opening chord, which is the aural equivalent of the four Beatles breaking through a wall and landing squarely in front of their instruments. It was a bold maneuver; the bleat of that guitar was a starting gun that shot the band forward into one of their most propulsive tracks ever. It's a wild rush, featuring Starr's cowbell-infused beat, bongos played by engineer Norman Smith, and a combination solo of guitar (played by George Harrison) and piano (played by George Martin) that was quickened in the studio to make it sound extra-breathless. The sound is thick but never sludgy; the rhythm section makes sure everyone is light on their feet so that no one gets caught from behind.

Lennon plays the narrator as harried rather than exhausted, because he knows he doesn't have time to be exhausted. This is one of the first songs where he displays his love for shut-eye (see also in this countdown "I'm Only Sleeping" and "I'm So Tired), but there's no chance for it during his busy day. Nor is there any desire for it when he gets home at night, considering that his desire is channeled elsewhere.

It's interesting how the group's chief rivals for British Invasion supremacy, the Rolling Stones, had some difficulties getting things by the censors, while the Beatles often snuck the same lascivious content into their songs with no trouble. A few years down the road, the Stones would have to change the lyrics to "Let's Spend the Night Together" to play it on American television. But the Beatles had no problems inserting overt come-ons from the narrator in "A Hard Day's Night" such as "And it's worth it just to hear you say / You're going to give me everything" or "But when I get home to you / I find the things that you do / Will make me feel all right."

One can take the innocent (read: naïve) point of view and assume that these "things" he's anticipating include a warm glass of milk. More likely, sexual release waits for him at home, a notion that seems to be confirmed by Paul McCartney's exuberant high notes in the middle eight.

In the closing moments of the song, the forward momentum of the music finally comes crashing to a halt with Lennon's last "all right," and it's followed by an unwinding guitar figure that eventually fades out. You could tie that sound to the film and hear it as the after-effect of the dizzying life of a Beatle. Or you can focus on the song and interpret it as the wonderfully woozy state of afterglow. In any case, "A Hard Day's Night" leaves your head spinning in every conceivable way, as fine a bit of ad hoc songwriting and recording as you'll ever hear.

20. "Yesterday" (from *Help!*, 1965)

When considering "Yesterday," and it's been considered probably more than any song recorded in the latter half of the twentieth century, it's important to remember that the Beatles were a bit sheepish about it. Although it was included on the album *Help!*, it's nowhere to be found in the film of the same name. They chose not to release it as a single in the United Kingdom, and they didn't even afford it the glory spot of the last song on the album. Instead, it was the penultimate track preceding a desultory cover version of "Dizzy Miss Lizzy."

People found it though. It was honored with awards in Great Britain at the end of 1965, and when it was released in America a year later as a single after inclusion on the *Yesterday . . . and Today* compilation—which included songs chopped off *Help!*, *Rubber Soul*, and *Revolver* by Capitol—it soared to No. 1. This was only the beginning of its overall ascent to being the most covered song of all time.

As with any song that gets played as much as "Yesterday," people start to get fatigued hearing it so often, which makes judging it against the group's body of work difficult. In addition, it was so groundbreaking in its marrying of the song structure of a rock ballad with the instrumentation of classical music that it naturally begat copycats, many of which were more ambitious in scope than the song that inspired them.

Yet it's the simplicity that makes "Yesterday" so wonderful. The story is basic and the music is subtly done. Everything is understated. It's hard to say what direction these kinds of songs would have taken had Paul McCartney and producer George Martin not been so restrained with their deployment of these new elements. And that's actually where that initial sheepishness about doing such a thing on a rock record actually came in handy.

Notice that the string quartet doesn't arrive until the second verse, allowing McCartney to establish his tale of woe on his own before the instruments come in to make their commentary. When they do, they mostly follow McCartney's melody around and harmonize sadly. A brief countermelody appears now and again, and in the final verse, for a little added drama, one of the violins squeals a high-pitched note above everything else. Martin's instincts as arranger were incredible; considering this was probably the first time a thing like this had been tried in a rock setting, and considering how influential the Beatles were, he could have set everyone on a self-destructive path had he been the least bit bombastic about adding the strings. (Heaven knows that many artists have gone down this wrongheaded path anyway, even with "Yesterday" as an example of the right direction to go.)

That leaves us with McCartney's song and performance. As for the actual writing of the song, his buddy John Lennon, who appears to have had nothing to do with it, took his digs in a 1980 interview at what he perceived as its dead-end nature. "Although the lyrics don't resolve into any sense, they're good lines," he said. "They certainly work. You know what I mean? They're good—but if you read the whole song, it doesn't say anything; you don't know what happened. She left and he wishes it was yesterday—that much you get—but it doesn't really resolve."[38]

To which the response should be "So what?" The whole point of the story is that it is left unresolved, as so many broken relationships tend to be. And what does it matter how it happened? The narrator searches for those answers because he's stuck in a cycle of replaying the past, in part because he can't face up to the present without her, in part because he hopes that there's something in there that he can possibly undo. But even if he finds some clues, he can't change the past, which is why his deep dive into it is only furthering his anguish.

As for the performance, McCartney gives one remarkably lived-in and tender, one that doesn't cross the line into melodramatics. Certainly you can envision how someone singing a song like this could descend into histrionics quite easily. (A few of those kazillion cover versions certainly have.) Instead, he lets the melody do the dramatic work. Both the verses and the bridge rise from the doldrums to a teetering edge, only to tumble back down into the pit of despair because he just can't hang on.

The song shouldn't be blamed for inspiring a million sound-alikes or for being so evocative in its depiction of regret that it still gets played a lot some fifty years after McCartney first crafted it from a dream. It's still as stirring and sad as it was then, and, if you believe in "Yesterday" as the narrator does, you might realize that almost every string-laden ballad since not only owes it a tremendous debt but also fails to meet its towering standard. Of course, we have a choice in believing in it; for him, it's his only resort.

19. "Within You Without You" (from *Sgt. Pepper's Lonely Hearts Club Band*, 1967)

We've talked several times in these pages about the rapid progression George Harrison made as a songwriter within the Beatles after lagging well behind John Lennon and Paul McCartney in the early days of the group. In much the same way he made stunning strides in terms of his incorporation of Eastern sounds, particularly those inspired by the music of India and Ravi Shankar, into the Western-based sound of the Beatles.

It began with him picking out a sitar melody behind John Lennon's main melody on "Norwegian Wood (This Bird Has Flown)" from 1965's *Rubber Soul*. Later that year he dove headlong into Indian music with the driving "Love You To" from *Revolver*. "Love You To" got the sound right, but Harrison didn't quite write a memorable song to accompany it.

But Harrison, in what was really just his second attempt, created a masterly fusion of two disparate musical philosophies on the stunning "Within You Without You." In the process, he also provided *Sgt. Pepper's Lonely Hearts Club Band* with a necessary air of thoughtfulness. You could imagine the song's narrator and his friends sitting on the grass in deep conversation while Sgt. Pepper cues his band, others head off to see Mr. Kite, the nervous suitor picks up "Lovely Rita," and so on. The song weaves its way seamlessly into that tapestry despite being completely unique from the others musically, except, that is, in its sense of daring.

Probably more than any other Beatles' track, "Within You Without You" works as a piece of music that needs no words to make an impact. On "Love You To," Harrison had employed the guitar-like sitar, the droning tambura, and the bongos aping tabla to approximate a rock-and-roll rhythm section in Indian fashion. "Within You Without You" includes those instruments but also makes prominent use of the squalling bowed dilruba and the harp-like swarmandal to lend the song a stately, classical air.

He then ups that ante by having violins and cellos on the track as well. The juxtaposition is fascinating; hearing these seemingly disparate elements complement each other in the long instrumental passage preceding the final verse, you stop getting hung up on what came from where and simply get lost in the hypnotic beauty of it all.

Harrison's melody is also a main contributor to the song's success. In the verses, the notes are drawn out and the tune takes a gradual dip before rising up again at the start of each line, creating a soothing effect that asks the listener to relax and consider the meaning behind the words. But there are also moments when the melody spikes in urgency, a call to attention that demands the messages be heard and understood, as if the consequences of ignoring them will somehow injure both the giver and the receiver.

Those messages manage to blend spiritual concepts with secular concerns strikingly well. Harrison isn't afraid to throw some lofty ideas around in the song, but he grounds those with the effects they have on life as we live it. "We were talking about the space between us all," he begins, and the musical context immediately makes it understood that "space" can be defined here by the seemingly unbridgeable distances people construct in their heads and hearts to isolate themselves.

The narrator calls out those who would build metaphorical walls, warning them that the damage will be done on a cosmic level after death. When he drops in Jesus's line about gaining the world and losing one's soul, Harrison also deftly shows how different religious beliefs can easily intertwine. That plays very well with the Hindu concept that "life flows on within you and without you."

What keeps the song from drifting off into airy philosophizing and even condescension is the empathy that Harrison displays for those on the wrong path. His vocals rise out of their trancelike intonation when he promises, "With our love / We could save the world / If they only knew." On the word "knew," he quivers between notes, the dilruba mimicking him, as if everything is hanging in the balance.

Harrison also switches back and forth between recounting this conversation and directly addressing the audience. In the final lines of the last verse, his concern crosses the boundaries from those whom he feels have gone astray and the person listening at that very moment: "They don't know / They can't see / Are you one of them?"

It's a wake-up call to anyone who hears the song, one that nonetheless comes couched in music of impressive ambition and breathtaking beauty. "Within You Without You" is instructive, questing, clever, and, more than anything else, heartfelt. Pretty much George Harrison the musical artist in a nutshell, which is just one more reason the song is essential.

18. "Please Please Me" (from *Please Please Me*, 1963)

The Beatles' story plays out as a fascinating combination of gradual steps and seismic leaps. For example, they trundled their way through about a half decade of low-profile shows and dead ends on their way to finally securing a recording contract; just six months or so after that, their name was on the lips of everyone in Great Britain. In terms of songwriting development, John Lennon and Paul McCartney took a huge bound from the relatively simple ditties of 1963 to the more mature, assured compositions on 1964's *A Hard Day's Night*, an album from which they would begin a steady ascent that peaked in 1967 before plateauing at that towering level for the next few years until their breakup. Even that breakup could be seen in those terms: in actuality, the rifts within the band had been widening for several years leading up to the dissolution, but it all ended officially with a full stop when Paul McCartney announced it to the world in the spring of 1970.

"Please Please Me" sort of falls into both categories, as it took some grunt work just to get it recorded but shot the band into the stratosphere once it was. It was just their second single, released at the tail end of 1962. The first single, "Love Me Do," was a modest success, reaching No. 17 on the British pop charts. That wasn't too bad considering the band's hardscrabble background, but it also could be attributed largely to the local following they had cultivated. The song itself was little more than a trifle; the band's charisma seemed immediately evident, but their mammoth talent wasn't.

What the modest chart success of "Love Me Do" ensured was the leeway for the band to record a follow-up, but their desire to stick to original material for their singles was nearly thwarted right there. Producer George Martin was understandably skeptical about the Lennon/McCartney songwriting team; if the pedestrian "Love Me Do" was the best composition they had, why would he risk releasing a second song that could have been even more mundane? And Martin's early exposure to "Please Please Me," which was conceived as a Roy Orbison–style number with a sauntering tempo by Lennon, didn't exactly sway him. He presented the band instead with "How Do You Do It?," a song churned out by legendary middle-of-the-road hitmaker Mitch Miller.

The rest, as they say. . . . After doing a demo of "How Do You Do It?" to get Martin off their backs, the Beatles supercharged the tempo of "Please Please Me" at his request and ended up on the dizzying top of the charts instead of the mediocre middle. (And Martin turned out to be only half wrong: although "How Do You Do It?" was the inferior song by miles, it did hit the top of the charts when rendered by fellow Liverpudlians Gerry and the Pacemakers in the spring of 1963.)

It all makes for a great story, but the story pales in comparison with the potency of "Please Please Me" as a song. And this is no door prize for being the first time the Beatles really got it right, because they got it right to the extent that the song remains one of the greatest rock-and-roll records ever released. The lyrics are catchy and direct (and more than a little mischievous), while the music somehow melds chaotic energy with graceful precision.

In terms of mischief, you can certainly read the song as Lennon's complaint that his girlfriend won't perform the same, ahem, favors that he grants her on the regular. More important than the meaning though is the way the lines flow and the punchiness of couplets like "I don't want to sound complaining but you know there's always rain in my heart / I do all the pleasing with you it's so hard to reason with you."

The vocal trading keeps things lively throughout. Lennon sings the main melody in the verses while McCartney belts out a one-note harmony. George Harrison joins the action in a call-and-response bit in the "Come on, come on" section, while the bridges feature harmony vocals from McCartney and Harrison in support of Lennon. The Orbisonian falsetto in the refrain adds one more surprising touch.

Ringo Starr had only just won the job as Beatles' drummer, but he already proves indispensable with both his ability to keep a perfect patter even at the quickest tempos and his snappy rolls in and out that connect the disparate portions of the song. McCartney's bass thumps along frantically, upping the sense of tension that only gets released in the euphoric chorus. Lennon adds a harmonica riff for some flavor, and it all ends with the back and forth of the vocalists in the closing moments. Just two minutes long, yet full of infinite treasures.

The song provided the springboard for the wave of No. 1 hits that the band would ride throughout their career. Martin deserves credit for his patience and stewardship so that the song could hit its full potential, and the band deserves credit for the spotless yet animated execution. "Please Please Me" stands out as the first inclination of how great the Beatles would be, but even if they had never recorded another note, it would still be an undeniable classic.

17. "Tomorrow Never Knows" (from *Revolver*, 1966)

One wonders what the state of rock and roll might be had the Beatles not been the band to lead the revolution, or if they hadn't been the restless innovators they were. It might be the case that most bands would repeat the basic sound with which they first scored success over and over again, thus making the world a little less special place to be.

But the Beatles were always pushing, even if they could have rewritten "She Loves You" or "A Hard Day's Night" or "Yesterday" or any of their groundbreaking songs ad nauseam and still likely have been the most popular rock-and-roll band in the world. Luckily, they were far more concerned with greatness than popularity, which is how we end up at a piece of music like "Tomorrow Never Knows."

The band clearly knew that "Tomorrow Never Knows" was something special and different, as they placed it at the end of *Revolver* in 1966 to make a pretty strong statement about where their music was headed. Since they were starting to tap into the possibilities of the album as an art form, the placement of the song seems to have been deliberately aimed at making it one of the first classic closing tracks in rock-and-roll history. (Even though the band had released several great LPs by that point, the previous closing tracks were often less distinctive numbers like "I'll Be Back" on *A Hard Day's Night* and "Run for Your Life" on *Rubber Soul*. "Tomorrow Never Knows" changed that for good.)

The genesis for the song can be found in a trip John Lennon took to a bookstore, where he found a copy of Timothy Leary's adaptation of the Tibetan Book of the Dead. Lennon paraphrased a line from it for the opening line of "Tomorrow Never Knows" ("Turn off your mind, relax and float downstream") and was off and running. The tune he concocted for his heady lyrics featured little modulation from the insistent main chord, which meant that the band would have to dress up the song to liven it up a bit.

That's where the experimental bent they had begun to show really rose to the surface. "Tomorrow Never Knows" is built off a thuddingly persistent rhythmic base. Ringo Starr's drums pop with unbending purpose as Paul McCartney drones on a simple bass pattern. On top of that are all manner of sonic miscellanea: a tambura wrapping itself around everything, an orchestra bleating slightly off-key, a flock of seagulls diving down with dire warnings. The tape loops used to achieve the latter effects represented the band's widening efforts to put aside rock instruments so that they could achieve the sounds they heard in their minds. Even when they do use a bit of electric guitar here, it's distorted and played backward to render it nearly unrecognizable.

Lennon's vocals are also altered as the song progresses. Initially he's just cutting through the mix with his pronouncements that somehow manage to be both ominous and reassuring. But when he returns from the instrumental break, he sounds as if he's become disembodied, a voice not quite beyond the grave but certainly beyond whatever plane of existence the rest of us mere mortals inhabit. With this effect, he appears to have realized the transformation the lyrics push us toward.

The lyrics also represent a bold step forward for the band. Even though they had begun to get away from boy-girl songs somewhat, the idea of one of them addressing the audience with cryptic messages and otherworldly koans went far beyond singing songs about being a "Paperback Writer." In addition, the use of mind-altering psychedelics to influence their work could no longer be plausibly denied to any reasonable person listening to this track.

Lennon starts many of the lines with the word "that," suggesting that the ability to cast off a single hang-up attached to the everyday world of thinking and doing inevitably creates a domino effect toward enlightenment. Being able to "turn off your mind" and "surrender to the void" will reveal what it means to be "being" and "shining" instead of "living" and "dying."

He brings things back around to the group's common theme of love, but it's represented here as more a state of mind than the affection one shows toward another. The alternative to letting go: "Or play the game 'Existence' to the end / Of the beginning." It seems to be a vicious cycle, one that cannot be undone, because most don't understand they're trapped within it. He repeats the final line into the surreal sonics until it disappears into its own void.

We've only been visitors on this journey, but Lennon's narrator appears to permanently occupy this nether region. The title of "Tomorrow Never Knows" was taken from one of Starr's famously off-kilter statements. But it proved quite apropos for this song, which was only possible because of the Beatles insistence on looking forward into the unknown even when the sure thing of the present couldn't have been better.

16. "If I Fell" (from *A Hard Day's Night*, 1964)

The Beatles took tentative steps toward their mastery of ballads. John Lennon and Paul McCartney proved they could deliver the soft stuff of others with their cover versions of "Anna (Go to Him)" and "Till There Was You" on their first two albums, even if they weren't willing to go all-in with their own original takes. *With the Beatles*, from 1963, contained "Not a Second Time," an original that was moody but probably a bit too up-tempo to be considered a ballad in anything more than temperament. "This Boy," from that same year, was a B-side that certainly took it slow and sensitive but leaned too heavily on a kind of doo-wop approach to be placed firmly in the ballad category.

This brings us to "If I Fell," a beauty from 1964's *A Hard Day's Night*, which you can safely call the Beatles' first five-star ballad and receive only the weakest of arguments against it in return. Showing some vulnerability in the midst of a fast tempo and full instrumentation is one thing; showing it amid a sparse arrangement is quite another, a different level of soul-baring intimacy that hits the center of the listener's heart without anything to deflect the blow. When done right, such a song allows for a wonderful kind of wallowing, either the vicarious kind or the "I've been there too" variety. And "If I Fell" does it so right.

The best guess, one that is clouded by contradictory statements between both John Lennon and Paul McCartney and McCartney and himself, seems to be that it's mostly a Lennon composition with an assist from Macca, especially with the little preamble to the main section of the song. "If I Fell" creates a world of hypotheticals for the participants in the song, a kind of choose-your-own-adventure that inevitably leads to someone's heart getting broken.

Regardless of who wrote what, both Lennon and McCartney make essential contributions to the song simply by joining in yearning harmony. "If I Fell" comes off a bit like an Everly Brothers song thanks to these harmonies, albeit one with less country lilt and more confessional angst. Those two voices conjure such potency, especially whenever they join back up after brief vocal leads by Lennon, that the music wisely plays it quiet behind them, just a supportive rim shot–heavy beat from Ringo Starr and the interstitial guitar trills of George Harrison occasionally flashing to the fore before quickly receding again.

The melody of the opening section is sweet and true, which is exactly what the narrator wants from the girl he's addressing. He says that his experience showed him how difficult love can be: "'Cause I've been in love before and I found that love was more / Than just holding hands." Since the Beatles weren't even a year removed from the release of their smash single "I Want to Hold Your Hand," the message of that last line seems pretty clear: They were growing up and out of a black-and-white world of romance into one of gray complexities.

When McCartney joins for the first verse, his somewhat mournful vocal spins the seemingly hopeful opening couplet ("If I give my heart to you") into bittersweet territory. The narrator says that he's still somewhat stung by the failure of a previous relationship, which explains his gun-shy approach to new romance.

When they repeat the word "her" in the second verse, the melody takes an anguished turn: "'Cause I couldn't stand the pain." The harmony here is fascinating. Lennon's voice seems to be taking a more measured approach to the situation, with slight baby steps toward the new girl. McCartney is letting his cards show, however, so much so that there is audible strain when he hits the word "pain." It may have been simply a struggle to hit the note, but the slight flaw in the vocal actually resonates with authenticity.

Even by the final verse, we're still not sure if the narrator is ready to take a chance. He takes the remarkable step of explaining to the new girl that his ex will be hurt by their coupling: "And that she will cry when she learns we are two." It seems to be his way of getting her to treat this new relationship with import, but it can't bode well for the future that he's still bringing his love from the past.

The song ends with the line "If I fell in love with you," the vocals putting a kind of declarative spin on a line that is usually read with the expectation of something to follow it. It's as if the repercussions no longer need to be spoken, so well have they been spelled out to date. The outcome of "If I Fell" is unknown and really irrelevant, because this song is all about the pro-and-cons list made by the narrator. That list likely won't lead to an answer that satisfies everyone though, unlike this milestone of a Beatles' ballad.

15. "For No One" (from *Revolver*, 1966)

With "She Loves You" in 1963, the Beatles learned how useful it can be to fool around with the perspective of a song so that it might sound fresh even if the sentiments were pretty well-worn. In that song, a third party advises a guy to make it right with his girl before it's too late.

If you wanted to be morbid about it, you could view 1966's "For No One" as a sequel to "She Loves You," one in which it's already too late and our omniscient narrator is now telling the guy that it's all over. You could even subtitle it "She Doesn't Love You Anymore" if you were so inclined.

Only three years had passed, but the 1966 Beatles were a far cry from their 1963 vintage. In '66 they released *Revolver*, an album featuring a kaleidoscope of sounds and fast-maturing views on a suddenly expansive range of subject matter. "For No One," featured on that album, tackles the old subject of relationships, but it does so with nuance and depth that the band couldn't have possibly approached in the early days. Their life experience was catching up with their talent and producing startling results.

Paul McCartney wrote "For No One," yet another one of his pristine miniatures. Around this time McCartney had a special knack for sneaking into the lives of his subjects and capturing the details and dialogue that tell their stories with startling efficiency. It's basically a show-don't-tell approach that gives credit to the listeners that they'll be able to discover the emotional content of the song based on the lyrical clues and the tenor of the music, and, when pulled off as brilliantly as it is here, it can be subtly devastating.

The music of "For No One" strives to maintain a certain dignity, in much the same way that the guy in the song attempts to hold on to a sense of normalcy even as his world crumbles around him. McCartney uses a clavichord to pluck out the rhythm in the verses as the bass line tumbles like the hopes of the protagonist. Some drawing room piano shows up in the refrains as Ringo Starr joins with some barely there percussion.

Proving once again the ability to choose the right special guest instrument at the right time, the band employs a French horn played by Alan Civil. The choice is inspired because, again, it's an instrument that tends to keep a stiff upper lip. And yet the melody it plays, soaring high before fluttering back down to earth, can't help but hide the disappointment and regret.

McCartney sings the song with extreme empathy for this poor soul who's watching his relationship deteriorate before his eyes, even though he can't bring himself to admit it. But the signs are everywhere, from her laxity in getting ready for the day to her decision to go out without him. It's no wonder his "mind aches"; he's taxing his brain trying to find different ways of avoiding the truth staring him down.

In the second verse, McCartney lays it all out for him: "You want her, you need her / And yet you don't believe her / When she says your love is dead / You think she needs you." It's a beautifully assembled series of lines that simply have to be gut-wrenching for this guy to hear. The French horn solo had to come right after that just to soothe the blow.

Her words continue to do damage in the final verse: "She says that long ago she knew someone / But now he's gone / She doesn't need him." The use of the third-person narrator really makes sense by this point; all the references to "she" and "him" make it sound much more impersonal and distant than it would have been with "I" and "you," and impersonal and distant is exactly where this relationship stands. And when the narrator does directly address the guy in the final line of the last verse, the horn blowing stately and sad behind him, it really twists in the knife: "You won't forget her."

The refrain makes clear the pantomime to which this relationship has been reduced, a daily drama in which he is invested but she is simply playing a part, devoid of feeling: "And in her eyes, you see nothing, no sign of love behind the tears / Cried for no one, a love that should have lasted years." "For No One" is one of those songs that appear almost unassumingly on Beatles' albums, in this case sitting amid all the big hits and showier tracks on *Revolver*. Then you listen, and you wonder what hit you. It's apropos, since that's just how the poor protagonist is going to feel once his lover takes her person out of his life to follow her heart, which has been clearly gone for quite some time.

14. "We Can Work It Out" (from *Past Masters, Volume 2*, released as a single in 1965)

It shouldn't take any detective work to figure out that "We Can Work It Out," part of the Beatles' double A-sided single released in December 1965, was conceived and recorded during the sessions for *Rubber Soul*. Just a simple listen should reveal that it's very much of a piece with the other songs on that album, one in which the group mastered the art of intelligent, stirring pop music.

You also might be able to tell because it's another song where Paul McCartney is singing rather earnestly and passionately about some stress in a romantic relationship. We've already seen on this countdown the appearances of both "I'm Looking through You" and "You Won't See Me," songs from *Rubber Soul* that featured McCartney playing paramours frustrated by the physical and emotional distance that separates them from their partners.

Both of those songs, although featuring buoyant music, featured lyrics a bit on the tart side. "We Can Work It Out" conveys a bit of a more hopeful outlook, one in which the protagonist wishes to put aside the differences that are coming between the two and find the common ground that leads back to warm, trusting, blissful love. With John Lennon contributing a bit of a cloudy outlook to McCartney's sunny forecast, the song manages to be both positive and practical about the possibilities of this relationship righting course.

"We Can Work It Out" is also notable for being the first single the band released in the United Kingdom that couldn't really be classified as up-tempo rock and roll. The other half of the single, the rocking "Day Tripper," certainly fit the usual mold for a single release, but by utilizing the double A-side, the Beatles were able to broadcast their thoughtful side to the radio-listening public for the first time, which made sense since the music they were producing was heading more and more in that direction. Even though it's rhythmically propelled by some rapid acoustic guitar strumming, the song is light and airy, probably closest to folk in sound and spirit, albeit embellished with the Beatles usual instrumental and arranging cleverness.

In this case, the rapid strum of Lennon and the steady tambourine rattle of George Harrison get weighted down by the sad undertow of a harmonium, also played by Lennon. In similar fashion, the first few bars of the bridge come galloping out of the chorus, only to be slowed down by a grinding waltz beat in the second half of each line. The push and pull of the music turns out to be just the right accompaniment for this relationship that seems to have trouble sustaining its momentum.

McCartney uses the verses to plead his case to this girl, contending that an argument that's left unmended can fester and eventually infect a relationship beyond hope of a cure. "Try to see it my way," he constantly pleads, hoping that when two sides of the story are told, good intentions and better selves will win out over pettiness and the need to win the argument. The alternative: "While you see it your way / Run the risk of knowing that our love may soon be gone."

He contends that it's difficult in the heat of a spat to see the error in judgment that can befall even the most righteous of arguments: "Think of what you're saying / You can get it wrong and still you think that it's all right." And, when all else fails, there's always the logic that says you shouldn't go to bed angry: "We can work it out and get it straight or say good night."

In need of some kind of second counsel to strengthen his case, McCartney turned to Lennon to compose the middle eight. And Lennon responds with a typically morose counterargument, sung in urgent harmonies by the pair: "Life is very short and there's no time / For fussing and fighting, my friend." In a way it's no direr that McCartney's pronouncements about the possible end of the relationship, but there's something about the tone of the melody and the sudden slowdown into the waltz that throws more weight behind his warnings. "So I will ask you once again," he concludes, as if he were a lawyer putting the question to a squirming defendant after damning new evidence has been produced.

McCartney keeps the positivity alive with his boisterous refrain of "We can work it out," singing it with gusto in the hopes that his lover can't help but be swayed by it. Yet even that is tempered by the wheezing of harmonium as the song comes to a close, one more bluesy touch to balance out the light with more darkness.

"We Can Work It Out" stands out as a track that's essentially spotless. There isn't an ounce of flab to be found on it; every instrumental move, every melodic twist, every last word of the lyrics has a purpose. Quite simply, it represents the very best of what pop music can be, and yet it says here there are still thirteen songs that top it.

13. "Dear Prudence" (from *The Beatles*, 1968)

The White Album contained thirty-one songs. "Dear Prudence" is the best of them, and it's the one that captures the spirit of the double disc most accurately, from its odd inspiration to the anything-goes aesthetic of the recording, to the acrimony that began the process of splitting this once-in-a-lifetime band up.

The album was conceived well before the days of reality television, which is too bad, because a show detailing all of the goings-on during the Beatles' trip to meditate in India with the Maharishi would have been a doozy. Despite the objective of learning how to achieve calmness and peace in the midst of everyday tumult through meditation, the crazy mix of personalities led to all manner of drama, much of which became immortalized in the songs for the White Album (à la "Sexy Sadie," "The Continuing Story of Bungalow Bill," "I'm So Tired," and so forth).

In the case of "Dear Prudence," Prudence Farrow, sister of actress Mia, apparently worried some in the camp with her constant retreats to her tent, from which she wouldn't emerge for long stretches. John Lennon was among those tasked with coaxing her out. This eventually became fodder for a song that would immortalize the otherwise lesser-known Farrow sister.

When they went into the studio later in 1968 to record the song, the Beatles were forced to do so without Ringo Starr, who had bolted the sessions due to the discomfort of the environment and some criticism of his drumming. The group soldiered on without him for both "Back in the U.S.S.R." and "Dear Prudence."

Since "Dear Prudence" was built around Lennon's gentle fingerpicking on acoustic guitar, it would have been easy enough for the band, already a man down, to keep it simple and stark on the recording. Instead, they came up with one of their boldest arrangements ever, one that threw everything including the kitchen sink into the mix in a steady-building manner. Had Farrow actually heard the finished product while she was still in her tent, it's hard to imagine her not being roused back into social interaction by the magnificent madness of it all.

The song begins with Lennon on acoustic guitar with an insistent arpeggio style, asking in dreamy fashion, "Dear Prudence, won't you come out to play?" McCartney butts in with some single notes on his bass before joining with a steady drum patter leading into the end of the verse, which crashes to a halt once he goes to the cymbals.

In the second verse, McCartney becomes more assertive on bass, and some moaning backing vocals show up to support Lennon's lead. The bridge features the first appearance of George Harrison's lead guitar, while the backing vocalists, which included McCartney's brother John, Beatles' roadie Mal Evans, and musician Jackie Lomax, follow Lennon's imperative of "Look around" with their own chorus of "Round, round, round."

By the time we reach the third verse, Harrison starts to punch in a bit more while some hand clapping accentuates the percussion. But nothing can prepare us for the crazed orchestra that comes to the fore in the final verse. McCartney starts hitting everything in sight on the drum kit for a wild slap-boom-crash beat, Harrison derives an ascendant countermelody on guitar, and a flugelhorn enters the mix for no good reason other than the pure insanity of it all. The whole band lurches together for the final drawn-out conclusion, reaching a thrilling crescendo before everyone departs and leaves Lennon once again to pick away at his acoustic as if he had never noticed any of the wildness that had joined him.

None of this would have worked had Lennon not provided such a sturdy melodic base. And, in a manner that the Beatles' songwriters were able to pull off time and again, especially on this album, the lyrics easily overcome the specificity of their origins to make sense and resonate on a universal level.

In Lennon's hands, "Dear Prudence" becomes a paean to all those who have wrapped themselves in a shroud of despair and darkness in the hopes that they can see the brighter side of the world right outside their self-made confines. Surrounded by the inherent serenity and yet still potent sway of the music, "The sun is up, the sky is blue / It's beautiful, and so are you" somehow becomes more than just greeting-card sentiment, but rather a cosmic truth. "The wind is low, the birds will sing / That you are part of everything," Lennon insists, making a great case for a brotherhood of a man (and woman) a few years before he would make it much more explicitly in a famous solo song.

"Won't you open up your eyes?" he asks to start the second verse, but when he says it again to end that portion of the song, it's done so more assertively, as if he has the ability to make it so. And that sort of sums up the strange power of "Dear Prudence," which contains within it the ability to coax us all out of the metaphorical tents, maximum occupancy of one, into which we all retreat now and again, and back into the wide, wondrous world.

12. "Nowhere Man" (from *Rubber Soul*, 1965)

We're back once again on *Rubber Soul* with another song that achieves perfection so effortlessly that it seems as if it were just waiting around in the ether for any band to pluck it and put it on tape, only the Beatles got there first. Of course, such was their special talent that they could make songs like "Nowhere Man" seem so automatic, especially in their mid-1960s heyday when they were operating on a level that few artists or bands could even claim to have approached, let alone equaled.

They had found a sweet spot around that time where the songs they recorded were catchy at first listen and every listen thereafter, yet the meanings of those songs seemed to deepen with every subsequent spin.

"Nowhere Man" is crystalline pop rock, gleaming so much that you can practically feel the warmth of the shine through the speakers. (And it's hard to believe it wasn't a single, so radio-ready has it proven over the years.) Within that, though, lies a fascinating portrait of ineffectuality.

In multiple interviews, John Lennon said that he wrote the song after suffering through a bit of writer's block. Practically giving up on the chance that he might be even the least productive, he went to lie down, and the song popped into his head nearly complete. We should all be lucky enough to have such inspiration out of the blue just once in our lives.

Lennon puts the song in the third person, although he occasionally breaks through and attempts to converse directly with the titular character even when it's questionable whether the "Nowhere Man" can hear or respond. It's likely that Lennon was stepping outside himself and viewing his own predilection for daydreaming and lolling about through his ever-perceptive songwriting lens. If that's the case, you can hear the song as a kind of conversation between Lennon the artist and Lennon the man, and perhaps an attempt to figure out when and if those twain meet.

Lennon can afford to keep the rhymes at a simple level of clever wordplay because the musical setting is so piercing that it lends those rhymes extra weight. Thus the "nowhere man" in his "nowhere land" with his "nowhere plans for nobody" ends up being a fascinating subject in the midst of those crisp guitars.

It also helps immensely that, in the verses, the foibles and follies of this interesting character are rendered by some of the most exquisite harmony singing the band has ever done. In these verses, Lennon lays out the character's lack of direction, selective blindness ("Just sees what he wants to see"), and missing perspective ("doesn't have a point of view"), but he also makes clear that the Nowhere Man doesn't seem to regard any of this as a problem. And, after looking closely, the narrator notices his resemblance to the rest of us: "Isn't he a bit like you and me?"

In the bridges, Lennon takes over on lead vocal, while Paul McCartney and George Harrison step into supporting roles. These are the parts of the song when the narrator tries to connect and offer his advice, suggesting that "the world is at your command." He also seems to sympathize for this guy's predilection for idleness, telling him, "Take your time, don't hurry" and "Leave it all till somebody else lends you a hand." Again, if this was Lennon singing about and to himself, these parts suggest that he's okay with the state of nothingness he occasionally occupies, especially since it's the state from which these gorgeous songs of his seem to emanate.

In that respect, you might even be able to liken Lennon's "Nowhere Man" to Dylan's "Mr. Tambourine Man." Both songs champion a mysterious character, although Dylan more overtly asks his title character to be his muse. Lennon is coyer about it and perhaps unsure if the isolation and untouchability of his "Nowhere Man" status is worth the positive benefits that come out of it.

The song allows you to dive into conundrums like that if you should choose to do so. Or you can simply groove along to the midtempo, melodic succulence of it all. A precise, piercing guitar solo from Harrison adds to the effect (some sources have it as a dual solo with Lennon, although the aural evidence is a bit inconclusive), while McCartney's bass gives this thing far more wiggle than it has a right to possess.

The intertwined voices of Lennon, Harrison, and McCartney repeat the final line three times, with McCartney going up extra-high the last time for a flourish that leaves us wanting more. On the surface level it's ear candy of the highest order, and at its core it ponders deep philosophical quandaries. It's quite ironic how this supposedly ineffectual "Nowhere Man" ends up making such a profound impact on everyone who hears his tale.

11. "She Loves You" (from *Past Masters, Volume 1*, released as a single in 1963)

Want to understand Beatlemania? Put on "She Loves You." It's all there: the chaos, the excitement, the chorus that starts the song, the "Yeah, yeah, yeah" refrain. John Lennon as the rebel with a heart of gold, Paul McCartney as the melody maker, George Harrison as the sly guitar commenter, Ringo Starr as the unwavering backbeat—all are evident here. It's hard to find anything in rock-and-roll history quite as thrilling and fun as "She Loves You."

Besides the obvious merits it possesses as a song, "She Loves You" also carries great importance in terms of the development of the Beatles' popularity. As the A-side to the group's third single, it followed "Love Me Do," a modest song that garnered modest success, and "Please Please Me," a true firecracker of a single but one that easily could have been a fluke. "She Loves You" came along in 1963 and silenced whatever doubters were still lingering on the fringe, by somehow improving on the towering artistic and commercial success of "Please Please Me."

It's been noted often how the group thought to change it up from the typical love song by writing "She Loves You" from the perspective of a confidant advising a friend about a relationship. But there are other, subtler features in the song that help it stand out from much of what came before it. The chord changes, for example, are constantly surprising, with minors unexpectedly appearing to provide the song with necessary hints of urgency and putting the outcome of the relationship within the song in doubt, thereby raising the stakes.

The vocals tap into that feeling as well, and when they do erupt into the "Yeah, yeah, yeah" refrain, the effect is one of young love's triumph over pride and doubt and all the things that might have otherwise derailed it. In this manner, the Beatles, at a ridiculously early age, realized that a hint of the blues makes the moment when one rises above them even that much sweeter.

"She Loves You" also provides an early example of the group's unique chemistry. There's no real blueprint for when McCartney joins Lennon for harmonies, but his choices make it seem like he's giving support to a friend instead of just playing a role. There's also that role reversal whereby Lennon provides much of the rhythmic surge on guitar while McCartney gives the song more melodic punch on bass. Meanwhile, Harrison on lead guitar and Ringo Starr on drums, the two showiest instruments in most rock bands, never succumb to excess and always play to the singer and the song. By doing this, they make essential contributions to the way the tune stands out and becomes so instantly memorable. That all these things were in place so soon in their recording career is a testament both to the sound the band had developed through trial and error during years of live performances and to some kind of innate compatibility that really could have only been provided by fate.

The showmanship from those years of playing live also bleeds into the way the song is arranged, from Harrison strumming out the melody of the "Yeah, yeah, yeah" in answer to the refrain to the way the group repeats the last phrase ("With a love like that you know you should be glad") three times at the end, really stretching out the last one so that the impact when they dive into those closing harmonies will be particularly overwhelming. And it is; when you hear that portion of the song, that brief moment of anticipation is almost as exquisite as the delivery when they come busting back in to finish things off with one more "Yeah, yeah, yeah, yeah."

Trying to compare the early songs of artists with any longevity to their later output is always a difficult task. The Beatles made it especially dicey because they made such huge leaps in terms of musical innovation and ambition in such a short span of time. The tendency is to make a knee-jerk reaction and say the later stuff is better simply because it's more complex and comes from a deeper well of experience.

Yet there's no denying the impact that the energy of youth can have on music, and that energy practically drips from "She Loves You." The Beatles weren't even completely sure of what they were doing or how they were doing it on the song, but that ignorance or naïveté or whatever you want to call it bred something pure and indelible, something that even many famous later efforts, which were understandably lauded for their cleverness and insight, couldn't quite touch. "She Loves You" was the Big Bang for modern rock and roll, and all who followed in its wake have not just been beholden to it and the group that created it but have also generally labored in vain to reach its exuberant peak.

10. "All You Need Is Love" (from *Magical Mystery Tour*, 1967)

So you've been asked to speak in front of a worldwide television audience and deliver a message that everyone watching will hear. What would your message be? What is it that you might say?

The Beatles had exactly that opportunity when they performed as Great Britain's representative for the *Our World* broadcast, one of the first satellite linkups that would allow a performance from one country to be seen in multiple others. An estimated 350 to 400 million people from all over the globe tuned in to watch it on June 25, 1967, so an unprecedented number of ears would hear whatever message they delivered.

"All You Need Is Love"—it's a message so simple and pure, so free of the other trivialities and nonsense that tends to occupy a life, that it seems almost divine. And, in a way, it is, since it's essentially the message that every spiritual leader of whatever religion you choose has delivered throughout the mists of time.

Yet the message needed to be distilled by John Lennon, who wrote the song practically days before it was needed for the broadcast, and the

Beatles, who gave a loose, charming performance of it both in the studio beforehand and on the live show. Coming on the heels of *Sgt. Pepper's Lonely Hearts Club Band*, which was released just two weeks before, it was perhaps the band's ultimate moment of triumph, the absolute peak when it all came together. Their popularity, their talent, their influence, the culture they helped create, and this perfectly timed and expertly crafted message of love over everything else: it all cohered as Lennon sang and chewed his gum.

"All You Need Is Love" required a bit of a high-wire act by the band to bring it to fruition. So that they weren't completely without a net during the live performance, they created a backing track with odd instrumentation: Lennon on harpsichord, Paul McCartney on double bass, and George Harrison on violin. That ramshackle base was embellished by the live performance, which included an orchestra cleverly arranged by George Martin. The strings and horns not only add some gravitas to the recording but also throw in playful teases of well-known songs in the intro and outro to feed into the anything-goes spirit of the time.

Lennon's verses contain a Confucian kind of wisdom that says anything is possible if you can set free the hang-ups that are essentially nonessential. In his hands, the word "nothing" is given its most positive spin, as it comes to represent the boundlessness and infinity of a love-infused existence. "There's nowhere you can be that isn't where you're meant to be," he sings, insisting that the world is borderless and welcoming to those who can maintain this amatory wavelength. (And, again, with the whole world watching and listening, what a timely thing to suggest.)

This simple song also gets a simple melody from Lennon; it's mostly single notes repeated. In the moments when the tune emerges from its flatline, the difficulty of what Lennon is proposing briefly comes to the fore. There is a little desperation in the way he sings, "It's easy," suggesting that it's actually anything but. And in the chorus, the third time he sings the refrain, the music takes a suddenly sorrowful turn.

By making that subtle melodic shift, Lennon seems to be hinting at all the things that prevent us from giving and receiving love, from the outside influences that would scoff at the song as being naïve and do everything in their power to make it seem so, to the unexpected circumstances of life that can complicate and confuse. But it's only a moment, quickly doused when he serenely sings, "Love is all you need."

John Lennon had a way of connecting with his audience that probably no other songwriter has ever possessed. Somehow he found the exact right things to say at exactly the moment we needed to hear them most time and again. It's one of the reasons why he's so missed: whenever a crisis arises in the world, we yearn for words of wisdom or solace or vitriol or whatever is required for that particular moment in time, even as we know the guy proven most qualified to say them in a song isn't around.

Luckily we can go back to the words he said before he passed, ones which have a way of resonating through time. That's part of the genius of "All You Need Is Love," in that he took this specific instance as the opportunity to deliver a message, using the Beatles as the ideal messengers, that is just as crucial now as it was then. On our behalf, Lennon rose to the occasion and said the words that we all would want to say in that situation, words by which our best selves still strive to live.

9. "In My Life" (from *Rubber Soul*, 1965)

"In My Life" is one of two songs written by the Lennon/McCartney team for which the separate recollections of the pair about who wrote what drastically differ. Both of those songs happen to be in the top ten in this list, so you can understand perhaps why both would want the proper credit on works of this magnitude.

John Lennon recalled it as mostly his composition, lyrics, and music, with Paul McCartney helping on the middle eight. (That confuses the matter more, since there isn't really a middle eight in the song; Lennon was probably referring to the musical shift in the lead-up to the refrain.) By contrast, McCartney recalls essentially writing all the music after being handed an early draft of Lennon's lyrics.

Perhaps the truth falls somewhere in between, which means that both men should be commended, because the words and music are complimentary and indispensable on this, one of the greatest love songs of any genre of music. "In My Life," the emotional centerpiece of *Rubber Soul*, the group's landmark album from 1965, is the ultimate testament to finding the one person who changes everything.

Although the Beatles would go on to find different ways of scoring their ballads that often took them closer to classical music than rock, their recording of "In My Life" is a masterly example of how rock instrumentation could be utilized on a slow song. The words and melody need to be at the forefront of a song like this for it to work, and the way the band massages these elements while adding touches that second the notion provided by the lyric can't be underestimated.

The opening is a beauty, with George Harrison's lilting guitar riff undergirded by McCartney's bass. Harrison's guitar tone, clear and gentle, is just right for the tenor of the song. Ringo Starr's drumbeat is a bit unorthodox for the material, almost aggressive, but it provides effective contrast to the cooing backing vocals. George Martin's baroque piano solo, achieved by speeding up the tempo at which it was played in the studio, brings a bittersweet tinge to the whole affair. When Harrison comes back in at the end to close out the whole affair with his initial riff, the symmetry is deeply affecting.

Lennon admits that the song was an attempt to write in a more literary fashion akin to his books, but he almost derailed it by getting too detail heavy in his opening drafts. The final version drops away a lot of the what and where and instead concentrates on the before and after of the narrator's life. The first verse of the song concentrates on all of the wonderful relationships he has cultivated and sustained throughout his life, memories of which are spurred by different locations, the places calling to mind the people.

He admits here that there have been rocky times: "Some forever, not for better," he sings, that Lennon wordplay working its magic. But overall, the happy memories prevail, as do the warm feelings for the faces from his past: "In my life, I've loved them all."

In the second verse, things begin to change for him, as he directly addresses someone who has cast all these recollections in a different light: "And these memories lose their meaning / When I think of love as something new." Although he promises that he'll continue to remember these people and places, they are now subordinate to something else: "In my life I'll love you more."

When you look closely at "In My Life," you'll see that it's a pretty short song, just a couple verses worth of lyrics. Yet the power of that last line lingers to such an extent that nothing more was necessary. Reflecting on it, it's a pretty bold thing for Lennon to have said. Surely many people would feel more comfortable compartmentalizing their affection based on who is receiving it rather than putting it in terms of greater or lesser.

Instead, this song proposes that ideal romantic love simply outdoes the love for family or friends or anything else in one's life.

Yet Lennon's intent here wasn't to say that the love of those other people in one's life needs to be eliminated or sacrificed in some way so that this new relationship can take over. But he does seem to suggest that, in order for a lifelong love between two people to really work, those other things do have to be subordinated in some fashion.

At the time he wrote the song (or at least the lyrics to the song, depending on your view of the songwriting split), Lennon was married to his first wife, Cynthia. And it doesn't appear that he followed its tenets too closely, considering the demands of his life as a Beatle and the extramarital affairs to which he later admitted. But you can certainly see the kind of devotion and commitment espoused by "In My Life" in his relationship with Yoko Ono, one that, through ups and downs, would define his life until his untimely passing.

Perhaps it takes finding that one person you love above all else to fully understand "In My Life." What's certain is that umpteen lovers have used Lennon's words over the many years since the song has been released to best articulate the totality of their devotion.

8. "Something" (from *Abbey Road*, 1969)

"Something" is the finest complete song on *Abbey Road*, the Beatles' grand finale of an album, which was released in 1969. It is also tops on the list of Fab Four songs suitable for slow dancing with one's significant other, thanks to the gorgeous sway of the music and the stirring pull of the words; you practically just have to stand there and this song will move you around by the force of its beauty.

Frank Sinatra often lauded the song with superlatives before performing it in concert, although it took him a while before he stopped referring to it as a Lennon/McCartney composition. No rock connoisseur was Ol' Blue Eyes, but you can partially forgive his mistake, considering that "Something" was actually written by George Harrison, who wasn't exactly known for proclaiming, with heart on sleeve, the wonders of love.

Love had been more of an abstract quality in Harrison's previous work, something that tended to unify the whole world rather than just two people. On "Something," he brings it back to a very personal level, invoking the kind of love that defies description. In fact, he's not even able to put his finger on the attraction in the song, but he knows it's there, drawing him to this other person. This song is all about the indefinable and the intangible aspects of love, the qualities so fragile that, if exposed, might disappear just as quickly.

Harrison took a line from his Apple label mate James Taylor as inspiration for the lyrics of "Something," built up a stunning melody around it, and fronted his first single with the Beatles as a result. (It was part of a double A-side with "Come Together" and topped the US charts.) Although his songwriting had vastly improved throughout his time with the group, he hadn't quite mastered the art of penning a three-minute song for the masses that says everything and leaves you wanting more. You can tell "Something" is that kind of song from his very first guitar notes.

The song logs great mileage from the instrumental wizardry of Harrison, Paul McCartney, and Ringo Starr, along with some carefully deployed orchestration. (John Lennon played only a little piano and guitar on the track, both of which are somewhat lost in the mix.) McCartney's bass work is staggering here, as he derives numerous fetching countermelodies that stand out amid the relatively stark instrumentation. Starr feels his way about, occasionally tiptoeing, occasionally building up to a forceful cymbal crash, always giving space for Harrison to sing.

There is a passage after the bridge in which Harrison plays a solo that seems to express every last bit of feeling he has for the woman he's describing in the song. McCartney bobs all around those guitar lines, and the pair comes off like two dancers on the same floor weaving in and out of each other's way without ever touching. It is one of the most breathtaking segments in any Beatles' song.

While Harrison might have given over to his sentimental side for the song, he keeps a healthy dose of cynicism in play. He seems aware of love's all too ephemeral characteristics, which tinge "Something" with just a hint of uncertainty. In the bridge, he sings, "You're asking me will my love grow / I don't know, I don't know." This is the most anguished part of his vocal, as if the possible negative outcome is too much to bear. Harrison always led with honesty first and foremost, even when it propelled him down prickly emotional paths, and that stands as one of his most endearing qualities as a writer.

Over and over again in the verses, the narrator attempts to put a fine point on what it is about his lover that endears him so. He keeps coming back to the word "something," as if that's the only answer that makes sense. And it more than suffices, because "she knows / That I don't need no other lover." The strongest couples have an unspoken bond that not even they can describe or define; "Something" pinpoints this elusive quality, one that you can't see or touch or name but can always feel.

In the final verse, McCartney joins Harrison on high harmony vocals for a little bit more testimony. Harrison then takes back the solo stage to explain that what really matters isn't the reason for the attraction, but the consequence: "I don't want to leave her now / You know I believe and how." His guitar returns, climbing once up the hill but coming up short of the destination before girding its loins and soaring to the glorious, resolved final note, the aural equivalent of a passionate embrace after a time of separation.

George Harrison couldn't have known for sure that he would need a springboard so soon into his solo career when he wrote and recorded "Something," but the song surely acted as one. It is his finest moment fronting the Beatles and stands proudly on the list of the band's greatest accomplishments. And how.

7. "She's Leaving Home" (from *Sgt. Pepper's Lonely Hearts Club Band*, 1967)

It might be somewhat odd to some to see something like "She's Leaving Home" so high on a list of songs by the world's most celebrated rock-and-roll band. The song doesn't even have a tenuous connection to rock as we know it. Even previous ballads by the band like "Yesterday" or "For No One" featured heavy orchestration that could be tangentially connected to folk music, which is a kind of studious cousin to rock. "She's Leaving Home" seems more like it was plucked out of some operetta from the nineteenth century.

It doesn't seem to have the temperament of a rock song either. Much of rock and roll throughout its existence has been fueled by a generational divide, young folks writing songs about their parents' lack of understanding, which, in a self-fulfilling prophecy, their parents couldn't possibly understand. With the bashing away of the guitars and drums, there wasn't a lot of room for rock songwriters to depict that relationship with any subtlety, nor did most of them show any desire to do just that.

Paul McCartney had the idea for writing "She's Leaving Home" after reading a newspaper article about a teenage runaway. He also had the inspired notion to cast John Lennon as the parents in the song, and Lennon's rejoinders (which he helped to write) help to render the song as both a balanced portrait of a family in distress and a moving treatise on the way generational miscommunication can develop into something that's equal parts tragic and liberating.

Much of the song's success comes from the way Mike Leander, who filled in for an absent George Martin, arranges the orchestration to comment on the lyrics. Listen for the way the cello in the opening verse stalks along stealthily as the girl silently makes her escape, the suddenly dramatic swing the violins take when the parents discover her farewell letter, or the sense of anticipation the strings conjure as the girl prepares to meet the man "from the motor trade" in the final verse, signaling the start of her new life. Everything works, even that harp at the start, which must have sent Beatles fans reeling the first time they heard it when they spun *Sgt. Pepper* back in the day. And McCartney's melody is worthy of any bold-faced classical composer you can name.

The lyrics effortlessly drop you into the middle of this domestic drama. Notice that the girl who runs away never utters a word in the song, leaving a letter to do her talking; her parents have long since lost the ability to hear her cries for help anyway. Yet she's not angry when she leaves, nor is she initially happy. The one brief glimpse of her mindset is gleaned from her "clutching her handkerchief" so that it's nearby when the tears fall. She's not just carrying it; she's holding on to it for dear life, perhaps as a sign of stress, perhaps to steel her resolve for what she's about to do.

In verse two, the parents discover the letter, and the scene of the mother standing momentarily frozen elicits sympathy for what in other rock songs might have been a clichéd shrew of a character. When the mom refers to her husband as "Daddy," it is the height of irony, since his parenting skills clearly left a bit to be desired. Further evidence of this comes from their first reaction, which is not concern for their daughter's well-being but rather rampant self-pity.

The neatest trick that Lennon and McCartney pull off here is the way they play with the sequence of events. The verses move forward in linear fashion, but the refrains keep the parents stuck in that moment in which they find the letter. As the girl moves forward to her new life, making progress just two days after her departure, the parents can only proceed internally, going through three stages of grief in the three choruses:

shock, denial, and then acceptance. That acceptance, which seems to be prodded along by Paul gently singing the title refrain until it sinks in, comes finally when the parents understand their mistakes. "Fun is the one thing that money can't buy," Lennon sings, the father getting the picture far too late.

Yet the point to take away is that they were not intentionally harming this girl. In their minds, they thought they were doing the right thing for their daughter. To their credit, the song doesn't show them frantically searching for her at the end. Instead, their last words are a heartbreaking farewell. Maybe they finally realized that the girl's freedom would be more beneficial to her than all of their monetary gifts. It's like the old maxim that says you should let your kid choose her own path, and eventually it will lead her home.

That may not be the anarchic message of your prototypical rock song, and certainly the method of conveying that message, via harps and strings with nary a drum, wasn't run-of-the-mill either. The Beatles understood that there was more to rock than guitars and drums (which is kind of the point of the whole *Sgt. Pepper's* project), just as they realized there was more to parents and children than just clichéd rancor. "She's Leaving Home" is the culmination of all of that foresight and insight. All rock music should be so accomplished.

6. "Strawberry Fields Forever" (from *Magical Mystery Tour*, 1967)

The Beatles recorded "Strawberry Fields Forever" at the beginning of sessions for *Sgt. Pepper's Lonely Hearts Club Band* toward the end of 1966. Some have bemoaned the fact that the song was released as a single and not included on the final album, but it was the right choice. This was a piece of music that needed to stand apart, so unique and groundbreaking that it even left behind the experimentation of the *Revolver* album, released earlier in 1966. And while it would have given *Sgt. Pepper's* listeners more bang for their buck, it wouldn't have quite fit in with the more straightforward tales of routine folk that dot that album.

"Strawberry Fields Forever" is an outlier, for sure. Had the Beatles recorded it with John Lennon simply strumming an acoustic guitar and singing it, it would have been a moving confessional. Had they simply released the music they concocted for the song as an instrumental, it would have gone down as an avant-garde triumph. By putting it all together, they created a song that will still hold powerful sway over its listeners well into the distant future.

John Lennon borrowed the title from remembrances of a patch of greenery near a Salvation Army home where he used to hide out and play as a child. In the song, Strawberry Fields becomes a metaphor for anywhere one can be who they are without fear of repercussions. The trick is finding out exactly who it is you are first, and that's what the song strives to discover, not just for the narrator/Lennon but for all the listeners as well.

Lennon's song nails a conversational tone that had rarely been attempted to that point. Most pop or rock songs were just a series of lines pieced together in the service of meter and rhyme, but the narrator sounds here like a man desperate to communicate his feelings while unsure of the words to use. Notice that the verses often don't rhyme and that in the last section the singer seems to be practically stuttering in an attempt to get his point across.

It's a very insecure narrative, as if Lennon doesn't want to offend or make any definitive statements on behalf of anyone, hedging his bets with all the "I think" and "I mean" qualifiers. For example, the enigmatic opening lines ("Living is easy with eyes closed / Misunderstanding all you see") seem to be a kind of reprimand to those who would refrain from exploring themselves fully. But he quickly pulls back: "but it all works out / It doesn't matter much to me."

This reticence reflects Lennon's own conflicted feelings about his status in life. "No one I think is in my tree," he sings. "I mean it must be high or low." He told David Sheff in 1980 that those lines were deeply autobiographical. "Well, what I was trying to say in that line is 'Nobody seems to be as hip as me, therefore I must be crazy or a genius,'" Lennon explained. "What I'm saying, in my insecure way, is 'Nobody seems to understand where I'm coming from. I seem to see things in a different way from most people.'"[39] And, again, that leads to a kind of shrug of the shoulders: "That is you can't you know tune in but it's all right / That is I think it's not too bad."

In the last verse, he really seems to be at war with himself, conducting a kind of self-argument. There's a kind of breakthrough when he finally says, "That is I think I disagree," as he finally appears to take a stand, albeit a measured one, and against what, we're not sure. The one area where's he's certain is his desire to return to Strawberry Fields, where all this inner turmoil is put to rest.

The music captures this push and pull between angst and ecstasy in the most imaginative ways. George Martin's masterful touch with translating Lennon's musical ideas into reality finds its quintessence in "Strawberry Fields Forever." The song contains elements of bluesy rock, symphonic pomp, and psychedelic reverie, often at the same time. Ringo Starr is charged with maintaining some semblance of rhythm throughout all of these disparate moods and changes, and he rises to the occasion with one of his finest performances in the group.

Lennon's vocals had to be slowed down in order to match up the different parts of the recording, but that necessity proved a blessing, as the effect produced a wobbly texture that suited the indecisiveness of the lyrics. Once the rock elements disappear after the first verse, the absence of a bass guitar makes the entire song seem to float about weightless in some heightened reality. The mellotron opening is both lovely and spooky, George Harrison's swarmandal interstitials add a mystic edge, and the strange, haunted coda seems to be the dark side of the fever dream. At no point can you predict what is coming next in this song based on what has preceded it, which is a tribute to the imagination of Lennon, Martin, and the rest of the group.

Through all of this mysterious, mesmerizing music, Lennon's desire to connect, a quality to which millions of young (and old, for that matter) people listening to the song could relate, holds it all together. The tendency is to say that this song was ahead of its time. It's been fifty years now, and we still haven't heard anything quite like "Strawberry Fields Forever," so it's pretty safe to say now that this masterpiece was a one-time deal.

5. "Eleanor Rigby" (from *Revolver*, 1966)

Paul McCartney claimed to have written 80 percent of "Eleanor Rigby," while John Lennon said that he wrote 70 percent of it. You don't need to be a math major to see the discrepancy there. Considering that interviews through the years with the principals have also noted that George Harrison and Ringo Starr contributed to parts of the writing, it's quite the confusing situation. It seems the likeliest guess is that this was a collaborative lyrical effort based on McCartney's original idea and music.

Now that we've got that out of the way, we can concentrate on the specialness of "Eleanor Rigby." By 1966, rock and pop songwriters were beginning to see beyond the typical songwriting subject matter, which was largely restricted to romance, and look out at the world around them. The Beatles not only lent insight beyond their years to these worldly matters but also, better than any others, found novel ways of expressing these issues in their music.

Having used a string quartet to score McCartney's "Yesterday" in 1965, the group upped the ante on "Eleanor Rigby" by utilizing an octet. As with most Beatles' songs, the structure of words and melody is so strong that it could have been delivered in basic terms and the point would have come across just fine. But the inherent drama of the strings takes the song to another level of tragedy, one where only the lonely dwell.

The main character is introduced all by herself in the aftermath of an occasion during which two individuals ensure themselves against loneliness, till death do they part: "Eleanor Rigby picks up the rice in the church where the wedding has been." What's so heartbreaking about this woman is that she still holds out hope that her isolated lot in life will change. We see her waiting for some kind of deliverance at the window and making herself up in the hopes that someone will see and notice. But the narrator knows better. "Who is it for?" he asks.

What escalates the song from a single character sketch to the probing of a widespread calamity is the introduction of the second lonely person, Father McKenzie. His sermons go unheard, and he works into the wee hours of the night mending socks—mind-numbing exercises both. Like Eleanor Rigby's actions, the futility is evident. The point the song makes is that every single moment of a lonely person's existence is wasted somehow; like the old adage about the tree falling in the woods, "Eleanor Rigby" posits that an audience of some sort is required for a person's activities to have meaning.

McCartney as narrator keeps himself as detached as he can, viewing these subjects as an anthropologist would some foreign tribe. He can come up with no unifying thesis though, just questions: "All the lonely people, where do they all come from? / All the lonely people, where do they all belong?" The refrain of "Ah, look at all the lonely people" is the one point in the song when urgency seeps into the vocals; not coincidentally, it's the one point when McCartney gets harmony support from

Lennon and Harrison, as if to drive home the point about the need for human interaction even further.

The menial duties the two main characters perform would be considered boring by most. But the staccato rhythm the strings form creates a suspenseful effect, which in its way gives import to the problem of their loneliness. You simply can't ignore either Eleanor or Father McKenzie in this setting, even if the rest of the world has, because the music won't allow you to do so.

"Eleanor Rigby" elides right through most of the title character's life. We see her at the church, and then we are told that she died in that same church; she has made no progress, and any time spent in the interval was clearly not worth mentioning. In the final lines the strings hit levels of tension from which even Alfred Hitchcock might shrink, when we find out that Father McKenzie, in a bit of symmetric irony, performs the service for the dead woman, these two lonely souls meeting but not quite. McCartney's final damning assessment suggests that no religious rites will change their destinies, even beyond the grave: "No one was saved."

If you were describing the song to a stranger, it would resemble the plot of some independent film that was a critical success at Sundance yet has no chance of catching on with audiences: a lonely spinster and an ineffectual clergyman lead lives of parallel isolation before finally being united at the grave. "Eleanor Rigby" succeeds because it does what all great pop songs can do better than even the finest movies: illuminate a theme or topic with detail and emotion and all in less than three minutes, guaranteeing an impact that a ninety-minute movie can't hope to match.

The Beatles' ability to have such impact is largely due to their willingness to experiment musically in ways others wouldn't even have considered. And the lyrics, clear-eyed but tender all at once, contribute a great deal as well. If we assume that it took a bunch of heads put together to create "Eleanor Rigby," one of the most lusciously sad songs in the pop music canon, we can at least be assured that the creators of the song enjoyed far more community than those within it ever did.

4. "I Am the Walrus" (from *Magical Mystery Tour*, 1967)

Describing "I Am the Walrus" on *The Beatles Anthology*, John Lennon said, "It's one of those that has enough little biddies going to keep you interested even a hundred years later."

Analysis of the Beatles' music has been a cottage industry pretty much from the late 1960s on, and the practice has only intensified since the band's official breakup in 1970. John Lennon eventually softened to the phenomenon, giving several interviews in which he answered questions about the songs of the group. But it clearly aggravated him somewhat in the early going, which seems to be the genesis of "I Am the Walrus."

Included on the soundtrack for *Magical Mystery Tour* in late 1967, "I Am the Walrus" serves Lennon's purpose brilliantly. It not only dissuades any kind of logical analysis (not that it ever stopped folks from trying) but also serves as a reminder that the best Beatles' music makes a kind of visceral impact on the listener. On hearing it for the first time, you tend to be attracted to it, even if you don't know exactly what's going on or why it has captivated you. You just know it sounds great, and that's enough to hook you into delving into it further.

This year, 1967, was also the prime year for the Beatles making what you might call headphone music, and "I Am the Walrus" is the glorious epitome of that trend. If you immerse yourself in it and listen closely with the rest of the world blocked out, you'll hear the myriad intricacies of the recording and the endless sounds floating around the persistent snap of Ringo Starr's drumbeat and Lennon's searing vocal. These are the "biddies" that the group inserted into their most marvelously madcap recording.

Lennon also dares us to drink in his wild and wooly wordplay, even as we know we run the risk of being ensnared by his traps. He starts benignly enough with the somewhat hippie mantra of "I am he as you are he as you are we and we are all together." As a matter of fact, the whole first verse allows us to get our feet wet without too much craziness, even if "like pigs from a gun" seems a little odd for a simile.

But it's not too long before he's throwing words at us that aren't even words ("texpert," "crabalocker") and ramming actual words together into phrases that even Dylan at his most fearless might have shunned ("elementary penguin singing Hare Krishna" or "Corporation tee-shirt, stupid bloody Tuesday"). There is no reason and very little rhyme to Lennon's approach, but it's catchy in a maniacal sort of way, especially when you put it all together with the music.

After the siren-like intro and the droll string section that hangs about it, Lennon sinks into the main groove, pulling us along with the intense fervor of his vocal. Starr's snares rarely sounded as potent as they do here, as if he were breaking a pane of glass with each rap. Throughout it all, orchestration is evident, but it's a different kind of feel here than on songs like "Yesterday" or "Eleanor Rigby." The use of strings and horns here is more random, as they enter the sonic picture now and again, alternately suggesting mirth, sarcasm, or disdain depending on where they appear and the nature of their commentary. The crazed choral backing vocals offer the same kind of effect throughout.

All of this could easily have spun out of control if Lennon wasn't such a charismatic ringmaster at the center of it all. His insane insistence in the chorus that "I am the egg man / They are the egg men / I am the walrus" is like a call to arms to anyone who can connect to this wacky wavelength. Even his call-and-response with a Shakespearean radio play makes perfect sense in this context.

At the end of the song, Lennon's nonsensical "Goo goo g'joob g'goo goo g'joob g'goo" chant is the signal for the orchestra, the choral group, and his entire cult of listeners to soar off into the heavens with him, beginning an ever-ascending chord sequence and series of wild catchphrases that don't stop until that radio broadcast of King Lear finally interrupts, as if in an attempt to bring back some sense of decorum. But by then, it's too late. We are all egg men in the service of the walrus.

If there is a message somewhere buried deep in the mania of this song, it's that we should remember to enjoy the music first before we get so caught up in thinking about it. Or maybe, it's just "goo goo g'joob." Either way, Lennon was being modest when he described "I Am the Walrus," because one hundred years of listening to it isn't nearly long enough to fully appreciate it.

3. "Hey Jude" (from *Past Masters, Volume 2*, released as a single in 1968)

It began with something very personal. John Lennon had separated from his wife, Cynthia, with a divorce forthcoming. Paul McCartney felt bad not only for Cynthia but also for her son, Julian, who was still just a little boy. Paul had become good friends with the lad, so much so that Julian would later recall spending much more time with McCartney than with his dad. So Paul decided to visit, and on the car ride over began to compose a simple song to try to cheer the child up.

From such a humble beginning "Hey Jude" was born, a song that is ubiquitous even today as we close in on a half century since its release in 1968. Yet it hasn't lost any of its impact, any of its power to uplift, to encourage, to sustain, to console. It has become nothing less than an anthem for anyone suffering from the immediate sting of loss, a song that pinpoints the part of us that hurts the most and begins the healing process almost immediately through the sheer force if its empathy.

Over the years, many people have tried to come up with possible inspirations for the song other than McCartney's obvious explanation. Lennon heard it as a song about him and his newfound relationship with Yoko; others heard Macca's song as a bit of advice to himself; and still others have come out of the woodwork claiming the song is about them. And they're all right. That's the beauty of "Hey Jude." It's constructed in such a way that it belongs to everyone when they need it most, a bastion of hope in the bleakest of hours.

Paul could have kept the song at the personal level and sprinkled in details that would have narrowed the song's focus, and it likely would have worked, but not on the scale that it did. The Beatles usually swung for the cheap seats with their songs, going for the broadest possible audience a large percentage of the time, especially on their singles. They did this not by pandering but by presenting their own takes on universal themes and doing so in novel ways, giving the listeners a perspective they might not have heard before, or even shedding a light on a feeling inside the listeners that they didn't even know they had. "Hey Jude," their biggest single ever, epitomizes these qualities.

Over the years the sound of "Hey Jude" has been so widely cannibalized by every rock ballad you can wave a lighter at that it's easy to forget it was one of the first of its kind, and certainly the most influential. Paul's plink-plunk piano style has, for better or worse, become the standard for every band or artist wanting to show their sensitive side. Such copycat moves come off as cynical, but for the Beatles it was what suited the song best.

The gradual introduction of each instrument is also taken for granted today, but again, it was something relatively new at the time. Most rock songs to that point came on full bore from start to finish, but on "Hey Jude," the Beatles found a way to let the song breathe and to allow each new sound to bring something novel to the table. Starting with just Paul's piano and vocal, the song eventually encompasses a gigantic orchestra blaring out the refrain in the coda.

Along the way, Ringo Starr's gently intuitive drums are a real standout; his drumming possesses what sports fans call "touch," that indefinable and unteachable ability to know precisely what was needed for each song in terms of loudness or beat. The backing vocals are understated but lovely, and leave it to Lennon to deflate the somber proceedings by dropping the F-bomb. (Listen real close for his voice in the last verse right as Paul sings "Then you begin," and you'll hear it.)

The song itself is deceptively simple once you take away all the ornate touches. The tune gets you right in the gut without being needlessly complex. The chords are pretty straightforward. And Paul sings right on the melody, allowing his direct lyrics to bring forth the emotion.

There is deep wisdom in those lyrics, and they don't ever get needlessly showy. "For well you know that it's a fool / Who plays it cool / By making his world a little colder," McCartney sings, suggesting that those too proud to ask for help will regret it down the road. When he sings, "Let it out and let it in," he is referring both to the simple act of taking a deep breath and the necessity of confronting the pain you feel in order to eventually unburden yourself from it.

This song illustrates a general difference in outlook between McCartney and Lennon in their songs. Whereas Lennon tended to accept loneliness and isolation as a part of the tapestry of life in songs like "Strawberry Fields Forever" and "Nowhere Man," McCartney strives against it and offers alternatives. But even Lennon could still relate to McCartney's point of view. When McCartney debated dropping the line "The movement you need is on your shoulder," Lennon wouldn't allow it. He knew what his partner was subconsciously suggesting: that even when all hope seems lost, there is always something to guide us. Whether it's God or a lost loved one or even just our own inner strength, it's there.

As for the coda, that cathartic round of na-na-nas that takes the song into infinity, it's the answer that McCartney has been promising for the entire song, the movement that will set us free from sorrow. Because the four band members are still jamming endlessly on those same three chords even as the song fades out, it's easy to imagine that they never really stopped. When we need them the most, we can always reach for "Hey Jude," and we'll find the Beatles forever taking our own personal sad song and making it better.

2. "Golden Slumbers"/"Carry That Weight"/"The End" (from *Abbey Road*, 1969)

The inclusion of three songs as one entry on this list may violate the spirit of this project in some ways, but there's a reason for it. There is no real way to separate the final part of the side 2 medley on *Abbey Road*, as the three pieces of music are interconnected in such a way that they would individually lose much of their meaning without tangency to the other two.

Throughout this list, many songs have been lauded for their ability to resonate on a larger scale with the listening public even if they were composed based on something specific occurring within the lives of the Beatles themselves. That ability to make the personal universal comprises a great part of their allure.

Yet the medley of "Golden Slumbers"/"Carry That Weight"/"The End" need not be anything more than what it is, which is a kind of emotional period to the Beatles' career-long musical sentence, to carry huge import for anyone listening. This was a group that meant and means so much to so many that a proper farewell is a good enough reason for this medley to exist; that it rises to the occasion as one of the most stirring and moving moments not just in the band's career but in the history of rock and roll is fitting, considering the band in question.

The other members of the Beatles complained after the fact about Paul McCartney's overbearing nature and tendency to bossiness. But one wonders how the group might have ground to a halt had he not possessed the foresight to be concerned about putting a bow on the Beatles' legacy, even while the group members themselves were at a time of extreme dysfunction. Although it was still somewhat up in the air, the general consensus among the band was that *Abbey Road* would be the last album they would record. Thus McCartney rallied the troops for an appropriately majestic send-off.

How fitting to frame it as a lullaby. He was, after all, putting the Beatles to bed. McCartney does an amazing job of saying so much with very little verbiage, as there are precious few lyrics sprinkled throughout the medley. Every one of those words counts, however, especially that killer opening line: "Once there was a way to get back homeward." This is the chilling admission that fans never wanted to hear, a line that speaks of chances lost, opportunities missed, and the heartbreaking feeling that the Beatles could not go home again. Once, maybe, but not now, not ever again.

After Ringo Starr clears a path with his snares, McCartney sings the refrain of "Golden Slumbers" with tremendous power, putting all of his pent-up frustration and anger into those ancient lines that he found in a musty volume of poetry. This is the rare lullaby that will actually wake you from any lingering dreams and leave you in the cold, harsh light of the unforgiving truth. Yet at the moment when there seems to be no consolation left to give, the booming refrain of "Carry That Weight" arrives.

There has been much conjecture as to whom McCartney was referring that needed to "Carry That Weight." Speculation runs from a self-administered pep talk, to a dig at Lennon, to a tacit admission that the solo careers awaiting the band would be endlessly and unfairly compared to the Beatles' legacy. There might be a bit of truth in all of those takes. Overall it seems like an acknowledgment that each of the four men would always have to carry the weight of being a Beatle, in terms not just of the shadow cast over his career but also in terms of the way he was viewed in everyday life. In many ways, no matter what he would do henceforth, his individuality was sacrificed forever, and he would always have to live up to the Beatles' standard, whether he was in the studio or just walking down the street.

Even while bearing the burden, the music and the melody is upbeat, as if the lofty brass in this section is spurring the afflicted onward. A reprise of "You Never Give Me Your Money" is next, a clear-eyed reference to the petty problems that had beset the group. In the face of all this pressure, they were breaking down, as the song spells out.

"The End" refuses to let things finish on any down note though. It acts as a kind of closing number to the figurative concert that the Beatles had put on for the dozen or so years since Lennon and McCartney first got together. As such, what better time to let their hair down and go to town on their instruments. After McCartney sets the stage with his feverish belting, Ringo Starr takes his first and only drum solo in the recorded history of the group, a moment of thrilling indulgence that he had earned through so many years of bowing before the songs. Following that the three remaining members take turns blasting through the boogie-rock beat with scorching guitar solos, taking it all back to the Cavern once again.

After Lennon's final fuzzed-out guitar blast, the air clears with some tinkling piano, and McCartney gives his final pronouncement, with Lennon and Harrison in bittersweet harmony one last time: "And in the end / The love you take / Is equal to the love / You make." Hollywood screenwriters would kill for a closing line so concise and profound. It somehow encapsulates everything the boys had been telling us since the beginning. It's not the end of a line but the completion of a circle of, what else, love, eternal and unbreakable, like a beautiful song that never fades out. The Beatles let out one final harmonized sigh, and their work is finally done.

The perfect symmetry of this medley would be messed up by the carcass of the Get Back project being dragged into the world as *Let It Be* after the demise of the group had already occurred. But enough time has passed that we can appreciate the "Golden Slumbers"/"Carry That Weight"/"The End" medley as the grand finale that it was intended to be and that the group richly deserved. It makes sense that only the Beatles could write the fitting ending to their world-changing story.

1. "A Day in the Life" (from *Sgt. Pepper's Lonely Hearts Club Band*, 1967)

"A Day in the Life" would have been No. 1 on this list of the Beatles' greatest songs without any kind of personal connection, and, as the author of four Counting Down books, I have made it a rule not to bring any personal associations into these works, for fear they would damage my objectivity. I am going to break that rule for this song, but you'll hopefully understand why at the end of this section.

I received *Sgt. Pepper's Lonely Hearts Club Band* from my parents as a ninth birthday present in 1981. I had annoyed the whole family by constantly nagging them to put the Beatles' 1962–1966 greatest hits album on the turntable (which I wasn't allowed to touch), and so they bought me *Sgt. Pepper's* on that long-lost method of conveying music, the 8-track tape.

I didn't care at the time about the annoying program switches on the machine, which sounded like a toaster burping, nor was I aware that the songs were way out of order from their intended sequence. All that mattered was that I could play the Beatles all by myself and get totally absorbed in this fascinating music while adding to the repertoire of Fab Four songs that I knew word for word.

Even with the jumbled order, "A Day in the Life" was still at the end, where it was always supposed to be. I put my father's headphones on, which threatened to tip me over, and listened to it over and over, absorbing every nook and cranny of the recording until I could play it in my head from start to finish when I had to be away from the stereo.

"A Day in the Life" captures better than any other song what the Beatles represented to those who listened to them. On that song they took the seemingly mundane ordinariness of everyday life and showed it in a different light, changed the perspective. Suddenly the drear of existence seemed flush with possibilities, even if those possibilities were only accessible via the corridors of one's own mind. While the lyrics drolly looked at the limits of reality, the music dared to suggest those limits were illusory and easily shattered.

Let's take it from the top, shall we? As the crowds cheer at the end of the "Sgt. Pepper's" reprise, the gentle acoustic strumming of John Lennon is heard. His very first line can't hide his lack of enthusiasm for the story he's about to tell: "I read the news today oh boy." The world-weary sarcasm is impossible to miss, even with Lennon's voice at its most ethereal. He then proceeds to tell an odd tale about a man who has "made the grade," which would seem to be a positive thing, at least until it's revealed that he's apparently been killed in a car accident.

Or has he? The car accident reading is backed by Lennon's later interviews in which he claimed to be referencing the death of Tara Browne, a young moneyed friend of the Fab Four, a few months before "A Day in the Life" was recorded. In the song, however, the narrator sounds like somebody who keeps changing his story in an attempt to keep the listener's interest. The line "Well I just had to laugh" doesn't seem like the proper response to a tragedy, unless the harsh truth of the situation inspired some typical Lennon gallows humor. As for "He blew his mind out in a car / He didn't notice that the lights had changed," that sounds like an impatient fellow honking his horn at the car in front of him, oblivious that the traffic light is now red. The whole verse plays out like a dream, and dreams play a heavy role throughout the song.

The second verse takes place in an entirely different scene with no connection to the first, again a dreamlike non sequitur. Here the narrator is watching a war movie that sounds suspiciously like *How I Won the War*, the film Lennon had just completed with Beatles movie director Richard Lester. The crowd of people suddenly has no interest and departs, which is perhaps a winking reference at the film's critical or commercial shortcomings.

Up to now, the music has been gentle and controlled, distinguished by Lennon's fragile acoustic strumming, Paul McCartney's steady bass, and the rumble and crash of Ringo Starr's drums. When Lennon switches to falsetto for the line "I'd love to turn you on," the music, as if on cue, breaks out of the stately restraint and begins to come alive.

What comes next is not your run-of-the-mill orchestral crescendo. It sounds like the instruments are racing each other in a feverish effort to get to the necessary chord first. This brilliant flourish, conceived by McCartney, is a marvel of shambolic grandeur that seems to mirror the entirety of the human race rushing to find a meaning to its existence. While the pretty opening verses lulled us into a lovely state of relaxation, that crescendo jolts us awake and alive.

McCartney takes over in the next section, a bouncy piano-driven jaunt depicting a typically harried weekday morning in the life of an average guy frantically trying to start his day. Listen to the way he describes every little task as a grind or a mishap: "Fell out of bed," "dragged a comb across my head," "found my way downstairs," "looking up, I noticed I was late." Nothing is easy on this morning, but the buoyant rhythm propels him, and us, along to get through it all.

Once arriving, the narrator has a smoke (you can decide for yourself what kind) and we're back in a dream, once again at the expense of the drudgery of routine. McCartney's voice floats above the horns so blissfully that it seems he wants to stay out there in the distance. Only the orchestra can drag us back for the final verse.

Now Lennon is at the newspaper again, but this time the peppier rhythm from McCartney's middle section is along for the ride. The absurdity of this final verse emphasizes the theme that the banality of the daily grind can drive you mad, as the narrator relates a true story about an excess of potholes in the town of Blackburn. This last item in this litany of the strange but true—that they, whoever they are that care for such a trivial item, can now ascertain the number of holes to fit into the Albert Hall—is so meaningless as to be farcical. He seems to be saying, "If that's the best reality has to offer me, I'd rather let my mind wander into another reverie."

And so he does, the crescendo rising again into the stratosphere, taking the listener along for the ride. Only this time the spell is broken by that unforgettable piano chord, thundering away all the useless detritus of this particular day, of this particular life, in awe-inspiring fashion. Finally, at this moment, after striving against the surly bonds for the entire song, for the entire *Sgt. Pepper's* album really, the Beatles achieve transcendence.

"A Day in the Life" is a groundbreaking piece of work that shattered any preexisting boundaries for what rock music could be. It is also the ultimate Lennon/McCartney collaboration, a song in which their disparate songwriting talents were so in synch that they seemed to be finishing each other's musical sentences. The song scores historical points as well, because it is arguably the peak moment in the the Beatles' career, the point to which all their joyous rock and roll from the early days ascended and from which circumstance, pressure, and personal animosity caused them to fall.

All those things are wonderful, but to me, the author of this humble list, "A Day in the Life" is the No. 1 Beatles' song because it is the epitome of the notion that all their finest music espouses: that music can uplift us from dark times like nothing else. As a kid who lost his dad just a year after I received that birthday gift from him, you can see why that notion would hold extra-special appeal.

This list has been my way of saying thank you to the Beatles for giving me, and every last one of their fans, that uplift for all the years since and for all those times they turned . . . us . . . on.

NOTES

THE COUNTDOWN

1. David Sheff, *All We Are Saying: The Last Major Interview with John Lennon and Yoko Ono* (New York: St. Martin's Griffin, 2000), 180.

2. Barry Miles, *Paul McCartney: Many Years from Now* (New York: Henry Holt, 1997), 175.

3. Sheff, *All We Are Saying*, 174.

4. Maureen Cleave, "How Does a Beatle Live? John Lennon Lives Like This," *London Evening Standard*, March 4, 1966, http://www.beatlesinterviews.org/db1966.0304-beatles-john-lennon-were-more-popular-than-jesus-now-maureen-cleave.html.

5. The Beatles, *The Beatles Anthology* (San Francisco: Chronicle Books, 2000), 22.

6. Miles, *Paul McCartney*, 270.

7. Jann S. Wenner, *Lennon Remembers: The Full Rolling Stone Interviews from 1970* (London: Verso, 2000), 83.

8. George Orwell, *Animal Farm: A Fairy Story* (London: Secker and Warburg), 1945.

9. Ray Coleman, *Lennon: The Definitive Biography* (New York: McGraw-Hill, 2000), 369.

10. Sheff, *All We Are Saying*, 189.

11. Andy Greene, "Read Previously Unknown George Harrison Letter from 1966," *Rolling Stone*, May 25, 2015, http://www.rollingstone.com/music/news/read-previously-unknown-george-harrison-letter-from-1966-20150525.

12. Wenner, *Lennon Remembers*, 159.

13. The Beatles, *Beatles Anthology*, 182.

14. Miles, *Paul McCartney*, 321.

15. Sheff, *All We Are Saying*, 182.

16. Ibid., 191.

17. Nicholas Schaffner, *The Beatles Forever: How They Changed Our Culture* (New York: McGraw-Hill, 1978), 220.

18. Sheff, *All We Are Saying*, 199.

19. Ibid., 192.

20. Miles, *Paul McCartney*, 490.

21. Ibid., 370.

22. Miles, *Paul McCartney*, 314.

23. The Beatles, *Beatles Anthology*, 350.

24. Ibid.

25. Miles, *Paul McCartney*, 273.

26. Sheff, *All We Are Saying*, 136.

27. The Beatles, *Beatles Anthology*, 337.

28. Ibid., 316.

29. Sheff, *All We Are Saying*, 177.

30. Wenner, *Lennon Remembers*, 9.

31. Sheff, *All We Are Saying*, 196.

32. The Beatles, *Beatles Anthology*, 339.

33. Miles, *Paul McCartney*, 271.

34. The Beatles, *Beatles Anthology*, 188.

35. Ibid., 206.

36. Miles, *Paul McCartney*, 485.

37. Sheff, *All We Are Saying*, 196.

38. Ibid., 139.

39. Ibid., 157.

BIBLIOGRAPHY

The Beatles. *The Beatles Anthology*. San Francisco: Chronicle Books, 2000. This is the book tie-in to the acclaimed documentary series and the three-volume CD collection of outtakes (along with two new songs from Paul McCartney, George Harrison, and Ringo Starr that originated from John Lennon demos). It's good that we get the story right from the mouths of the group members, and the book is so mammoth that it goes into even more detail than the docs. It tends to skim over some of the harder moments in the group's time together, but you can get lost for hours in this thing.

Dowdling, William J. *Beatlesongs*. New York: Simon & Schuster, 1989. My copy of this paperback is barely holding together, so often have I consulted it over the years. Dowdling collected numerous sources to provide information on the recording and release of every Beatles' song. It provides endless trivia and unearths some rare quotes from the Fab Four on both their songs and their albums.

Miles, Barry. *Paul McCartney: Many Years from Now*. New York: Henry Holt, 1997. McCartney's remembrances as told to Miles gave him an opportunity to tell his side of the story in terms of the songs and music of the Beatles, well after Lennon's interviews had been the definitive word on the situation. Many Macca skeptics had a problem with what they felt was revisionist history on some of the group's most famous songs. But the depth and specificity of McCartney's recall make him a pretty convincing source.

Sheff, David. *All We Are Saying: The Last Major Interview with John Lennon and Yoko Ono*. New York: St. Martin's Griffin, 2000. Sheff actually conducted a series of interviews for *Playboy* magazine with Lennon and Ono as they were in the midst of finishing up *Double Fantasy* in 1980. The interviews are collected in this volume, and the final third or so of the book is devoted to Lennon's recollections about the songs of the Beatles. He is as candid as ever and isn't afraid to criticize either his bandmates or himself, but he has far less of an axe to grind than when he first left the band in the early 1970s. That makes this a somewhat reliable source for Beatles fans looking for info on the music, as long as they both understand that Lennon's recall was faulty at times and can handle the almost overwhelming poignancy of knowing that he was just weeks away from his death as he spoke with such a clear head and tender heart.

Wenner, Jann S. *Lennon Remembers: The Full Rolling Stone Interviews from 1970*. London: Verso, 2000. Wenner, who had founded *Rolling Stone* just a few years prior, interviewed Lennon with Yoko Ono in 1970 right after his primal scream therapy and in conjunction with the release of his searing solo debut, *John Lennon/Plastic Ono Band*. As such, Lennon's agenda to put the Beatles behind him led to some raw putdowns both of his ex-bandmates and the work they had done together. So you have to take a lot of this with a grain of salt, especially in terms of his Beatles criticism, but it's still riveting stuff.

INDEX

ABOUT THE AUTHOR

Jim Beviglia is a featured writer for *American Songwriter* magazine, reviewing new albums and looking back at classic songwriters and songs for both the print and online editions. This is his fourth book in the Counting Down series, following 2013's *Counting Down Bob Dylan: His 100 Finest Songs,* 2014's *Counting Down Bruce Springsteen: His 100 Finest Songs,* and 2015's *Counting Down the Rolling Stones: Their 100 Finest Songs,* and he continues to maintain his blog, *Countdown Kid* (countdownkid.wordpess.com), where he delves deep into the musical libraries of rock's finest artists. Jim was born and raised in Old Forge, Pennsylvania, where he currently resides with his mom; his daughter, Daniele; and his wife, Marie.